Ninachka

The Making of an Englishwoman?

Nina Murray

Edited by Jay Underwood

Hamilton Books
A member of
The Rowman & Littlefield Publishing Group
Lanham • Boulder • New York • Toronto • Oxford

Library of Congress Control Number: 2007933979
ISBN-13: 978-0-7618-3791-6 (paperback : alk. paper)
ISBN-10: 0-7618-3791-4 (paperback : alk. paper)

∞™ The paper used in this publication meets the minimum
requirements of American National Standard for Information
Sciences—Permanence of Paper for Printed Library Materials,
ANSI Z39.48—1984

One ship drives east, another drives west
With the selfsame winds that blow;
'Tis the set of the sails,
and not the gales
That tells them the way to go.

Like the winds of the sea are the winds of fate
As we voyage along through life;
'Tis the set of the soul
That decides its goal
And not the calm or the strife.

(Ella Wheeler Wilcox 1850–1919: The Winds of Fate, 1916)

This book is dedicated to the memory of my late beloved husband Admiral Leonard Warren Murray, through whom these beautiful words reached me; and to my father, Sergei Shcheyteenin, whose courage and boundless spirit live on in me.

Contents

Introduction   vii

1 Russia   1
   Pontoons   1
   Journey from Istanbul   3
   Early History   4
   The Crimean Exile   8
   Young Family Life   15
   Turbulence Starts   20
   Leaving Tuapse   24

2 Manchester Days   27
   Winmarleigh   27
   Birth of the Studio   33
   College   39
   Medical Training   42
   Into Careers   46
   Early General Practice   52
   Businessman Sergei   54
   Riviera Visits   55
   Moorfields   57

3 War   62
   War and Nicolas   62
   Prisoners of War   65
   The Long March   71
   A Woman's War   74
   Royal Naval Voluntary Reserve   79

A War Wedding   83
Penelope   88
Homecoming   92

4   Post-War Years   97
    Blood Trail in the Snow   97
    Guardian Angels   102
    Mighty Manxman Sonny   107
    Buxton   109
    Home Life   114
    The Holidays   116
    The Canadian Connection   118
    A Greek Romance   124
    Historic Buxton   126
    "Madame" in Retirement   130

5   Kaleidoscope   133
    Leonard's Brief Buxton Life   133
    Pinner Troubles   136
    A World Cruise   138
    Herefordshire Story   142
    The Young Classicist   144
    A Valiant Struggle   146
    The Huxleys   151
    Working in Worcester   154
    Father and Daughter   158
    Wide Horizons   162

6   Later Years   165
    Windsor   165
    Swallowfield Park   171
    Essex   179
    Rising water   183
    Epilogue   188

Index   189

Introduction

This book, originally dedicated to the loving memory of my Russian parents, Sergei and Vera Shcheyteenin, was started in the late 1980s or early 1990s on my long delayed retirement from a British medical career.

It was intended for the benefit of the members of the family born in England of mixed émigré and natural born British parents, for that generation to have an idea of the history of their forebears. These young people rightly feel truly British, but whether or not they are proud to accept as an asset the burnish given to them by the characteristics of their other nationality depends on, and varies with, their ages.

During the course of the project, however, several other components of my story came into focus, not the least of which is the controversy that is often created when one assumes a new course.

These were made clear to me by the author of another book on the plight of Russian émigrés, who wishes to remain anonymous. I sent him a rough draft of my original work, and was rather severely criticized for the title.

Indeed, he wondered how I could do so, since the England to which my family came in the 1920s had, in his words "gone forever . . . as had the old Russia."

This comment is helpful, because at no point did I make a deliberate decision to become English! There is nothing feigned in what I hope are the qualities I now have as a result of my experience, that typify what many would see as being truly English. According to my critic, my transformation was ". . . just something you did and not what you became. Would you have become Chinese were you to have lived and been brought up in China: I doubt it. And the fact that refugees sometimes know more about a country and its people (and often the language), and frequently better than the locals, has nothing to do with the question."

But it does have something to do with how willingly any immigrant, not just refugees or exiles, becomes assimilated with their new surroundings, and makes the most of the opportunities that are made available to them.

Too often, in any country that accepts large numbers of immigrants, the criticism is that these new citizens arrive and collect in large ghettos of their own creation, and appear determined to impose a cultural imprint that reflects the nation they left, the nation that failed them so badly they were forced to leave it.

Thanks to my critic's helpful observations, my focus has shifted in part, to offer an example to any immigrant of how to become a citizen of a new nation, without necessarily having to sacrifice their heritage.

As an émigré parent who has grown up in England from a young age I cannot really regard myself as truly Russian. My knowledge of that country consists only of hearsay and early childish memories. Nor did I feel really English as my early years in England were spent in the Russian atmosphere of my parents' home and an English out and about one; a condition I recognise as one of the difficulties facing a great many recently arrived émigrés of latter times. Though the need for the thought of nationality has arisen less and less with the passage of time and I have become totally and loyally British, when called upon, the pride of that long Russian lineage has only added to the short new English one.

My heritage was given to me through the courage of my parents, I shall always treasure it, and hope to pass it on through this work.

My critic's other observation was that my story contained too much "domestic detail" to be of real interest to a general readership. This was countered for me by my male editor, who brought to my attention a point that I had overlooked.

For the past few decades, since the 1980s at least, a great deal of social comment has been directed toward the development of the single mother/professional woman, and the problems they face in what is still considered to be a male oriented society.

My editor pointed out, however, that I—and many women of my era—was a pioneer of this trend long before it became, well, trendy! What is today a choice made by many women, was something forced upon us by the exigencies of war and an unrelenting male control of society that many of today's young professional women cannot appreciate.

My editor further noted that my critic's comment about domestic detail only underlines the depth of male misunderstanding of the situation still faced by single mothers and professional women; that "domestic detail" is as important, prevalent, and unavoidable a part of their life as the demanding details of their work and career. It cannot be escaped as the traditional father might escape it, by insulating himself with the demands of his job.

As my life has been involved in many of the events of much of recent English and world history I feel that the widely ranging story might be of special interest—perhaps even of some help—to the many newcomers who are perplexed by their complex circumstances. It is my hope that others in similar circumstances around the world, be it Britain, Canada, the United States; anywhere an immigrant might choose to find a home and start a new life, will find the account interesting, and that single mothers and professional women today will find it encouraging.

Nina Murray

Chapter One

Russia

PONTOONS

Early in December of 1920 Tsarist Russia was finally conquered. The remaining 250,000 men of the Imperial forces—and their families—faced brutal extermination, and needed to leave the country.

Throughout the four devastating years of Russia's revolution, the Imperial forces had fought valiantly, but having been thrust back repeatedly by the Bolshevik 'Red' army, Crimea, that huge peninsula jutting into the Black Sea and joining Russia's south coast by a sinuous isthmus, became the 'White' army's ultimate stronghold.

Crimea normally basks in the southern sunshine of its Mediterranean climate, but that year an exceptionally hot summer was followed by an unusually severe winter that gripped the Black Sea's northern coast with unaccustomed ferocity. For the first time in centuries, vicious frosts froze the marshes around the isthmus and enabled the Bolsheviks to penetrate inside the strongly fortified peninsula. Attacked from behind, the White forces were routed and Imperial Russia had to admit defeat.

Every seaworthy vessel in Crimean waters was mustered to Sevastopol, Russia's southernmost naval port on Crimea's south coast, where distressed families, carrying little more than hand luggage, awaited to be launched into exile. Crowding too hurriedly on to the port's pontoon bridge to board their allocated vessels, some overloaded pontoons tilted perilously. Frantically clinging to railing chains, despairing people could not prevent their precious luggage from slithering off the wet boards only to bubble volubly and slowly sink before their owners' anguished eyes.

1

Amongst this sorry throng my father, Major Prince Sergei Orestovitch Shcheyteenin clasped his two terrified children and their mother to him, as the righting pontoon rocked violently. Glad to have been on an upraised edge of their pontoon Sergei, a deserving forty-five-year-old, fair-haired and blue-eyed Cavalier of the Order of St. Stanislas and St. Ann, with his young brunette wife Vera and their children—my eleven-year-old brother Nicolas and me, then seven years old—were bidding sad goodbyes to Aunt Natasha and our beloved Nanny Liza. These ladies, neither being immediate service family members had no evacuation permits and had to be left behind.

Sergei's permit was for the floating dock *Kronschtadt* where we were allocated space enough for each person to lie down; the adults on the floor, the children on top of the ventilation shafts. Marie, Sergei's mother-in-law with her youngest son Shoura—Sergei's fellow officer and brother-in-law—were given an adjoining area.

As the family boarded, exhausted by the hours of facing the agony of being irrevocably thrust into the unknown, Sergei was astonished to be handed a tattered obviously long-travelled letter. This was an unexpected spontaneous response to a very out-dated business message of Sergei's, in which his friend Frank Reddaway was inviting the family to England. Dazed by their good fortune Sergei and Vera continued to seek their allotted space with unbelieving hearts.

With all the folk accommodated, the heavily laden vessels cast off as darkness fell that grim night, and sailed out to sea with no surety of any destination. Whilst the bizarre flotilla sailed hopefully towards the Black Sea's only outlet, urgent negotiations went on anxiously as to whether Turkey would let the ships through the Bosphorus, and which countries would be willing to accept the refugees. Though England had declined, France and the Balkans agreed, whereupon Turkey graciously allowed transit.

In the confusion of the hurried exodus some ships collided, and some sank. The slowly moving *Kronschtadt* was rammed, but mercifully only shuddered ominously and went on to accommodate drenched and shattered survivors from the other lost vessels.

On board the overcrowded craft, with little for anyone—especially children—to do in their cramped conditions, I lay on my stomach on the air duct ledge, chin cupped in my elbow-propped hands and gazed dreamily through the porthole. The deeply imprinted pictures of the distant Bosphorus coast as it slowly passed by in all its sun lit beauty have stayed in my mind for many years. My brother happily took interest in the activities of the sailors.

When, some days later, the bedraggled convoy anchored in mid-Bosphorus to allow for temporary accommodation to be improvised for Balkan-bound refugees, Sergei arranged for the family to disembark direct to Constantinople where Frank had arranged for visas and £100 to await us. As the *Kron-*

schtadt's anchorage was out of sight of land, Sergei was dismayed when the arranged for transport turned out to be a rough tub of a wooden rowing boat manned by two burly Turks.

His alarm proved to be well-founded; once out of sight of the *Kronschtadt*, as the flimsy boat was tossed about and lifted high by giant waves, the men demanded exorbitant excess fares from my father, on pain of throwing overboard not only their precious luggage, but the children too!

JOURNEY FROM ISTANBUL

The relief of at last being on dry land and away from the villainous Turks was immeasurable, but being in Istanbul, as Constantinople was by then known, was not the end of their troubles.

The long wait at Pera, the bustling station through which Europe connects with Asia, was long and tedious and a new peril suddenly loomed. While squashed up against a long barrier in a dense crowd waiting to pass through a ticket check, to my mother's horror, a swarthy man from beyond the barrier lifted me out from the long queue and, holding me firmly in his arms, backed determinedly away. With the boatmen's threats vivid in her mind my mother immediately visualised "KIDNAP" and though she had never in her life before screamed at anyone, in that instant she did so without restraint. In the ensuing commotion the man tried to explain that he had only meant to help the family get through all the pushing and squabbling surrounding the turnstile, but my mother felt her anguish had not been without cause!

With Frank's miraculous invitation accepted, and the precious papers located, verified and honoured, and with tickets bought, our family boarded a ship bound for Marseille. As the vessel began to leave port, an angry crowd gathered on the promenade deck noisily protesting against the presence of a bundle of peacock feathers attached to a pile of someone's luggage; indeed a portent of doom for a vessel at sea. As the crowd grew larger and more insistent, the owner of the offending object sadly let the lovely coloured plumes flutter from the ship's rail into the waves while the anxious spectators, glad to see the 'evil-eyed' feathers go, jabbered excitedly between themselves.

Watching the coast recede into the distance, everyone enjoyed the luxury of eating tangerines, a fruit not native to Sevastopol, but as the ship gathered speed and entered the turbulence of more open waters our childish delight began to fade. We had never experienced sea-sickness before! For many years the smell of tangerines brought on a vague nausea for me. The passage was indeed rough, and it was only as the ship entered calmer waters on nearing Marseille some days later that my mother and I were able to accept the offer of food made by our cabin steward. Dutch Gouda cheese with its big holes, fancied on that occasion, still has a great attraction for me. How Nicolas fared in my father's care was not discussed.

A few days were necessarily spent in Paris buying clothes to replace our tatters, and as Nicholas and I had long been without toys, we went to Lafayette's toy department. Though fussy French sales ladies paraded large gaudily-dressed dolls before us, a little simply-clad golden-haired china doll, with brown eyes that opened and shut, won my heart. Though my parents could ill-afford the cost of this dainty toy, the delight the little object gave me was a joy to them all. Nicolas's treasured possession was a Meccano set.

The next phase of the journey brought the family to the Channel crossing that presented little problem compared with the rough Mediterranean passage, but the scratchy horsehair-covered waiting room seats at Euston station were difficult for us tired children to accept. After a long wait the midnight train eventually took our weary group to Manchester, from where we were to contact our host.

Arriving there at four in the morning on January 1st 1921 my parents were astonished to find all the town's hotels filled to capacity for New Year celebrations. After weary fruitless combing of the city for accommodation we all eventually fell into longed-for beds out in the suburbs, just as winter's late murky dawn began to glimmer. Eventually, after Sergei had spoken to Frank, the family was courteously collected by the Reddaway chauffeur and driven in the comfort of their Rolls-Royce to join the closing days of a Christmas and New Year house party at Winmarleigh Hall, Frank's home.

Arrival at this comfortable, gracious Victorian country house, standing in its own park and farmlands in the Fylde district of Lancashire, was indeed very much a long delayed homecoming for Sergei and Vera. It had been some four years since the Shcheyteenins had lost their real home, and though some English ways were strange, and language difficulties were a complication, we were—at last—at ease.

EARLY HISTORY

My father first met Frank Reddaway in the United States in the early 1900s. They were both attending an American geological society meeting in Baltimore; Sergei there as a junior minister for the Russian Imperial Mines and Minerals ministry, and Frank just pursuing his own interests. Sergei, a warm-hearted moustachioed young man with a pleasant military bearing about him, liked Frank, the broad-bearded Englishman who was interested in Siberian gold mines. As this was a subject in which Sergei was well-versed, a lasting family friendship soon developed.

Some years later—a little before the outbreak of the First World War—Frank arrived in St. Petersburg intending to extend his thriving British Industrial Belting business to Russia, and contacted my father. He planned to set up factories in St. Petersburg, and was about to build himself an appropriate house nearby. As time went on and revolution threatened, Sergei advised the Reddaways to leave Russia, and eventually—when the war had started and means of leaving the country were no longer possible—he managed to conduct them over the frontier into Finland.

My father, who started his days in July 1875 in Tashkent in Western Siberia, was the only surviving member of a long line of militarily-minded Russian nobility who proudly trace their origins to Rurik, the Nordic prince who—in the year 861 AD—had been Russia's earliest recorded ruler whose dynasty preceded the Romanovs, and whose sword-bearers the Shcheyteenins are reputed to have been.

Sergei's father, Major-General Prince Orest Vassilievitch Shcheyteenin, was a kindly Russian gentleman who had been born in 1836 in the family home at Kuntsovo near St. Petersburg. My grandfather had followed the family tradition of military service, and became a member of the Imperial General Staff. In the early 1870s he was appointed Governor General of Western Siberia and Russian Turkestan, which meant that he and his wife Sophia went to live in Tashkent, the capital of the province.

In 1879 Orest, Sophia and their two young sons, Oleg and Sergei, set off from Tashkent for a short stay in St. Petersburg to attend to the family home and affairs, and arrange for the boys' future education. On their return journey tragedy struck them. While visiting a small provincial town where a civic reception had been arranged in their honour, the two small boys escaped their governess's travel-wearied eye and rollicked in a dining room.

Inevitably a samovar, the traditional Russian charcoal-fired urn, fell over and quickly set fire to tablecloths and hangings. Six-year-old Oleg, who tried to protect his small brother Sergei from the quickly spreading flames, soon had his clothes on fire and died painfully several agonising days later from his horrific injuries.

The grieving family, with a very lonely four-year-old Sergei, eventually reached Tashkent where saddened years went by. Eventually time came for Sergei, who was to follow the family tradition, to start his education in the Corps of Pages. Harrowing goodbyes were exchanged between the tender seven-year-old and his sorrowing parents as, escorted by his tutor, Sergei set off for St. Petersburg. The Corps of Pages, though the most elite of Russia's educational establishments, was harsh, spartan and militaristic, where Sergei was not happy. Besides the minor injustices and general austerity of the regime, he felt he never had enough to eat, and later blamed his relatively

Prince Orest Shcheyteenin (1838–1898), my grandfather

short stature on the under-nourishment of those growing years. With his parents at the other end of the world in Tashkent, there were no 'tuck boxes' or gorging 'days out' to supplement the deficiencies.

Sergei's days in the corps were followed by the Imperial Military Academy, from which he graduated as an artillery officer. He devoted himself whole-heartedly to the welfare of the men he commanded, and strove to enlighten them, but was perpetually disappointed by their low morale. Though he spared no effort in trying to improve their views and conditions, he was discouraged by the general inertia he encountered, and in time transferred to the Marines.

In Tashkent Sergei's parents, who missed their beloved Sergei and mourned the early loss of their elder son, devoted their energies faithfully to the arduous duties of their post. One unfortunate day, whilst accompanying Orest in Semi-palatinsk on a formal inspection of the southern region of Western Siberia, Sophia attended a display of oriental carpets in a caravanserai, and picked up erysipelas, a virulent and rapidly spreading skin infection that killed her.

Sergei and his father were deeply distressed by their loss, and Orest was eventually glad of the move when he was appointed commander of the fortress headquarters of the Imperial Russian Southern Forces at Bendery, which lies somewhat inland from Odessa on the northern coast of the Black Sea. His memorial stands there to this day.

Orest spent several lonely years at Bendery, but ultimately married a comely lady from nearby Ochakov where she had been teaching German to a colleague's young family. In 1893, Sergei's half-sister Olga was born.

Sergei's half-sister Olga, in her young days at Ochakov

After Orest's death in 1898, Olga and her mother moved to Odessa where, towards the later years of the 1914-1918 War, the old lady died, disclosing her original nationality and revealing Olga's half German ancestry. As just about anything connected with Germany was a very inflammatory topic at that time, Olga was soon dubbed *Nemka* (German woman) and was subjected to undue humiliation and victimisation.

Although she was a beautiful, svelte young brunette, who had been a kind and very able volunteer nurse from her early adult years, she was made to sweep streets and hew stones for road-building. After many backbreaking years Olga was ultimately exiled to intensive agricultural labour in Siberia. A many-hundred-mile-long journey in cattle-truck conditions took her and many others to the grim life of a *kolkhoz*, the nucleus of USSR collective farming.

She arrived at an encampment of corrugated iron huts scattered over miles of desolate agricultural land near Karaganda, north of Lake Balkhasch. The inadequacy of the housing—which offered no protection from the burning heat of summers and piercing cold of deep-continental winters—made the hard labour demanded of her all the more difficult to bear. Olga's only solace was that she could write letters for many of her illiterate fellow exiles. Much later, when restrictions had eased a little, she earned permission to cultivate a strip of land for her own use.

Unfortunately she couldn't keep the same strip from year to year, and had to cultivate from very rough ground each spring. She managed, however, to grow crops of cucumbers that she trundled in an old discarded perambulator to the nearest town some miles away, and bartered her produce for such luxuries as a jersey or a piece of rough cloth that she later cobbled into a skirt or dress. Her letters ceased in late 1979.

THE CRIMEAN EXILE

At the end of the Crimean War—which raged from 1853 to 1856—France appointed a senior naval officer, architect Jules Victor Elysée, to conduct postwar reparations to the Sevastopol, Balaclava and Inkerman areas.

In 1857 Jules and his frail young wife Matilde arrived in Sevastopol, where they were welcomed by the commander of the port, Captain Paul Vassilievitch Protopopov and his wife Nadezhda. A warm friendship soon developed, and the Protopopovs grew to love the little lady from Lorraine, who it sadly proved, was not destined to live long. Their grief at Matilde's early death in childbirth in 1860 was deep, but when that tragedy was followed by Elysée's sudden death, they were happy to adopt the orphaned Marie Josephine.

Marie Josephine Elysée, adopted daughter of Admiral Pavil Protopopov

Marie grew to be a charming and attractive young woman with many winning French ways about her. She was petite; brown-eyed with glowing chestnut hair and soon enjoyed the busy social hubbub of her adopting parents' naval entourage. Amongst her many friends, her closest companion was Natasha (Natalia Alexandrovna) the daughter of widowed Admiral Alexander Matousseyevitch, a talented member of a long-established Imperial Russian naval family who traced his ancestry to the early princes of Russia's Polish borders.

Natasha's three young brothers Ossia, Vassia, and Nikolai—all naval officers—soon became fascinated by Marie. Of the three, the one most captivated was Nikolai, who happily was Marie's favourite from the very start. He was the tallest and best looking of the three handsome, bearded, tall young men, and as he absolutely adored Marie they soon planned to marry.

Their marriage in 1879 brought about a warm friendship between the two families and a very contented and expanding kinship grew between the various relatives. In time Marie and Nikolai had a young family of their own.

It was started with daughter Vera, my mother, who was born in September 1881, soon to be followed by two brothers, Nicholas and Paul, and a little later by a third brother, Alexander, known affectionately as Shoura, the usual Russian affectionate diminutive for that name.

The advent of these junior Matousseyvitches promoted the benevolent Natasha and her brothers to warmly loved, unmarried aunts and uncles.

At about the turn of the century my father, Sergei, by then a well-established dapper young Marine officer with somewhat receding fair wavy hair, a friendly face and perfect manners, was posted to Sevastopol. Nikolai Alexandrovitch Matousseyevitch, by this time an admiral and Senior Naval Officer of the port of Sevastopol, welcomed Sergei and introduced him to his home, where his elegant petite French wife Marie, his sons: budding naval astronomer Nicholas (Nikolayevich), aspiring submariner Paul, young cadet Shoura (Alexander Nikolayevich) and their hazel-eyed sister Vera (Nicolaievna) all quickly involved Sergei in their family activities.

My father had in fact met Vera in St. Petersburg while he was at the Academy of General Staff, and she was a pupil at the Smolny Institute, Russia's supreme school for young ladies. Captivated by her in those early days, he was now more than delighted to meet her again. No longer just the attractive child she had been earlier, she was now an alluring, slender beauty. Her large hazel eyes showed the alertness of her mind which, with its roguish sense of humour and expressive face, easily held the centre of attention and overwhelmed my father's young emotions.

Vera, her father's darling who had grown up amongst considerate and affectionate brothers, was very content with her life, and was as charming with Sergei as she was with everyone. She had seen enough of her mother's repeated annoyances at recurring pregnancies and other inconveniences of married service life, and had become wary of marriage. She paid Sergei no special attention, seeming to regard him as some kind of adopted brother or long-established family friend. Sergei, however, was deeply interested in her and was distressed that his loyal devotion was making no headway. His gallant attempts at enticement showed little result. They went riding on the best of horses, attended theatres, enjoyed picnics and every other suitable and fashionable lure including drives in his state-of-the-art de Dion Bouton motor car, but Vera was still reluctant to submit to a romance.

Vera Matousseyvitch, my mother, in 1900

Unbeknown to him, Sergei had a secret ally in Vera's mother Marie, to whom his whole-hearted adoration of her daughter was obvious. This little lady, who relished the limelight that her husband's rank endowed her, had begun to realise that daughters should be married and away, and she was growing impatient with Vera's persistent independence. Regarding Sergei as a very suitable match for Vera, and worried by her daughter's indifference to him, Marie decided to take advantage of her husband's impending posting to Vladivostok where, as Vice-Admiral, he was to take command of the Far Eastern Fleet.

Marie had always been of the belief that long stays in continental spas and holiday resorts were essential for the benefit of her delicate health and, as she disliked the frequently recurring demands of service life to move house, her husband usually encouraged her to entrust the management of removal to naval personnel, and take her vacations at these times.

On this occasion she planned to stay in Nagasaki, renowned for its mineral springs and thermal mud baths. Vera, as the unmarried young daughter, would naturally have to accompany her mother. So, choosing an appropriate moment in the pre-move bustle Marie enquired: "Verochka dear, are you going to accept a proposal from this charming young man?"

As Vera's big eyes looked at her mother in sudden fear and uncertainty, she added: "You realise, dear, that you will be coming to Japan with me when we follow your father to the Far East" thus stressing the urgency of decision for Vera, and hopefully opening a welcoming door for Sergei to take the matter from there.

Fortunately for both their sakes Vera preferred Sergei to the other prospect, and their marriage in 1901 proved to be a very happy union.

Married life, and joining Vera's extended family, suited Sergei's outgoing nature. He proved to be a very genial host, and thoroughly enjoyed the contacts of naval social life and the company of all the many relatives and friends. Though not himself an accomplished musician, he was able to indulge his love of music with the help of the newly invented 'Pianola' device. He had this mechanism built into his Bechstein grand piano, and gladly arranged musical and card-playing evenings besides other such occasions. He did not, however, feel fulfilled in his service career, and ultimately resigned.

Having spent his early years in Tashkent, Sergei was very conscious of, and interested in, the enormous geological resources and possibilities of Siberia and Russia's many other vastnesses, and decided to take up geology and mine engineering. As in the early 1900's the wide scope he needed in his chosen subjects was only available at the Freiberg University in Dresden, the young Shcheyteenins set off for Germany.

Sergei's studies gave him great satisfaction and ultimately enabled him to become a man of great value, both to the armed force and the government of

Imperial Russia, in each of which he went on to hold highly responsible appointments. Vera too was very content in her new life. She studied art and painted porcelain in Dresden, and took part in many kinds of applied art including tooled leatherwork, a craft revived in Germany at that time.

Vera had originally accepted Sergei's proposal of marriage on the condition there were to be no babies, but soon responded to his gentle devotion and quickly understood the beauty of the full expression of the deep mutual love of a happy marriage. Both she and Sergei felt very blessed when, in due time, they had a lovely daughter, Ariadne who, in the miraculous way of nature, soon grew into a brown-eyed and golden-haired enchantress who quickly walked and talked her infant way into the hearts of all who knew her, and gave her parents great joy.

Vera's contentment was, however, soon disturbed by anxiety for her father in Vladivostok when Russia's conflict with Manchuria heightened.

When the Russo-Japanese War was declared in 1904, her father as Commander-in-Chief was indeed deeply involved, and calamities befell him. The north-western squadron of the Imperial Russian Fleet—engaged in manoeuvres in the Baltic at the time of the outbreak of hostilities—was urgently summoned to the support of the Far Eastern Fleet and although it set off immediately, it faced a very long journey. The Far Eastern Fleet, however, even pending the arrival of reinforcements, was making good progress and the battle for Port Arthur was going remarkably well. Alas, at the precise moment when Nikolai, who commanded operations from the flagship *Tsezarevitch*, ordered the Victory signal to be hoisted, a Japanese shell demolished the flagship's bridge.

In the incredible devastation caused by the this disaster; with the C-in-C lying unconscious and the second-in-command blown to pieces, the third officer, without knowledge of the nature of the signal silenced only moments earlier, ordered the signal for surrender to go up. Nicolai's wounds were relatively insignificant and he regained sufficient consciousness just in time to see the wrong signal going up, but he was not yet alert enough to be able to countermand it.

For the rest of his life Nicolai could not forgive himself for not having revived just that instant earlier, just soon enough to correct the monumental error of the final signal hoisted, the gravity of which was so blatantly obvious to him and which did so seriously affect the outcome of the war. The whole of European history could have been different without that shell and its consequences at precisely that crucial moment; but that is what wars depend on. Had Russia been the acknowledged victor then, her ultimate destiny is likely to have been shaped differently. History now endorses that Russia's defeat in the Russo-Japanese war was, to a very great extent, instrumental in the

My father and mother and their first daughter Ariadne

beginnings of the downfall of the Tsar, the start of the Revolution and the end of the Romanov dynasty.

In view of the admiral's rank a special concession was made to enable Nikolai, who subsequently became a prisoner of war in Japanese hands, to take continental treatment for the physical and psychological wounds he had sustained. Paroled on condition he would not re-enter Russia during hostilities, he was ultimately allowed to go to Italy where Marie had rented a house at Nervi, near Genoa for her husband's convalescence.

This house, described by the Italians as a *palazzo*, had terraced gardens overhanging the cliffs at the edge of the sea, where—accompanied by their young cadet son Shoura and temporarily by Sergei on leave from Freiberg with Vera and toddler Ariadne—they settled resignedly into exile. This, to their distress, proved to be longer than anticipated as negotiations dragged on for more than a year. Peace with Japan was not established until the Treaty of Portsmouth was signed on September 5th 1905, on somewhat humiliating terms for Russia.

YOUNG FAMILY LIFE

Fully qualified by the end of the Russo-Japanese war, Sergei returned to Russia and took up government service. Appointed to the cabinet as junior minister for Imperial Mines and Minerals, the empire's gold mines formed a large portion of his portfolio. This entailed many trips to Siberia and to different parts of the world, including the U.S.A. where he had first met Frank Reddaway.

The stays in Siberia tended to be long. This was a vast territory that Sergei knew well, but which held sad associations for him from his young days: his young brother Oleg and his beloved mother had both died there. The tragedy that befell my parents there devastated them totally. Their adored little three-year-old daughter Ariadne had picked up meningitis somewhere on their travels, from which, to their utter inconsolable desolation, she died in a matter of only a few shattering hours.

Back in St. Petersburg, my mother grieved and ailed. She was unwell for so long that tuberculosis was suspected, but after nearly four years of care and Sergei's devotion, though still downcast, she began to recover and by 1909 it was medically agreed that she was well enough for them to hope that a new young life might heal the wound of their loss.

To everyone's delight, and bringing great happiness with him, young Nicolas arrived in November of that year. Busy, contented years unfolded for the young family. Devoted relatives and friends surrounded them; proud grandparents Nikolai and Marie came for long visits, as also did the now considerably aged great-aunt Tatiana, still surrounded by elegance appropriate to her age, and devotedly accompanied by her genial husband.

These family visits were enjoyed by everyone, especially Aunt Natasha, who was an almost permanent member of the family, and whose warm personality beamed through her friendly face. Uncles Vassia and Ossia in their

Proud grandfather Admiral Nikolai Matousseyvitch with my brother Nicholas in 1910

smart uniforms, bedecked with well-deserved medals and decorations, enjoyed the considerable company on their long and frequent stays. The house
in the Royal Park of the Imperial Summer Palace of Tsarskoye Selo near St.
Petersburg was a comfortable home with its own extensive gardens. The men
pored over long games of chess in well-tended conservatories where the
ladies embroidered intricate tapestries, or read exciting books between
leisurely walks and admired the be-flowered pagodas and summer houses.

The new member of the family came in for a lot of affectionate admiration
as he was proudly held in Nanny Liza's loving and contented arms. She too
had grieved over the loss of her earlier charge and, having devotedly cared for
my mother in their sorrow, was now glad to have resumed her real duties.

Four years after Nicolas, a little sister arrived in 1913 adding to the family's happiness and to the boy's great pleasure. Nicolas regarded the baby as a special present for him, and eagerly awaited the arrival of the moustache to which he felt he was entitled 'like all fathers'. When asked what name he would like for the baby, he thought she should be called like the big waist-high marguerites amongst which he liked to play, but since he could not remember the real name of his favourite flowers, she became Antonina in honour of an earlier pre-Orthodoxy member of the family.

According to the custom of Russian Orthodoxy a child on christening has to be dedicated to a saint, whose name is bestowed on the baby. As there is

Aunt Natasha with me and brother Nicholas at Tsarkoye Selo near St. Petersburg

no St. Antonina, the little sister, though named Antonina was dedicated to Saint Nina. It seems she was a young girl who had brought Christianity to southern Russia and was said to have been 'almost equal to the apostles' and it is her name that I carried into the sun-kissed life that rolled smoothly and happily along.

My father's busy life absorbed him rewardingly, and my mother enjoyed her palace duties. These, by that time, involved little more than reading to the older members of the imperial family when in residence.

Before long, when Sergei took on the necessary technology for Moscow to draw water from artesian wells, the family moved to a tall, balconied house with views over the linking lakes at Ozerki (Little Lakes) near Moscow, where we children enjoyed being rowed by one or the other of our parents over the still and glistening waters.

Although by this time Sergei had resumed military service, amongst his various discoveries and inventions, his involvement in the production of smokeless gunpowder resulted in his being given control of the imperial government's production of explosives. This resulted in the family moving to the Alexandrov Mills, referred to as *Zavodi* (mills) that, although also near Moscow, were in a very different terrain.

Life was now centred in the midst of dense forest camouflaging a remotely positioned government gunpowder production centre. It consisted of research establishments and extensive factories, mills and housing for operatives, and

My mother, Nicholas, and me picking fruit in the garden of the house at Ozerki outside Moscow

A gunpowder mill at Zavodi

was served by an intricate, sprawling tree-hidden railway system on the edge of which we lived.

Our house was a solid single-storey, newly built timber dwelling with rows of tall heavily shuttered and richly curtained windows in vast inter-communicating parquet-floored rooms. These provided wonderful facilities for Nicolas's toy railway systems. Convoys would take many minutes to complete circuits, and cause great delight when a busy little sizzling-sounding train suddenly immerged from around the corner of an adjoining room.

Both of us enjoyed being driven along rough tracks through the forest in the donkey-drawn governess cart, or a bell-bedecked sleigh in winter. At other times great pleasure was derived from visits to the domestic regions of the house where brief glimpses into the icehouse, and feeding the chickens, were great pastimes. As the chickens soon became our friends, Nicolas had to assure me that the chickens that came roasted for the table had nothing to do with our pets: these were specially made for eating.

TURBULENCE STARTS

As political unrest intensified, my father began to grow anxious about his family. As 1917 approached and conditions deteriorated even in our remote area, he felt it was time to arrange for his family to move to a safer region, and he and Vera decided that Pyatigorsk (Five Hills) in the Caucasus would be suitable.

Pyatigorsk was a small town they had known in a peaceful area of hilltop resorts, sanatoria and spas in the mountains inland from the Black Sea's eastern coast. My parents had often stayed at nearby Kislovodsk (Sour Waters), another hilltop health resort where they had spent long periods of convalescence while Nicolas recovered from the damaged heart that rheumatic fever had left him, and Vera regained her strength after the strain of the boy's illness.

Having made the necessary arrangements Sergei took leave from his service duties and supervised the methodical packing of the household for the move to the Caucasus.

Duly packed items were loaded into suitable long-distance removal wagons at a convenient railway halt near the house and, once filled and securely sealed, the wagons were moved on for their further main-line journey to Pyatigorsk. The family; Vera, Nanny Liza, we two children, widowed grandmother Marie and Great Aunt Natasha—both of whom now lived with us most of the time—were to follow as soon as everything was packed. While the family assembled the personal travelling items usually regarded as necessary for a normal long passenger-train journey, Sergei anxiously wished he could be seeing the travellers to their destination. He did not know how serious his foreboding was.

While all these preparations were busily going on, conditions amongst the mill workers were beginning to get difficult and, to Sergei's horror, havoc and insubordination were spreading and began to run riot amongst the removal men as well as the mill staff. Items still in the house, such as his beloved

My father, Nicholas, and me in happier times before the Revolution

grand piano, were suddenly brutally smashed before his anguished eyes. Other treasures too were being flagrantly destroyed instead of being packed.

Surrounded by the rapidly spreading anarchy it was now imperative for the family to get away, but they were stunned to learn that all railways had come to a standstill. It soon became apparent the only hope of any means of possible transport would be the few incompletely loaded removal wagons. The few remaining loyal mill transport men assured Sergei that the establishment engines would still work.

Having no other choice, Sergei helped his family into one of the so-called house-moving trucks, only to find that all the wagons were filled nearly to capacity with mill operatives and their families. With nothing but his confidence in Vera's good sense to bolster his fears for the family's immediate and future safety, and after anguished goodbyes were exchanged, a distraught Sergei briefly returned to the shattered house in grief and anxiety before rejoining his unit. He did not know until much later that all the family possessions and those of the various relatives and retainers — so seemingly sensibly dispatched to would-be safety — were never seen or heard of again. Nor did he know that his little family group had been marooned in the middle of nowhere with only what they carried for sustenance.

He did, however, learn much too soon that the whole of the Caucasus was now a vicious theatre of war, and that he was virtually destitute. His resources;

bank securities, property, lands and personal goldfield involvement and whatever ownership he had anywhere, were all summarily confiscated and annulled.

Squashed into a corner of the overcrowded removal wagon, the four weary
and benumbed ladies and we two children huddled dozily in the slowly
trundling train, and faced the unpredictable. Liza had wisely brought some
travel provisions which, rationed, sustained us until the train's eventual final
halt some days later in an unknown part of the country. Though the ghastly
journey had dragged on a long time it had in fact covered little distance, and
our little group found itself in alien territory with no known destination.

In a desperate search for shelter the group trailed forth, each carrying what
they could of their dwindling hand luggage. By happy chance a modicum of
elementary comfort was found in an empty house. Settling themselves as best
they could my mother, Marie and Aunt Natasha endeavoured to find out
where they were, and to work out what to do next. Their only hope of refuge
in the bleak prospects facing them was Marie's house in Sevastopol many
thousands of miles away in Crimea.

In the absence of public or private transport, even when eventually a degree of public transport revived, without money for either, the only way to get
anywhere was to walk: a daunting trek to undertake. The women realised they
would need courage, endurance and opportunity to move toward their goal.

My mother soon grew to expect the worst in any situation, and was not surprised that even in our first chance haven the family was subjected to searches
by 'the Reds' who, under the guise of officialdom, plundered valuables from
people's homes. Because body searches were included in these raids, my mother
soon realised she must hide the few valuables she had secreted about her person.

She found an opening small enough to exclude anyone except a small child
into the foundations of the house and helped Nicolas squeeze through it to
bury her small bundle. She hoped he would remember the spot well enough
to retrieve the treasure later.

Eventually we moved on, but progress was indeed slow and hazardous.
There were times when, in the absence of other chance accommodation, we
all huddled together in forest clearings with my mother and Liza taking turns
at keeping a bonfire burning throughout the dark hours. *Kasha* (buckwheat
porridge), made on the embers of the fire in the enamel jerry-pot that had
been a child's travelling companion in earlier times, was a welcome beginning for uncertain days. Later in the year when the weather eased, such
bivouacs were occasionally highlighted with cobs of sweet corn snipped off
surreptitiously at the edge of a swaying field of maize, and boiled in an old
bucket balanced on stones over a brushwood fire.

The precious old bucket was our main cooking utensil. In it water was
heated for the luxury of brewing tea. This was made from treasured sun-dried

slithers of carrot. Occasionally a farm cart might give us a lift on our weary and uncertain way. Although it would be much appreciated, Vera tended to distrust the motives of any assistance offered; though on the whole, we encountered a great deal of kindness as, in the disorganised conditions everywhere, like-minded people were willing to share and shelter, and there was much give and take.

With shoes soon wearing out or becoming too small for her children, my mother managed to devise footwear from strips of canvas and chunks of wood. In time she learned how to make real shoes, and was able to earn some 'keep' by fabricating people's relatively suitable material into what had to serve for shoes. As winter approached we had the good fortune to manage to share part of an abandoned *dacha*, someone's summer holiday bungalow, where we stayed for a considerable period. Scattered wood was gathered for fuel, and oil—in a saucer with a bit of string lying in it for a wick—supplied light.

As time went on and we got further south, our small convoy fell in with migrating refugee Cossack families who were fleeing from war zones that seemed to spring up in unpredictable areas. Distant gunfire and the "whoosh" of shells overhead varied in direction as we plodded on. This was either the result of opposed troops repositioning themselves, or by independent interchange of gunfire between contesting bandit groups who fought for their own ends.

Finding shelter on reaching anywhere that looked like a town or hamlet, was even more difficult than in the country. Most dwelling houses were tightly packed with weary families in every room. Many such overfilled houses got burnt down because, needing warmth and cooking facilities, exhausted ignorant occupants inserted flues for their improvised braziers into random holes they made into wooden walls without looking for any evidence of a chimney. Other fires resulted from stray shells. 'In and out' shell holes in the opposing sides of pitched roofs of semi-demolished houses were to be seen everywhere. The glow of conflagrations lit up night skies following distant gunfire, and the catastrophic firework displays of exploding ammunition dumps were a common accompaniment to the family's progress, leaving indelible scars in both our young minds.

Nearly twelve months of trekking eventually brought our little family to Tuapse, a small seaport on the lovely, sandy Caucasian east coast of the Black Sea, from where ships plied across to the Crimea.

Since Aunt Natasha had at one time lived in Tuapse, we were able to find shelter in what had once been her home. As the area was at that time still held by the White army, and Sergei's and Shoura's units were serving in the Caucasus, we stayed there nearly a year in comparatively civilised conditions. We were vaccinated, and Oxo cubes and corned beef were available thanks to British Red Cross relief supplies.

Though the White army valiantly fought many long and fierce battles throughout the country, the Red army advanced and forced the Whites down towards the coast. When eventually Novorossiysk fell in March 1920, Crimea—with its isthmus fortifications further reinforced—became the White army's last stronghold on the anniversary of "Red October."

With overland access severed, the only means of reaching the Crimean peninsula was by sea. As Marie's house in Crimea was our only hope of sanctuary the men hastened to Tuapse to pick up the family hoping to take a ferry from there to Sevastopol. Assembling portable essentials we all set off for the pier only to find it solid with people anxious to leave the Caucasus.

LEAVING TUAPSE

Hampered by their bundles the family faced having to elbow their way through the crowd to reach the landing stages at the end of the pier. With my hand in Marie's, and Nicolas's in my mother's, we followed my father and Liza. Shoura and Aunt Natasha, more heavily laden, had even greater difficulty in making headway.

The ladies with the children were better at squeezing between people, and got to the boats first. They were aghast to see how the moored vessels were rapidly overfilling and having to cast off to prevent getting dangerously overloaded. Marie and I managed to board an almost full boat, but when Marie realised that it was about to cast off—and that my mother and Nicolas were still on the jetty—she quickly insisted; on the strength of being "the widow of Admiral Matousseyevitch," that her daughter and grandson must be taken on board. As the ship was still within arms' reach of the dock, the captain ordered the sailors on the quay to pick up the lady and the boy bodily, and hand them across the rapidly widening gap to the outstretched arms of the perilously positioned sailors at the rails of the rocking and progressively receding vessel.

Mercifully no one fell into the churning water. My father and Shoura and the two other ladies, only managed to get to the landing stage as the last ship was casting off and though grudgingly, Liza and Aunt Natasha were allowed to scramble on, but the two men were left behind.

During that day while the greater part of the townspeople had been trying to leave, Tuapse had fallen into the hands of an unnamed and unknown mob of bandits. These people allowed any women left on the pier to filter back into the town but pronounced all the men to be prisoners. These they hustled off somewhere for some incomprehensible trial; no one knew where they were taken, nor why, except that as they had been trying to leave they were regarded as enemies.

The men's captors, who announced themselves as 'Greens' proceeded to set up a so-called court in some building they had commandeered, and began to question the twenty or so of their captives. They sought knowledge of the strength and disposition of both the Red and the White armies. Just when the inquisition was becoming intense and ugly, the lights failed. In the ensuing confusion my father and Shoura volunteered to mend the lighting:

As the fault proved to need radical repair, the trial proceedings were moved elsewhere, and by the time the two men finished the work there were no other prisoners about. To their surprise and relief the Green officials told my father and his brother-in-law to "just go." With quick thinking and feigned self-assurance, my father calmly claimed their earlier confiscated watches and rings, and clenching the unexpectedly returned property in their fists, both of them eagerly slipped out of the building.

As they emerged, cringing against a raging snowstorm, they were hailed by the carter who was returning from the gruesome task of having removed the other prisoners. Barely able to speak with disgust at what he had witnessed, the carter told them of the fate the two of them had escaped: all the removed men had been stripped naked in the snow and had had their eyes pierced with bayonets before being shot.

Realising the mercy of their amazing good fortune Sergei and Shoura hurried away not knowing where they were going. Eventually, gathering together their shattered thoughts they found their way to Sochi, a bigger port just a little further south along the coast where the British Cruiser *HMS Calypso*, having completed her delivery of Red Cross Relief supplies to beleaguered Russians, was getting up steam for her journey back to England. Mercifully, on hearing the two men's story, the captain gave Sergei and Shoura passage to Crimea.

On this journey, needing to send essential business information to Frank Reddaway in England but unable to do so in the absence of any postal services, my father wrote his friend an overdue letter and entrusted it to the captain.

When my mother and the rest of the family—all desperately anxious about Sergei and Shoura, whom they had last seen in Tuapse—eventually managed to reach Sevastopol they found Marie's house full of refugees squatting in it. Fortunately Uncle Vassia, who was still in his official apartment in the Admiralty buildings on the heights of the northern arm of the port, was able to accommodate all the family temporarily where, at long last, the two bewildered men eventually reached them.

Overjoyed at their return, but stunned by the account they heard, the reunited family waited for room to be made for them in Marie's house. Only when the squatters were eventually reshuffled enough for the family to fit in, were they able to occupy a part of it.

The house had been the Matousseyevitch home for many generations, but was by then in considerable disrepair. It was a typical Russian town dwelling, extending far into grounds behind its long low frontage on Bolshaia Morskaia, one of the main roads of the southern arm of the port. Wide carriage gates at the side of the house opened on to a drive that passed the intricate side of the main building to a descending series of wide quadrangles, at the bottom of which broad wooden double gates opened into gardens. Old orchards and neglected former flower gardens reached down to a wide south-facing deeply-walled kitchen garden where I loved to day-dream amidst the bee-humming peace into which the faint, mournful *Azan*, the Muslim call to prayer, occasionally drifted from far-distant minarets.

Stables, carriage sheds, grooms' and coaching staff quarters, barns and storehouses lined the various quadrangles. All these buildings were now filled with refugees. Since these people had fortunately not taken advantage of the land, Sergei and Shoura dug the gardens that soon rewarded them with generous crops of tomatoes and every vegetable sown. As the mature peach and apricot trees yielded luscious crops, food was no problem during 1920, the year they spent in Sevastopol, and from where they ultimately reached England's Manchester.

Chapter Two

Manchester Days

WINMARLEIGH

In contrast to the dismal hours of our first arrival in Manchester, the stay at Winmarleigh was bliss. The fact that the house was full of guests did not surprise any of us because in our 'normal' lives families were made up of different branches and generations.

The actual Reddaway family consisted of Mr. Reddaway and Mrs. Turner—Frank and Annushka—and three adult daughters Constance, Frances and Edith (whose husband Tom Warburton was away in Australia). Annushka was the delightful long-standing and beloved family friend who became the second Mrs Reddaway when Frank's first wife died after many invalid years spent in a Southport nursing home. Harold, the only son who had long set up his own home, was not there.

With January safely launched, the house buzzed with the busy comings and goings of departure. Heartfelt thanks and affectionate goodbyes were being exchanged as the family station wagon and the Rolls-Royce conveyed groups of departing guests to their various trains.

When the last visitor had been warmly waved away, normal family routine resumed the smooth flow of its measured pace into which Vera, Sergei, Nicolas and I quickly settled. Afternoon tea, served in the drawing room by Rawlings the butler, was followed by leisurely walks in the gardens before dressing for dinner. The evenings were spent in conversation, embroidery and a little piano playing by the daughters while the men played billiards and reminisced.

My brother and I had meals in the morning room, served by a plump little uniformed parlour maid supervised by Bridges, the housekeeper, who occasionally enquired whether we were content. In fact we badly missed the wise

Frank Reddaway, our benefactor in England

and patient presence of Nanny Liza, who had been our guide and guardian since our earliest days. When faced with bananas—another fruit we had not seen before—we decided to slice them like *kalbasah* (German sausage), but the bitter taste of the skin of these discs convinced us that the curious curved yellow items could never have been intended for eating!

The rabbits on the extensive lawns around the house enchanted us, and though we adored the lambs and calves at the home farm, we could hardly be dragged away from the carpenter's shop, where the foreman shaped up stumps, bails and a cricket bat for Nicolas.

Winmarleigh eventually came to be the virtual home where Nicolas and I did the most important part of our British growing up, since we and our parents were guests there during practically all the school and bank holidays of our early lives in England.

It was as "guests", or as the immigration authorities termed us "exceptional guests", that we were isolated from the myriad Russian émigrés who were congregating in London at the time.

For my parents this "guest" status imposed conditions that obliged them to "stay put" with the Reddaways until such time as we became eligible for naturalization. They were happy to comply; the alternative was to risk being returned to Communist Russia, which could have resulted in my father's execution, and our disappearance into some *gulag*.

Staying at the Reddaways imposed some isolation on us. There were very few Russians in Manchester, other than a couple we met occasionally; the woman was a singer, the man a former employee with Mather & Platt, a machine-making firm with a factory in Russia.

In any event, socialising was largely precluded by my parents' need to work. They had landed in England with Nansen passports—the temporary identity cards issued by the League of Nations to stateless refugees—but with no money. Social activities like the theatre, or gallery visits, even the solitary comfort of books all required money, as did the simple pleasure of toys.

Winmarleigh Hall, the home of the Reddaways, and our shelter on arrival in England

The Reddaway family's old retired motor cars, brick-mounted in the various former carriage-sheds, and lovingly cared for by the two family chauffeurs, occupied us for hours on end, taking us on endless wild and hair-raising imaginary jaunts. Our special favourite was the old disused Ford station-wagon which, nosed-up against a dark brick wall, took us up the Amazon, across the Sahara and into many of the fiercest battles; not to mention the big-game hunts we conducted in it, vanquishing Zulu warriors in the process.

On other occasions, strictly confined to the estate boundaries, well supplied with picnic provisions and accompanied by Mr Reddaway's ageing fox terrier, Nicolas and I went on country explorations. As we grew, we accompanied the family on stately tours of special areas of the estate and joined them for croquet and, in time, were allowed to try playing tennis. The billiard table, however, was taboo.

Sergei enchanted the ladies with the superb photographic studies he made of all of them. He had fortunately been able to salvage and bring with him his wonderfully accurate concertina-fronted Kodak camera that used bromide quarter-plates. Photography having been his favourite hobby, he developed the plates himself and could show results without delay. Vera painted, embroidered and talked French with Annushka and the daughters in the afternoons, occasionally joining Constance in singing to Frank's accompaniment on his Steinway grand in the evenings.

As my family's first visit began to draw to a close, the question of our immediate future and accommodation in Manchester had to be decided. Frank was confident that "all this nonsense in Russia" would soon blow over, during which time Sergei could get a thorough knowledge of industrial belting manufacture and become a well-equipped key man to restart the Reddaway businesses in Russia. In the meantime he was to share an office with a Mr. Murphy, the works manager at the Pendleton factory, who was commissioned to find rooms for the family.

Immediately hostile to the presence of this Russian man being foisted on him, Murphy proceeded with his commission with all the malice that smouldered in his mind throughout the long and difficult period of his association with Sergei. He arranged for our family to take two barely-furnished top floor rooms in a shabby house in the Bury New Road part of Cheetham Hill, a badly run-down area of Manchester.

The happy stay at Winmarleigh had not prepared us for the conditions that we now faced. The rooms chosen by Murphy were rented from a Mrs. Jenkinson, a shrivelled scrooge of a woman, who flapped about in broken bedroom slippers clutching at a much-stained apron. Her young teenage son Clarence, in a peaked tweed cap with a button on top, gawked at us, while a

Sergei in 1931, resplendent in his suit, in Mr. Murphy's office in Pendleton

seemingly ill-treated wisp of a Mr. Jenkinson—whose celluloid dicky preceded his every movement in spite of his occasional attempts at repositioning it into the confines of his ill-fitting jacket—scuttled away into the back regions of the house. Whilst showing the bewildered new tenants into their prospective quarters, Mrs. Jenkinson briefly opened the door into a small room next to the one due to be ours and pronounced menacingly: "I didn't think you'd want this one."

The glimpse of a bed piled high with coloured papers, the recently dismantled Christmas decorations and paper chains, convinced me, (I had never seen coloured paper decorations before) that there was a dead body on that bed. Many spook-haunted unhappy days had to pass before I could be reassured to the contrary.

Education was promptly arranged for Nicolas and me at the local church school, and although years earlier in St. Petersburg, on hearing the Reddaways speak 'peculiarly', we had twittered at each other in what we called English, we actually knew none.

One day Sergei and Vera were perplexed to find they were the centre of great interest to nuns in a convent in nearby Bury, who suddenly showered my brother and me with beautifully knitted tiny dolls' cotton clothes and many other such delights. The interest, however, ceased as abruptly as it had begun when the nuns realised that Russian Orthodoxy was more akin to Anglicanism than to Catholicism. A young novice, who did not complete her noviciate, did continue to keep up a friendship with my mother, who enjoyed occasional visits with the little lady in her Forest of Bowland home. Later Vera also derived great pleasure from her several happy stays with Annushka at her lovely London home.

The difficult Cheetham Hill stay ended when Sergei had the good fortune to find pleasant rooms within easy reach of the Reddaway Pendleton factory, in a place called Eccles, now a part of Greater Manchester, and from where Eccles cakes are reputed to have come. Oddly these puff pastries are stuffed with Greek currants, so perhaps they were the product of other earlier immigrants to the city.

Promptly starting at the Eccles Clarendon Road Council School, Nicolas was put into a class according to his age, where his language problem made learning difficult. Fortunately my class mistress, a Mrs Roughley, took great interest in the two small newcomers and their disorientated parents. On hearing of the boy's troubles Mrs Roughley offered to coach him. A very satisfactory arrangement was quickly arrived at in which, in return for Nicolas's English lessons, Vera taught French to Mrs Roughley's son Charlie. Before long this arrangement led to Vera starting French classes for other neighbouring children.

Though both Nicolas and I soon picked up English, overawed by the cheeky behaviour of some of the rougher children, we continued to feel strange and out of touch with our new companions. Though Sergei and Vera wished they could send us to other schools, it was just not possible. Some considerable time later, however, and to our great delight, a Christmas came when our wonderful presents proved to be a Pendleton High School hat band for me, and the little Oxford and Cambridge blue-striped Manchester Grammar School cap, with its silver owl badge, for Nicolas.

The joy of the prospect of going to the high school was temporarily clouded for me when, proudly dressed in the white blouse and navy blue gym-slip uniform of the new school, I was taken to an empty classroom and faced with an incomprehensible long-division sum. Dismayed that my ignorance was going to debar me from that school, I was relieved to find that the test was just to gauge my class placing. But for Vera and Sergei the problem of the cost of two schools had been daunting for a long time. Four guineas per term for the high school, and eight per term for the grammar school, together with tram and train fares, came to quite a lot of money to find, and had spurred them to ceaseless efforts to create additional income.

BIRTH OF THE STUDIO

As those bewildering early days wore on, my mother began to hear that England's ladies were starting to experiment with tooled leather work. As this had been part of the applied art in which she had dabbled during her time in Germany at the beginning of the century, she wondered whether her past experience might prove useful. With this in mind, she went to an evening leatherwork class. To her delight, as soon as her expertise and abilities were discovered, she was invited to become a teacher, and long evenings of 'night school' teaching began. Her 'charming English' also proved to be quite an asset.

Needing to buy materials in order to make a leather bag as a 'specimen' for pupils to copy, she borrowed five shillings from Violet Winks, our friendly landlady. With the borrowed money Vera bought 'calf' (the leather that can be tooled), 'skiver' for lining, and cut thongs of 'persian.' She worked out how to 'frame' a purse, with a little friendly help from a tool-shop salesman, and proudly made her first handbag. Having launched the pupils on making various versions of the specimen, the bag was anxiously bought by one of them, enabling Vera to buy tools and materials for further 'specimens' and widen her scope.

The fact that the Art Deco style was coming into vogue at that time, and department stores did not yet have fancy goods sections—and people wanted to beautify their homes—my mother's various craft accomplishments were soon in demand. She quickly realised she needed to find rooms in which to give lessons. After a long search, Settle Speakman, a Manchester coaling firm agreed to rent her a small upstairs office for one afternoon a week on their city premises at 100 Deansgate. As this happened to be in the heart of Manchester's smartest shopping area, it suited Vera well.

This arrangement, however, soon proved to be inadequate, and a long busy scouring of the town ultimately led her to consider a small ground floor room. Although small—and with little in the way of facilities—these shortcomings were outweighed by the fact the room was in St. Mary's Street, a busy side street branching off Deansgate near her first rented room, and had a window on to the street. The window was suitably low to be used as a shop window, so my mother took the lease and bravely launched "The Studio."

My mother, Nicholas, and me, ready for school at Monton

In the later 1920s and early 1930s England, together with the rest of Europe, was descending into the Depression. As factories were forced to lie idle the Reddaway "Camel Hair" Industrial Belting business was becoming less prosperous, and as Russia—deep in her own troubles—was not likely to have the hoped-for prospects, Frank Reddaway was forced to review his business situation. To his deep regret, but coerced by his main managing staff who had long been irked by the 'Russian connection', Frank was compelled to include my father in staff cuts.

Unfortunately Frank had been involved in a gun accident at one of his shoots just at the time when the official notices were due to go out, and so had not been able to break the news to Sergei personally. This resulted in a very official notice terminating Sergei's £25 monthly 'marking-time' salary being presented to him very starkly. My father, unaware of Frank's accident, was more shattered by his friend's silence than by the distress of the sudden financial drop. He had frequently made tentative requests for some degree of responsibility in the firm, without stressing the tedium and degradation of his existence with the barely competent Murphy at Pendleton, but his ideas had always been countered by Frank's reassurance that he would soon be required in Russia. Nor had Sergei spoken much about his and Vera's efforts at regaining some degree of independence by teaching languages and the developing Studio.

Though dismayed by the sudden loss of his regular income, my father welcomed the release from his useless and demoralising work-time enslavement. He took a more active part in the development of the infant Studio and was glad to devote more time to his Russian language teaching, for which there was a growing demand. Russia's immense cultural wealth was becoming better known in Europe as a result of the dispersal of the greater part of Tsarist Russia's most cultured population into its various capitals. This, together with the grandiose promises of Communism — which were conjuring up visions of the revival of great industrial and commercial prospects — gave people wild hopes. As some knowledge of the Russian language was essential in all these developments, people were clamouring for instruction, and my father was glad to teach them.

The Studio, now with a display window, besides teaching crafts was able to sell the articles it produced. Making stock for sale became quite an industry. Nicolas, my father and I were soon quite adept at making small items such as decorated comb-cases, leather key containers, purses, artificial flowers and painted glassware, while my mother created pewter vases, leather blotters and address book covers, as well as other such articles that people were glad to buy. To help the business grow Vera arranged pre-Christmas exhibitions, much along the lines of the present-day charity sales. Held in a rented suite of rooms in one of Manchester's smartest hotels, these Christmas sales soon became yearly 'friends-meeting occasions'.

As Nicolas and I grew, the family needed more space than we had sharing Miss Winks' Eccles house. My parents were glad to learn about council housing. A small development of these had just been built in the adjoining village of Monton; the next railway station along the line from Manchester and several stops on the tram route, but securing one of these was no easy matter. Doing his best to further the family's claim, the local parish curate, a Mr. Oliver, took me in the rickety sidecar of his motorcycle to call on a friendly lady councillor, a Mrs. McIntyre, who gave us tea and seemed very sympathetic.

My preoccupation in the proceedings was whether, if my parents got a house, we would be able to have a little dog. Happily we were eventually allocated a three-bedroom end-of-terrace house, and a little dog materialised. Duly named *Druzjhok* (Little Friend) but more easily said as Droogy in English, to both of which versions the friendly little Springer spaniel puppy responded with a joyous wagging of the tail and body, to everyone's delight.

My father, Nicholas, and me with dear little Droogy

Though sorry to leave Eccles, we were glad to have a whole house to live in. Gradually my parents bought simple well-made furniture on the instalment system, and slowly proceeded with home-making amidst the wilderness that surrounded them.

Galvanized wire and concrete posts subdivided the rubble-filled ground into plots around each of the newly-built houses. These areas took much subduing before they roughly resembled elementary gardens. Though most roofs were festooned with aerials, peace was not disturbed as wireless telephony was only at the crystal set stage in the mid-1920s, and the rarely received transmissions were confined to earphones.

Soon settled in, the family's life progressed. Nicolas and I grew, the Studio expanded, and my parents' daytime and evening teaching increased.

As Droogy had to be left alone all day, my father devised a splendid contraption, a precursor of the cat or dog flap, which gave the young pup access to and from the scullery. The difficulty with this arrangement was that it did not prevent the devoted young animal from following members of the family as we left the house for school or work. To begin with this was a great trouble, but in time the sensible creature learned he could follow as long as he turned back when told to do so, either at the bottom of the railway station steps or at the tram stop. Occasionally, however, he was known to try following by taking the next tram!

As I was the first to get back from school, Droogy's ecstatic welcome with tail and body wiggle and face-licks soon dispelled the dismay that engulfed me in the chilly, untended house; the previous day's cold ashy grate and the morning's breakfast table disarray staring at me, together with unmade beds upstairs and emptiness. Having done household shopping on the way home, the smell of a warm cob loaf very often tempted me to postpone setting about the obvious tasks that cried out to be done, by sharing a buttered crust with Droogy: bad for both our figures!

Vera did her best to pre-prepare food for the family. She assembled stews and Lancashire hot-pots, recipes taught to her by our good friend Miss Winks in those bewildering early days. Rice puddings and baked apples, dishes well within my ten-year-old cooking capability, were soon on the family's regular menu, though in the process my fringes and eyebrows often got singed off by flashes of exploding gas! Homemade cakes and steamed puddings were the envied fare only met at other people's homes. As by this time my mother was teaching in Manchester most weekday evenings, our family's main meal took place on Sergei's six o'clock return from Pendleton, Vera's portion being kept for her return.

After a while, when my parents began to feel they could just afford to do so, to everyone's delight, they arranged to employ Millie, a highly recommended part-time housekeeper. Alas, Millie's first morning brought not her smiling face, but a note saying she wasn't coming. The tears which I had to bite back were very bitter; all the cared-for clothes I had hoped for, the ironed blouses, clean stockings, made beds, warm house and dusted staircase were not to be. Fairly soon after that sad flutter, on hearing that the house next door to our earlier shared Eccles home was 'To Let', we gladly settled into it.

One of Eccles' salient features, besides its cakes, is its lovely old square-towered parish church. Built on a hill above the steeply descending main street, it towers nobly above the village, displaying its Norman arches. Although we children had been christened Russian Orthodox, we attended the children's three o'clock services held every Sunday in the church's lovely nave, by Canon Ross, the rector. These services were actually a shortened version of Evensong, with ceremony and ritual geared for young minds, fully respecting their understanding and stimulating their interest in, and feeling for, religion. As a consequence of these services Nicolas began to feel that the church could be his vocation.

Though Canon Ross had encouraged him, he wisely ruled out the idea on discovering Nicolas to be tone-deaf, but he continued to be interested in the family. This friendship enabled Sergei to have many happy chats with the canon's daughter Lesley, a tall, late-teen-age girl as good-humoured and sociable as her father, who enjoyed hearing Sergei's accounts of life in Russia. As Lesley was about to launch into medicine, a very unusual career for a woman at that time, the information she imparted about medical training eventually proved very valuable to Sergei when it came to deciding on Nicolas' future.

As all Sergei's careers had been disrupted by outside influences, he wanted his children to have careers that no political situation could destroy. As a medical qualification provided an entry into a universally-needed profession, my father wished he and Vera could see their way to finance the cost of such an education should either Nicolas or I—perhaps even both of us—choose medical careers.

Just at that time, following the Dental Act of 1921, dentistry (formerly regarded as a craft) became a profession. At that time the cost of university training was the responsibility of parents, but some universities, including Manchester, were offering places that carried the possibility of small bursaries to encourage suitable young men to take up dentistry. Art and drama had interested Nicolas, but as kindness and the urge to minister to people began to determine his bent, the idea of becoming a dentist had some appeal for him.

Calculating very carefully, Sergei and Vera decided that as long as their various work projects continued they would, especially if helped by a bursary, be able to meet the situation, and in 1928 Nicolas entered Manchester University Dental School.

Very able with his hands, he would have done well in dentistry, but as time went on his interest in medicine began to outweigh that in dentistry. Because the pre-clinical courses are the same for the two professions, and are run concurrently, students had the option of transferring from one school to the other at the end of the first year. Nicolas, eager to transfer to medicine, asked his parents whether he might change. By this time the Studio was growing, and the demand for both Vera's and Sergei's teaching continued to increase, so they felt they could face the costs of the longer training, and were happy for Nicolas to make the transfer. They also calculated it would be cheaper for them to live closer to the university.

After much searching, and many anxieties, they found a pretty, medium sized semi-detached house with four bedrooms in Victoria Park, a residential area near the university where many of the formerly privately owned large houses had become Student Residences, hotels or apartments. Although the £350 asked for the house they liked was a lot of money for them to find, as it suited them and was within easy walking distance of the Medical school, and only a short bus ride from the Studio and evening schools, they decided to buy it. After many delays and risking unduly costly loans, 38 Park Range, Victoria Park, became the family home for the next thirty-three years.

COLLEGE

From our early childhood Nicolas and I were a closely-knit team; Nicolas, as the older, was boss and I became 'the troops'. So, when 'boss' was doing medicine, 'troops' automatically expected to follow suit especially as, like Nicolas and most teenagers, I too was fired with the urge to help people, heal sick animals and generally overflowed with warm humanity.

In the family's uprooted circumstances Vera had, from my earliest adolescence, impressed on me that careers and independence were to be my goal in life, vaguely hinting enigmatic warnings against the subject of marriage: something my juvenile mind regarded as story book and magazine material.

Still vaguely imbued with the schoolgirl notion of irreconcilable animosity between boys and girls, as depicted in the *Just William* stories of Richmal Crompton, the idea of marriage seemed a totally incomprehensible sphere, and one which—I was told—was apparently not to encompass me.

Conversations with the Reddaway ladies on the subject of any advanced education for me had been frowned on as unwomanly, and the thought of a woman going in for medicine was regarded as totally unseemly; marriage, pre-ordained by social standing, being any woman's obvious but unmentioned aim. As these ladies' views came from the security of established af-

fluence; a condition no longer available to my mother's family, and accorded
with customs that were beginning to be out-dated, their ideas only endorsed
Vera's feeling that women needed a new status.

Daunted by her own insecure, new, un-classed and penny-pinching position, she trusted that a university education would adequately equip her diffi-
dent and ingénue young daughter with the required emancipation.

Totally immersed in the need to work to provide essential funds, Sergei and
Vera were unaware of how out of touch they were with their career-intent but
un-self-assured children. The idea of the 'modern' behaviour of women,
which was by that time beginning to be generally accepted if not wholly expected, was totally alien to them. Due to these strictly Victorian views—in
which both parents had been brought up without mention of the rightness of
sexuality and its place in people's lives—both Nicolas and I were inade-
quately prepared for the prevailing conditions.

Full of teenage benevolence, but with the deeply ingrained belief that independence was the only mode of life to be embarked on, perplexed, defen-
sive and self-deprecating, I eventually plodded doggedly into medicine some
three years behind Nicolas's jaunty launch into the career.

Nicolas, a handsome, dark-haired, hazel-eyed, agile young man with an
aura of mysterious past glories of a lost imperial Russia around him, was thoroughly enjoying university life. He took up fencing, in which he did well, but
was ignorant of the fact that "getting husbands by degrees" was the current
trend for post-World War One young ladies. He did not know that prospective
doctors were regarded as 'good catches,' nor did he realise how clever and determined some of these young women were in achieving their ends.

Student days are a time when young romance flourishes, and Nicolas' first
love soon became a dark-eyed and alluring Armenian girl. There was nothing
of the scheming young woman about Adrienne, who came from a large happy
family of many affectionate brothers and sisters. She was just a young girl
bounding with energy and fun, who was as truly captivated by Nicolas as he
was by her.

Adrienne had, in all genuine innocence, also won John Bardsley's heart.
John and Adrienne were botany 'freshers' together. John was a tall, slightly
stooped young man whose kindly face looked down from above hunched,
broad shoulders, and conveyed an attitude of a 'gracious standing back to observe.' From the moment Adrienne walked into the lecture theatre for the first
session of their course, John knew that for him there would never be any other
woman.

John and Nicolas had been friends from early grammar school days and, as
a true loyal friend, John watched silently but caringly as matters took shape
in their expanding youthful student group. When, after some time (and as no

surprise to John's observant eye) Adrienne was very hurt to find herself ousted from Nicolas's interest by a determined colleague, John's gentle devotion enveloped her in his patient love.

Adrienne's rival was Kathleen; a comely Yorkshire lass, the daughter of a worthy north-country doctor, whom Adrienne mistook for a bashful 'fresher,' and welcomed into the botany group. In actual fact Kathleen had been sent down from a geography course at Reading University for various misdemeanours, and had come to Manchester to make a new start. Gladly joining Adrienne and her friends, Kathleen soon enjoyed various student union functions and dances where Nicolas was very much in evidence. Ignoring, or unconscious of Adrienne's interest in Nicolas — or simply going on the basis that 'all is fair in love and war' — Kathleen, whose aim in life was to become a doctor's wife, decided from the first encounter that Nicolas was the answer to her prayers, and launched into her project diligently.

Her apparent familiarity with all things associated with the medical world, gleaned from her home life, was an insidious attraction for Nicolas: an ingénue in the sphere he was entering. Perturbed by Nicolas's complicated surname, Kathleen had impressed upon him that in medicine he would be wise to use a simpler name. Indeed, in the early 1930s, foreign names were not as accepted as they have become of late, so Nicolas was easily persuaded to take the name of Seaford; a change that hurt my father deeply, though he understood the reason for it.

On first arrival in England, Sergei had tried to simplify the family name Shcheyteenin by spelling it Shtetinin and, in the prevailing humbled circumstances, had not used his inherited title of Prince. Later the family came to realise that the fully phonetic version of the name, though frightening in its length, might not have been quite the spluttering stumbling-block the simplified version proved to be, and would have been less liable to be associated with the German town of Stettin, an unintended consequence.

Kathleen's parents knew and liked their daughter's young friend Nicolas, from the earliest days of their association. Both he and I had enjoyed visits with Kathleen's family at their home where her parents, just as mine, could not have entertained any idea of marriage during student days. But in the emotional fervour of youth, and using woman's oldest wiles, Kathleen achieved her aim upon which, complying with the conventions of the time, Nicolas was honour-bound to marry her, though secretly.

Though 'married,' Kathleen was genuinely terrified of evoking her strict and old-fashioned, downright Yorkshire father's inevitable anger, and to prevent the risk of any rumours reaching home, she tried to hide her condition by vicious tight-corseting. This she carried on to such an extent that the baby did not survive its premature birth. With the problem solved, Kathleen and

Nicolas eventually announced their "nuptials" while attending the local hunt ball in Kathleen's hometown.

MEDICAL TRAINING

With the marriage acknowledged, a part of the upstairs of the Victoria Park house was made into a pleasant flat in which the young couple lived quite separately. Nicolas went on to qualify, and took up his first house-officer post at the Infirmary, whilst I, by this time in my fourth year, continued my studies.

My parents were very concerned that a considerable portion of the family housekeeping and catering, simple though it was, seemed inevitably to fall on me, as I was able to shop on my way to and from college. Cooking too, somehow seemed to get done in some elementary way. So when my parents learned that their good friend Nanny Liza had eventually been able to leave Russia and was in Tallinn, her hometown in Estonia, they wondered whether she would consider coming to them in England. They had been very distressed to have to abandon her and Aunt Natasha in Sevastopol when they left, and thought that perhaps, besides the joy of having her with us, it might be to Liza's advantage to come to England.

To everyone's delight the kind creature agreed to come, and arrived eagerly bringing with her the few family treasures that had survived in Marie's Sevastopol house where she and Aunt Natasha had stayed on, sharing a small back room. The family all listened sadly to the brave tale of how the two ladies had managed; how they had had to struggle, and that Aunt Natasha had soon died.

Under the new Soviet state of affairs Liza, who was born in Estonia, was entitled to repatriation and, on being left alone, applied for the appropriate privilege. With the permit in her hand she was able to apply for the costly visa, so essential before she could start the lengthy process of ordering a railway ticket to Estonia. Because the cost of fares rose continually, by the time she had earned enough money for the ticket the visa expired and the cost of renewal used up the travel money. By the time this sum was again earned, a further new visa was needed. The process repeated itself again and again, resulting in more than ten years elapsing before she was able to get to Tallinn. Her arrival in Manchester, dealt with—of course—by Sergei, was very warmly welcomed, her devoted presence immediately creating an aura of orderly contentment for all of us.

Liza, however, found her inability to speak English a great disadvantage and eventually began to feel homesick. On hearing that the brother in Tallinn (whose existence had enabled her to leave Russia) was ill, she felt bound to go to him. So it was again with great sadness that farewells—likely to be final this time—had to be said to the most genuine of true friends anyone had ever had, and whom we all sadly escorted to the station.

"Liza, Liza," my mother said with tears welling in her eyes. "You and I have been through many difficult times together, no sister could have been as good a friend as you have been to me in all these years." They clasped hands and then embraced each other warmly. Drying her face, my mother tried to smile as the train whistle sounded, making Liza scramble into her compartment as Sergei embraced her saying: "Thank you, Liza dear, for all your good care, we will miss you. Bless you and all your loving deeds, Goodbye!" Gently the carriages began their slowly accelerating creep on and away, tears dimming the last any of us could see of that serene face.

Medical studies, a difficult undertaking for anyone, were proving to be very hard work for me. Latin and mechanics needed special tutoring; chemistry was highly complicated, physics seemed rational, and physiology fortunately proved to be interesting. Botany, however, led to a friendship with the lecturer, Bertram Miles, and his pretty Canadian wife Mary, who happened to be learning Russian from Sergei.

Bertram was a tall man with a twinkle in his eye, a charming Gloucestershire accent, a shapely crop of chestnut hair and a moustache. The occasional need to use spectacles only added to the charm of his military appearance. He had met Mary in his very young army days at the end of the First World War, when she, as a slip of a Canadian nurse, had gently tended his painful wounds. They were now both entomologists and Mary's research into the lifecycle of the Psoar fly had contributed towards some degree of control of that fruit-tree pest.

Bertram, who had actually been christened Bernard, had unexpectedly been renamed Bertram when he was appointed as the new 'Natural History Uncle' on the Children's Hour radio programme of that time. The BBC producers decided that Uncle Bertram sounded 'crisper' than Uncle Bernard, and the name had stuck. Except for a lively, long-legged Springer spaniel, Bertram and Mary had no family, and as they enjoyed the company of young people they soon included me in their circle of friends, and often invited me to their Canadian-style log cabin up on the Westmorland fells. A true and long-lasting friendship was soon established.

Because there had been no chance of any schooling in the turbulent circumstances we had lived through, Nicolas and I—though fluent in spoken Russian—could neither read nor write the language. So, hoping to fill this void, we attended Sergei's evening classes. Besides managing to grasp some degree of the language's complex grammar we made friends with some of the other pupils.

There was a seemingly bright young man named Henry Best whose behaviour seemed somewhat strange. His interest in the language was dimmed by his zest for Sergei's accounts of life in former Russia.

Another of Sergei's pupils with whom a friendship soon started was Henry Bedford, the pharmacology lecturer at the Manchester Medical School. Henry was a tall, pale-skinned, shy man of indefinable age, with a sprinkling of silver in his black hair. I frequently enjoyed talking with Henry as he hurried about the medical school with his characteristic heel-dragging gait, and looking smart in his crisply laundered white lecturer's coat, that hung behind him from his somewhat hunched shoulders.

Besides attending classes Henry, as a near neighbour, was invited to the family home and was doubtless charmed by Vera. He took every opportunity of calling at the house to ask questions about Russia, or to drop in with books he had come across. For my part, however, oblivious of the possibility of his interest in my mother, I gloried in these visits and adored him with schoolgirl devotion and embarrassment, and treasured the many letters he wrote to me on abstract subjects to which I was delighted to reply by dropping in to his office at the school.

Some years into this association, when I was doing my resident midwifery stint at Queen Charlotte's Hospital in London, after a stilted invitation, Henry took me to lunch at the Blue Cockatoo in Chelsea's Cheyne Walk. How I was to dress for this auspicious occasion had caused me immense anxiety. My self-conscious awkwardness, however, more than matched Henry's when we met and—lasting throughout the meal—was painful to both him, and crippling to me. Our conversation was just a series of 'full stops'.

"How do you like your course?" from him would get no more than; "Oh, very nice," accompanied by hurried insistent nods. My; "Do you know London well?" which of course neither he nor I did, was followed by his; "I think this is a nice place," to which my reply was lost in fruitless searching for evidence of the Blue Cockatoo of the restaurant's name.

However tasty the meal may have been, its end was bitter for me. I did not know what I had expected, but we just parted with my polite thanks when he saw me to an appropriate bus stop, leaving me feeling bruised and very alone in the big city.

Still hankering after the idol whose feet of clay I was not willing to acknowledge and, without the sense and resilience of an older woman, I failed to appreciate the unexpected attention I found being showered on me during those London days by George, my sister-in-law Kathleen's schoolmaster brother.

George and I had spent a lot of time together the previous summer when Nicolas and I had visited the Longbotham family home in North Yorkshire. I had enjoyed George's warm friendship very greatly. This he now seemed to want to resume and extend; but I was not mature enough to recognise his interest, nor young enough to weep my broken heart on his willing shoulder. George on his side, not conscious of my problems, felt rejected and soon married a barely suitable chance acquaintance.

Back in Manchester, though anatomy, physiology, chemistry, botany, zoology and pharmacology milestones had been laboriously passed, I had found anatomy very difficult to face. On the journey home after my first morning in the dissecting room, the sight of a display of half-cloven animal carcasses hanging in a butcher's window—looking so like the formalin preserved human bodies I was beginning to study—left a more lasting impression on my mind than all the anatomy books I ever studied.

In spite of trying very hard, clinical medicine, surgery, dermatology, gynaecology, ophthalmology, otology and laryngology, together with psychology and orthopaedics had so overfilled those following clinical years that, overwhelmed, I failed finals and had to join the following year of students.

In the final year of a medical curriculum, tutorials and clinical sessions occur in small groups, whose members all become good friends in their various ways. From among my new group, Roger Jackson seemed to be the odd one out. A loner, he was perpetually rushing determinedly from one university site to another in a great and serious hurry, head thrust forward and books bundled under a hooked arm. Though he was forever bumping into me, he remained aloof and preoccupied.

My family as a whole were so involved in the pressing need to work that they did not have any social life, and did not go in for any recreation; a deprivation that my father, basically a sociable man, found very trying. Throughout my school and growing-up years I, like my father, would have liked to have had guests in to teas and the like, but such occurrences were very rare.

Had it been possible for Vera to make herself more available to welcome and encourage friendships, and less stressful in her misogamistic influence in those early days, my many awkward moments might have been less long-lasting and confusing. Perhaps it had been Henry Bedford's frequent out-of-hours visits and persistently repeated references to the Russian word "*semya*"—which actually means "family" but literally translates as "seven of me"—that may have alarmed my mother, making her wary of any English man, and over-protective of me.

Fortunately the friendship with Bertram and Mary Miles chanced to play an important part in my development.

Mary, needing to be away in Canada tending to her ailing parents, enlisted my well-established friendship in looking after Bertram during her absence. Having long missed Nicolas's company I was glad to welcome Bertram's easy big-brother companionship. He too was glad to share his solitude, and ably and willingly provided the necessary 'mix' for the two of us to arrange simple, easy groups to go to student union dances and theatre matinees, and enjoy other similar occasions.

We arranged small gramophone sessions at Victoria Park, to which Bertram invited his and Mary's friends, and where we all enjoyed listening to the soul-wringing Russian songs and other enchanting pieces from the then well-known Russian musical called *Chauve Souris*. Sometimes Bertram struggled to play his flute to my faltering piano accompaniment. That fortuitous period of Bertram's company and unassuming moral support, gave me the self-confidence I had long lacked, and I began to mature.

Our group was soon joined by the unsmiling loner Roger Jackson. Roger was a deep-voiced, serious-minded young man with gold-flecked grey eyes, and slightly wavy light brown hair that swept back from his high, permanently knit brow. Like Bertram, he danced well. Though tall, Roger was dwarfed by Bertram, especially as his slender body with its sloping shoulders seemed to be streamlined as it followed his forward thrust 'path-finding' head. After a time Roger began to invite me to the bigger, end-of-term dances. These proved to be family events attended by his sister and mother, all of whom Roger escorted gallantly, if a little awkwardly.

In due time Mary Miles returned and soon Bertram became principal of a horticultural college near Bristol. From there he went on to become Professor of Horticulture at Wye College in Kent, and contact with him and Mary became quite rare, but the friendship with Roger persisted.

Roger approached medicine very academically and took the prospect of exams very ponderously. As it is helpful for two students to work together, we began doing so quite frequently at my home conveniently situated nearby. We would check each other's memorised lists of medical names of various kinds, between times going for brisk walks to freshen up.

As time went on I felt I was getting very behind with my medicine reading, and arranged to have tutorials from a very kindly, rather religiously minded young man called Reggie Luxton, who was a tutor in medicine at the Infirmary. He was very reserved and correct, and a perfect teacher whose friendship I soon felt I wanted to cultivate, and had hoped to do so after finals. As 1937 drew on, however, and exams approached, I buckled down to serious study. When, to my delighted surprise I passed the dreaded finals, the thread of student contacts and interests was superseded by the pressure of post-college life.

INTO CAREERS

Eventually qualified, both Nicolas and I were very grateful for the opportunity given to us by our parents, and conscious of the privilege with which our prospective profession had endowed us. Equipped with the essential certificates and a modicum of knowledge, we now both had splendid careers to pursue. Though it had been no easy undertaking for either of us, for Vera and

Sergei sees Nicholas off to his "finals," with help from Droogy

Sergei the task of meeting the protracted financial demands of the years needed for training two students had called for supreme and unrelenting application to their work. This they were glad to have achieved, and were content to continue the intense work they had come to undertake.

In the 1930s medical training was rounded off by doing hospital 'house' appointments or by taking on 'locum' work as a temporary substitute. As Nicolas was interested in doing orthopaedics, he took the post of orthopaedic house surgeon at the Manchester Royal Infirmary with Sir Harry Platt, a world authority in the subject.

During his term of office Nicolas's co-houseman was one John Charnley, the now world-famous devisor of the early artificial hip joint. The two housemen had together pondered deeply and often as to whether, or how, the excruciating suffering that growing numbers of people had to endure could be relieved surgically. The smooth surfaces of plastics, that were being devised just then, beckoned as a possible solution to the problem if only human flesh and bone could be persuaded to accept so alien a substance.

Though Nicolas was eager to continue in orthopaedics, his wife Kathleen longed to be a housewife in a home of her own. She and Nicolas could have gone on staying in their flat in the Victoria Park house, from where Nicolas could have continued his training. Eventually he was persuaded and agreed to go into the more immediately lucrative work of general practice. So, abandoning his ambition on completion of his promising first year of orthopaedic training, he started doing locum work while deciding where to settle.

Meanwhile I had duly qualified in July of 1937, and began to realise that I was now a doctor, and needed to get an idea of what doctoring entailed. Whilst pondering as to how I should set about the matter, I was surprised to get a call from Nicolas who, having developed jaundice while doing a locum in Westmorland, was asking me to take over from him.

Having that very morning acquired a little Singer 9 car, I soon found myself in the craggy picturesque Lakeland town of Grasmere in the midst of wild hills and the resting place of the poet William Wordsworth.

I was soon facing a surgery full of quarry workers and farmers, where I had to take my first plunge into doctoring. As women doctors were almost unheard of at that time, these country folk eyed me very critically.

"I wonder why she's here?" said one portly lady into the air between the waiting folk.

"Happen our young doctor's ill? He looked pretty seedy when I saw him, Saturday," came from another waiting lady who cradled a wide basket on her ample knees.

"D'you think she be a nurse?" whispered another conspiratorially, just as, with my courage braced, I called for the first patient.

"P'rhaps she's one of these new-fangled women doctors they have down south," conceded a quiet little lady who was rather hemmed into the corner of the wooden settle on which the patients sat.

Some of the men, on seeing a woman and young at that, chose not to stay, but others decided that 'at least she was a lady'.

Being a lady was of no real comfort to me when I had to climb a dark mountain path in the small hours of the night, having been called out urgently to one of the flint cottages perched high on the hillside. As the cottage door opened I was faced with steeply rising, dimly lit narrow stairs at the top of which stood a solitary, bare, artificial leg. This was the indispensable possession of a haggard old miner who, only just still alive, was propped up in the big bed that so filled the tiny room that the leg outside the door was easily within his reach were he well enough to need it. He was dying from pneumonia, a common occurrence in the days before antibiotics.

After doing a few more locums in various parts of the country I decided that I should take an assistantship.

Nicolas, who had soon recovered from his jaundice, and had experimented with further locums, also decided to take an assistantship, and finally chose one that was to lead eventually to a partnership in the Harrow district of Middlesex.

He and Kathleen occupied a house provided by the practice, where Kathleen delightedly settled into house pride, applying her artistry very effectively, and Nicolas devoted himself to the practice with his winning charm and impeccable bedside manner, both of which appealed to patients. Though the assistantship eventually graduated to partnership, as the demand for Nicolas's gentlemanly and heartfelt attention grew to be embarrassingly popular, it was eventually agreed that the partnership would be dissolved.

Considerably experienced by this time, Nicolas took on a single-handed practice in central Harrow and was glad to find that his success continued. A successful solo practice is very demanding, and Kathleen soon found that she was left alone more often than she liked.

Mornings started with; "Darling, must you really go?" She would wail as Nicolas grabbed his car keys whilst swallowing a half-cup of black coffee, and stuffing cold toast into his mouth. He knew that he was already late for the surgery, and that he had promised to look in on the sick child he had seen in the night.

Pursued as he raced away, the plaintive; "Darling, you haven't given me a kiss!" would be countered by a distant; "I'll give you two at lunch time," as he rushed headlong for the car, which sometimes started obligingly but often only added to his desperation. But lunchtime would go by in dealing with emergencies with no time for home, and only a quick cup of coffee in the surgery before starting a considerably delayed afternoon surgery that needed to be followed by more visits. What could he do?

The practice was growing; but so was Kathleen's solitude, and with it anger and resentment simmered in her. She tended the house lovingly, and it really was as lovely as it could possibly be. None of the latest magazine pictures were as tasteful as the decors she devised, but Nicolas was rarely home to admire her efforts, and she really felt more than disheartened and sorely disappointed, almost to tears, much too often.

"Darling, have you seen how I have done the drawing-room windows? I've put up those American curtains, with those frills."

"I'll see them later, darling; I'm sure they're just lovely. You do it all so well!" but he was off on his way, full of anxiety for a seriously ill child who needed a hospital bed, and there were none to be had.

Kathleen's frustration soon grew into discontent. In her early schemes she had visualised Nicolas as part of her father's practice. On home ground she would have seen to it that her husband was a privileged partner in the group, but Nicolas, rightly, had to be his own man. Before long Kathleen's dissatisfaction, and Nicolas's inability to curtail his work, began to cause a rift that gradually widened, and Kathleen began to have minor breakdowns in which nothing was of any comfort. She would spend whole afternoons weeping, and on a morning following such a distressed day, she would refuse to get up.

Though a present from Nicolas of some valuable bauble, and a meal at their favourite roadhouse would restore life to its full verve, in time even such measures lost their power. Longer stays in bed were resorted to, and tears were replaced by periods of deep gloom that could no longer be dispelled even by her chosen pep pills.

Sorely lacking contentment in his own home, and sensing accord in many a friendly patient's surroundings, Nicolas—glad of the peace and serenity—often tended to prolong his visits. He also enjoyed the homely company of his various receptionists at the surgery, thus putting further strain on his home situation.

His inborn military instincts having long taken him into the Territorial Army (another bone of contention) Nicolas was not surprised to find that, when war threatened, the prospect of active service appealed to him very strongly.

Nicolas and Kathleen had wondered whether a child might bring them together and though Nicolas was uncertain as to the wisdom of starting a family in view of Kathleen's recurring depressions, young John Nicolas arrived in September 1939, just as war was declared. Nicolas, as a Territorial Army reservist, got his overseas posting as those first sirens sounded and, entrusting his practice to a locum, was off and away. This meant that he missed the period when Kathleen was an elegant young mother who made a very pretty picture with John, an alluring copper-headed and brown-eyed babe who soon became a charming toddler.

Meanwhile John Bardsley, Nicolas's faithful friend moved to London soon after leaving university. He had taken control of the London end of the Manchester textile business in which he and his father had long been involved. John and Adrienne married in London, and after various periods of flat life had settled in Twickenham and were glad to find that Nicolas and Kathleen were in nearby Harrow.

John, who had been widely interested in photography from early school days, soon found that there was great scope for his hobby in London. He made great progress in the art, and having written various articles and published a textbook on the subject, he was ultimately elected president of the Royal Photographic Society. When war broke out, anxious to serve his country, John had volunteered, and was disappointed to find that the importance accorded to textile production precluded him from military service.

Because he had long been a reserve member of the London fire service, whose work he greatly admired, he was promptly absorbed into it. As an experienced officer he was detailed to Oxford, which had become strategically important and needed efficient protection. His photographic ability was soon discovered in his work upon which, besides his fire-fighting duties, he willingly added his skills to the work of the photographic unit of this gallant and insufficiently appreciated service.

With the two men away, the two young women; both mothers with small children by this time, were glad to be near each other in those early war days. As Nicolas's practice house had to be occupied by his locum, Kathleen stayed for a while in a pleasant flat on Harrow Hill, but soon moved into London without Nicolas's approval. She took a third floor flat in one of the city's tall terraces on Westbourne Grove, a tree-lined road immediately to the southwest of Paddington Station.

Toddler John, who had not heard air raids in his Harrow days, faced London's bombing bravely, but with a blanched little face and his huge brown eyes bigger than ever. During a nasty blitz raid, when bombs fell nearby on a day when I happened to be visiting, his trembling little person belied his reassuring statement that: "Soldiers like me and my Daddy are never afraid."

Sergei and Vera, John's devoted grandparents, rightly insisted that, with no need to be in such a dangerous situation, Kathleen and the boy should not be living beside so prime an enemy bombing target, and offered them hospitality in Manchester. Eventually Kathleen grudgingly agreed to come for a short time during which she arranged for the tiny boy to go to a preparatory school at Windermere in the Lake District.

Having settled the solitary waif in what was at least relative safety, she returned to the glamour of London, where she was surrounded by Canadian forces and was much feted by a so-called distant relative of some friend of hers, a Canadian Philip Rawson who was glad of her company.

Although I was doing eye work in London by 1944 and sometimes paid brief visits to Westbourne Grove, Kathleen and I did not meet again until many years later as my life, and that of Nicolas, took us into different spheres.

EARLY GENERAL PRACTICE

In the autumn of 1937 after taking over Nicolas's Grasmere locum, and doing a few others, I chose an assistantship in Stockport, a small Cheshire town contiguous with the east side of Manchester. The post carried a yearly salary of £600, was near Derbyshire and the Pennines, and was convenient for Victoria Park.

As assistant in the partnership of doctors Shankland and Broughton, I had two gas-fire-heated rooms over the surgeries and dispensary in the practice house in Higher Hillgate, in the nucleus of the town. A Mr. and Mrs. Bolton lived in the house, and acted as practice caretakers, who handed out medicines, were a liaison between the doctors and their patients out of surgery times, and hosted the assistant.

The usually cheery, plump Mrs. Bolton kept an eagle-eye on the degree of gas heating, and got annoyed if ever I kept a low flame burning overnight in the fire in my chilly bedroom. Mrs. Bolton usually brought me an early morning cup of tea, when her eyes went straight to the minuscule gas heater to check whether it was on.

"Doctor, you've got that fire on again," she would say in a very reproving tone.

"You would too, Mrs Bolton, if you had to get up in the middle of the night," to which the usual reply was:

"You don't know, doctor, how much that costs me."

After many repeated sallies on this theme I plucked up enough courage one morning to say: "Why don't you discuss this problem with the doctors?" Nothing was done, and the grumbles continued.

Quite early in the assistantship I found that my foreign surname had been reduced to 'Seccotine' (a glue, used to stick insect specimens to cardboard mounts) and other embarrassing versions, so I reluctantly followed my brother's example, and took the name of Seaford. This proved to be much easier; it prevented a great wasting of time and energy in explanations of the original name, and long discussions about recent world history.

My duties consisted of sessions at the main surgery in the centre of Stockport, and attendances at branch surgeries in outlying parts of the town. One surgery was in the front room of a row of back-to-back cottages near some mills, another was in a semi-detached house in a more prosperous area, and a third in a bungalow on a new development. Each surgery had a cupboard with a basic supply of rudimentary drugs, bottles, labels and a phone, a commodity very rare in the majority of homes at that time. Night call-outs were allocated on a rota system between the principals and the assistant.

All the landladies who staffed these outposts were nice, kindly souls, who acted as twenty-four-hour receptionists for the practice. Through these ladies, patients were able to ask for help if they were in trouble, upon which one of the doctors would come out promptly.

There was no National Health Service but, if employed, the man of the family got some degree of insurance benefit called the Panel. His family, however, had to pay for their own medical care.

A subsidiary but unofficial scheme was run by most doctors, whereby perhaps two or three old pence a week—though a lot of money out of a very small wage—covered the doctor's attention for all the family, and for their medicines that were dispensed by the doctors. In the absence of a wage in the widespread unemployment of that time, the situation was pretty desperate

Soon after I started at Stockport I was delighted to have an unexpected visit from Patrick Muir. He was the son of friends of Vera's, who lived in the area. Patrick, a big, soft-featured, broad-faced, warm-hearted and good-tempered Scotsman with fair curly hair, had called as a result of the recommendation of some other friends of Vera's who lived in the area, and a friendship soon developed. Like numerous young men intended for the business world, Patrick was unemployed and was in the painful position of going from door-to-door trying to sell vacuum cleaners. On the frequent days when thick smog stopped public transport, and prevented people from reaching their work areas, Patrick, unable to get to his work, would lead my car in which I hoped to reach my morning's surgery, by walking ahead of me, carrying his large pocket handkerchief as a white flag for me to follow.

Patrick came from a good family, and was a kind and generous young man, whose gentle and faithful devotion I enjoyed much on the basis of a continuation of my friendship with Bertram without appreciating that the situation was different, and how genuine his interest was. An only son, he lived with his widowed mother who found herself in considerably reduced circumstances as a result of the recent economic depression affecting the whole country.

Mrs. Muir only just managed to keep up the substantial family home in Davenport Park, a pleasant long-established residential part of Stockport, and may even have had to take in lodgers—to her shame. This may have been the reason why I was never invited to Patrick's home.

This happy and undemanding friendship continued into the next assistantship I took in Disley, a picturesque village on the border of Cheshire and Derbyshire. As assistant to Drs. Boyle and Titcombe, I now lived in their branch surgery house at High Lane, a residential hamlet between Stockport and Disley. Patrick and I often met for tea in the welcoming Ram's Head Roadhouse at Disley where, especially on cold winter afternoons, Patrick's friendly company and the tempting warmth of big log fires were little interludes to be treasured, and frequently delayed me from getting on with the afternoon's list of visits, a fault pointed out to me by my employers.

Long letters continued between Patrick and me during my well-earned trips abroad and various later posts, right up to the September 1939 declaration of war when Patrick proudly joined the army. On his way home on his first leave he was killed in an early London air raid.

BUSINESSMAN SERGEI

Although my parents' all-engrossing application to work had enabled them to launch both their children into professional careers, the web of work they had woven for this purpose still needed to be continued, if only for their own sustenance, and required their full-time attention. Their finances were still very limited. There had been no scope for any savings, nor were there any pension prospects. Furthermore Marie, Vera's mother, had become their total responsibility from the time of the early threats of war, and lived with them in one of their upstairs rooms.

Unlike business, manufacture and high finance, where much can be delegated, the personal nature of handcraft and teaching in which Vera and Sergei were valiantly engrossed—though they employed a few key people—carried only an earning power governed largely by the number of hours in the day.

Although their expanded work took all their energies, they had satisfaction in their hard-earned success and were glad to be able to press on. Their strict routine continued relentlessly. After a speedily pressure-cooked meal for themselves and Marie on returning from evening school, Vera and Sergei would 'beaver on' with their many undertakings until bed-time, setting off again to earnest work next morning.

They had gradually reorganised and modernised the house and had ultimately arranged for their own living quarters to be on the ground floor. This enabled them to rent out what had been Nicolas's flat to a widowed acquaintance, a Mrs. Luckhurst, whose friendly presence in the house was an asset in that Marie was not alone in the house all day.

Though limited means and transparent honesty precluded Sergei from being an entrepreneur, he established a workshop in Moss Side, Manchester's well-known soccer ground area, where he employed an able joiner named Lloynds, and from where he supplied the Studio with little occasional tables, waste-paper tubs, standard lamps and the like, and did picture-framing.

The Studio, by then, was a boutique-type of shop with a wide, elegantly curved staircase sweeping down to a lower-ground-floor second showroom on one of the town's main streets. It had a small screened-off workroom area, and was situated opposite Kendal Milne, Manchester's branch of Harrods, London's top department store. Though modest premises, they adjoined Waring and Gillows, another prominent London and Manchester emporium from whom Vera had been fortunate to rent a little section.

My mother, known as 'Madame,' now had a staff of three assistants, one of whom was mainly occupied in the making of much sought-after hand-sewn silk lampshades, an industry very little developed at that time.

Knowing how hard-pressed my parents were, I did what I could to help in my off-duty times. I sometimes filled-in for absent assistants, but my main help to Vera was taking her by car to trade fairs and on other business expeditions, the two of us spending exhausting days in huge exhibition halls in Blackpool, Harrogate and London. Although both of us would be nearly dead from fatigue, we usually came away contented and with new business contacts and useful information. Sometimes this information was obtained by me, furtively memorizing names and addresses that were not generally disclosed by certain firms!

RIVIERA VISITS

Entitled to a holiday from my Stockport post, I spent two weeks in early 1938 with my grandmother Marie, who was then living in Menton in the South of France. Years earlier in the late 20's, as a young teenager, I had stayed with Marie during her short sojourn in Marseille. At that time this kind little lady, full of good will, had abandoned her beloved Menton and taken a fragment of a small-holding in the rural outskirts of Marseille where I joined her during a school holiday. Marie had intended to run this minimal establishment with the help of young ex-naval officer Mitya, (Michael Matousseyevitch), a distant Russian cousin, and her son Shoura's young friend of former days, who badly needed a home and a job.

Mitya, in the way of many Russian émigrés, had found his way to Paris and had married a somewhat senior and well-established French lady there, who owned a renowned Fashion House called Vioné. This, I was recently surprised to find, still exists in 2006. Mitya soon found he could not stand the hectic pace of the fast-and-furious lifestyle of his French wife's set, and had gone to pieces.

Wanting to help her son's friend, Marie had thought up the scheme of a self-supporting rural existence for herself, which would also solve the young man's problems. To everyone's disappointment the primitive agricultural experiment proved to be a fiasco as Mitya suddenly vanished mysteriously from

Marseille, and, to my knowledge, was never heard of again. Marie and I wound up the adventure as best we could, me feeling like a traitor to the chickens whom I had to hand over bodily to the rough farmer who was buying up the livestock. When all was completed, and having put her young granddaughter on a northbound train, either disappointed or relieved, the brave and well-meaning Marie retraced her steps to her beloved Riviera and I resumed school with a widened view on life.

By the time of the 1938 visit my grandmother was sharing a flat in the centre of Menton with an English lady, a Madame Young. Marie, who had no ticed an increase in the size of a shadow in one of her eyes, was glad to share her anxiety about her eyes with her doctor-granddaughter. She had first noticed the shadow years earlier when admiring the lovely murals and painted ceilings in Italy's famous churches and museums on her then-frequent European visits from Russia.

On hearing of eye trouble Mme.Young quickly recommended a Turin ophthalmologist who visited nearby San Remo once a month. As the eye condition was not then urgent, the matter was left in abeyance and I returned home after a happy holiday.

For my holiday the following year, I again stayed with Marie who, by that time was living in San Remo, just over the frontier into Italy and had started a recommended treatment for her eye. Dr Michele D'Azaro Biondo, Marie's eye doctor, was a handsome pale-skinned Sicilian with black curly hair who went out of his way to charm me, saying things like: "*Signorina* cannot be a doctor; she is so young; so enchanting!"

He took me to the casino, after which we visited the pre-dawn San Remo flower market where he showered me with masses of carnations. Although I was very taken with the captivating Michele—having had it drummed into me, in more ways than one, that I was not a scheming go-getting young woman—I behaved so much to the proscribed effect that even if budding romance had been there, I did nothing to encourage it.

Michele insisted that Marie should have an intensive three-month course of treatment for her cataract, for which she would have to stay in Turin. As my disillusion in general practice had begun to chafe, I wondered whether 'eyes' might be a career for me and, having pondered on the matter a few days, I wired my resignation to my annoyed employers, and accompanied my grandmother to Turin.

From there it was soon arranged for me to go to Rome to do a course in ophthalmology with a Professor Bietti. I was to stay with an émigré Russian admiral and his wife who had a small flat in one of the huge apartment blocks in one of the beautiful, wide, tree-lined central city boulevards. The lady eked out her family's meagre finances by serving as a private, common-sense-trained assistant nurse, who worked with a physician whose clientele was mainly amongst deposed or émigré royalty and their complex families. The lady's main duties consisted of giving injections of the then fashionable health-giving vitamins like Cytamin 1000 that the physician prescribed to bolster the frail condition of many of these sad people.

For a period whilst my hostess was ill, I deputized for her. The various visits this entailed gave me an unexpected insight into the amazingly lowly living conditions of some members of the social circles amongst whom no-one would have expected to see such privations. These delightful, highly cultured people—such as the dowager former Queen of Greece and other senior members of formerly ruling families—were often clothed in threadbare and much-mended apparel, huddled in tiny cold, dark and poorly ventilated accommodation amidst remaining salvaged treasures. These were put about here and there between inessential hangings, strategically positioned to hide and protect these precious relics in the event of an emergency.

On returning from that protracted holiday, needing to put money in my empty purse and gather my considerably scattered thoughts, I undertook a locum for a lady doctor in Blackpool. Besides medical duties, I was asked to care for the lady's pink-eyed fleshy Bull terrier. During one early windy morning on Blackpool's bleak Promenade, the dog had difficulty in disposing of something strange from its bowel. Unable to deal with the situation, I took the terrier into a nearby chemist's shop where, to my relief, the owner, a Mr. John Dodd, soon dealt with the matter.

On hearing my story, and that I was interested in doing 'eyes', John Dodd exclaimed providentially: "You must get yourself to Moorfields!"

Surprisingly I had never heard of the world's prime teaching centre for ophthalmology, the renowned Moorfields Eye Hospital and Research Institute for Eye Diseases. I promptly arranged to take Moorfields' 1939 March ophthalmic training course, that was due to start in a matter of some weeks. Little did the Bull terrier know what fates his distressed hind quarter had sealed!

MOORFIELDS

I secured a convenient part-time general practice assistantship in London in Red Lion Square. In those days this was a quiet green backwater in the corner between Southampton Row and Theobolds Road, and in the centre of "Dickens land". My doctoring visits in the district soon showed me that the dank and rancid smells of that era, so convincingly portrayed in Dickens' stories, still persisted as late as 1939 in the murky impoverished conditions of that area.

Moorfields proved to be a happy place. Robert Davenport, the Dean, was a rosy-faced, fatherly man with a reassuring air who was ably assisted by his smiling secretary, Miss Winder.

Four outpatient clinics were held each morning by different honorary eye surgeons who each explained the day's cases to groups of students. The lectures that followed in the afternoons added to the 'back-to-college' atmosphere, except that the students were all self-assured post-graduates and mostly came from overseas. One gentleman was from Orange, but whether that was South Africa or Holland, I never discovered.

Of the others, one I knew as Charlie soon paid quite considerable attention to me. He was on leave from the Indian army, was a smallish, energetic young man with a perky grin on his moustached face, and was mainly famed for having been to Tibet. He had learned the phrase: "*Sta Yobe?*" which he said meant "Are you virgin?" and curiously, appeared to be a question Tibetan men were said to exchange on first encounter.

Besides his Tibetan connection he was a good sportsman, renowned for taking part in camel races, and came from Cambridge. He had two brothers, a slightly backward young sister, and a mother who regarded herself as a wronged woman.

There had been a notorious case in the popular press, very shocking at the time, in which a Cambridge doctor was said to have had an affair with the local greengrocer's wife, but reconciliation was said to have taken place, with promises of good behaviour. Great, however, was the family's dismay when, on the day following the truce, the papers flashed pictures of the delinquent doctor on board the smartest liner bound for South Africa accompanied by the greengrocer's lady. The doctor in question was the errant husband of Charlie's wronged mother. Naturally, the scandal had been very difficult for the family to live down.

All this, however, was well in the past by 1939 and though Charlie and I had not spent much time together, I had gradually become quite fond of him, and had even accepted his unexpected engagement ring on his sudden instantaneous recall to his unit when war threatened. Quite early in the friendship Charlie had taken me to meet a couple of his very prim elderly aunts. They lived in a beautifully-appointed picturesque Cambridgeshire cottage furnished with antiques and other family treasures. These ladies had scrutinised me very critically, presumably to ascertain my suitability for admission into the family, as I was 'not quite English.'

Very conscious of the cheapness (of necessity) of my clothes, I quickly sensed their lack of approval. Nor had I sensed much approval from Charlie's legally-minded uncle, at whose house somewhere in Chelsea I had been scrutinised over tea some weeks earlier. They need not have been anxious on

Charlie's account, as I was not connected with any greengrocers, nor would my Russian pedigree have brought any disgrace to the family. Perhaps at that time, being a woman doctor was not yet quite acceptable, but in any case the whole association from the start had been too nebulous and soon evaporated.

As Charlie was out of the country, I returned the engagement ring to his mother who sent it back to me, suggesting that I keep it as a memento. Some forty or more years later, when in Cambridge with some Canadian guests, I went in to a bookshop in Green Street at the family's former address. I was surprised to find that it was run by Charlie's brother Edward, and that Charlie was now a sedate and humourless old man: so different from the dashing, pink-faced, crisp and cheery colonel of those early war days.

Whilst in London for that Moorfields course in 1939, Charlie lived in a flat at Castellain Mansions in Maida Vale. He shared the flat with four other young men; Peacky a young solicitor whose parents lived in smart Kensington Square, Harry who came from Halifax in Yorkshire, Neil Pinsent who was being groomed for the diplomatic corps, and George Brammer whose Danish mother and half-Danish sister lived in Oxford.

I continued a friendship with all these people after Charlie's regretted departure. The friendship with George was the heartiest. He was a kindly, short young man with a faint lisp and a big head, who did night duty as an air raid warden in the district whilst awaiting call-up to the army. George and I enjoyed considerable explorations of London in someone's open-top car with the wind snatching away the silly songs we sang at the top of our voices.

When I needed a short spell of accommodation to tide me over a change of lodgings George, who did his off-duty sleeping during the day, offered me temporary use of his unoccupied bed for the nights. The brief cox-and-box arrangement, however, appeared to be 'improper' to Neil's mother, who promptly removed her son from the apartment. The friendship with George and his mother and sister continued for years and was very helpful to me in my later Oxford days. Eventually George got his commission. As George's father had been a British army general and had served in Denmark, where the children had been born and were fluent in the language, George had rather seen his bilingual ability in Danish as useful in the War Office, but got posted to Iceland. There he eventually married, and when a daughter came along she was named Nina: perhaps a future 'car-singer'.

A less turbulent friendship, formed during the Moorfields days, was with Emmett Lee Jones, and was one that lasted with him and his wife Virginia to the ends of both their lives. Emmett, an eye surgeon and—in the usual custom of the United States—an ear surgeon as well, came from Crofton in Maryland. He was doing the Moorfields course as a refresher so as to increase his ophthalmic work with a view to reducing his otology.

He was a medium-sized, medium-aged smartly dressed typical American man with a comfortable manner and—being bespectacled, round-faced and kindly—reminded me of my father. Emmett missed his home and usual companions, and was as glad of my easy unquestioning companionship as I was of his undemanding friendship. The simplicity of the relationship enabled us to spend a lot of time together very pleasantly, and Emmett frequently invited me to simple *table d'hote* dinners at his hotel on Southampton Row, very near my Red Lion Square perch.

As the London area and the Home Counties were as new to me as they were to Emmett, we enjoyed exploring at weekends in my little car. Petrol at that time was no more than one shilling and five pence per gallon; seven new pence a gallon and something like one-and-a-half new pence a litre, though the metric unit was not then in use in England.

One sunny Saturday afternoon, approaching Ware in Hertfordshire, after several amused misunderstandings between 'Where' and 'Ware,' and much laughter, we came upon a pretty country spring-time wedding being photographed in front of a squat-towered country church with apple blossom trees in full bloom. As this seemed so typically an English scene, I stopped the car so that we could watch and enjoy it and the spring sunshine. As we sat, Emmett began to fidget and look awkward until at last he blurted out: "I'm married." I had never thought along those lines, but quickly realised that Emmett must have suddenly thought that I might be beginning to have 'designs' on him.

My prompt reply of: "Of course you are. Why—?" gave place to peals of laughter and much relief. But as his subsequent: "I didn't know I looked as married as all that?" sounded a little rueful; as if middle-age had suddenly surprised him, I felt that my rejoinder needed to be gentle. Fortunately my genuine: "Goodness no, it's just that you are too nice not to be married," sealed a friendship which continued happily.

Emmett's wife Virginia, who may have had doubts about this friendship, joined Emmett towards the end of the course and I was glad to see that their reunion was totally whole-hearted.

Virginia had arrived in an entourage of several very smart, prosperous looking American couples, and I soon found myself involved in much elegant entertainment at undreamed of places like the Savoy, with the visiting ladies in long gloves and the gentlemen looking stunning in their midnight-blue tuxedos. Besides the Savoy we dined at the Ritz and other such places into which my humble circumstances had never before taken me.

Several of the fashionable 'Revues' to which I went with them, were above my full appreciation in their nuances. Shows like *Ten Sixty Six and All That* were a great joy to me, as were the many other delights that London then offered. The splendour and the smart guests, however, vanished quickly with the threat of war.

Besides the many happy memories that I associate with Moorfields, I cannot but chuckle to myself when I think of how, in the very early months of the ophthalmology course—when my ignorance was more than abysmal—I had offered to deputise for the dean who was trying to arrange for a short absence. He must have been very amused!

When on September 3rd 1939 war was declared, I promptly volunteered for service in the Royal Army Medical Corps (RAMC) but was not immediately called up. I marked time doing general hospital locum work much of which involved tuberculosis. I would have been wise to have stayed at Moorfields, but at that time I had done what I felt I should do.

Chapter Three

War

WAR AND NICHOLAS

Having inherited service instincts from our parents, both Nicolas' and my immediate reactions to the war were to enlist. Doctoring, a directing of ailing people back to health, is indeed a service within the service, and Nicolas's career utilised his talents to the utmost.

Nicolas was at summer camp at Aldershot with the 2nd/7th Middlesex Territorial unit when war was declared on September 3rd 1939 and, as he was instantly on active service, he was immediately detailed to defence posts in London. From there, after various re-routings, training and collecting of equipment, as captain in the RAMC he proceeded overseas with the No 7 General Hospital. It continues to amuse me that the photograph of Nicolas' handsome aristocratic Russian face was chosen to represent the young British army officer for the United Services Club. (Perhaps it was there because the portrait was by John Bardsley, then president of the Royal Photographic Society!)

After two years of various distressing destinations, Nicolas's unit was stationed for a welcome break in the prestigious Citadel at Cairo. This happy respite, however, did not last long, as the hospital was suddenly detailed to Crete for the intake of casualties from Greece. The vast hospital was duly set up on the island with all its tents displaying well-defined Red Cross markings on sides and roofs, and awaited action in full preparedness. Marking time between duty rotas, medics relaxed on a remote part of the beach, either playing bridge on a curiously cleft table-topped rock or sprawling in the sun around it.

Captain Nicholas Seaford

Charlie Searle enjoys a camel ride near Cairo

On May 20th 1941, Nicolas was enjoying a spirited game of bridge on the beach, and was somewhat annoyed when, some minutes before the normal 1300 hours rota changeover time, he was suddenly detailed to do an unscheduled tour of duty. As he hurriedly dressed, a German aircraft, the first of Crete's *blitzkrieg*, streaked from the sky spraying the hospital area with bombs. It was not until much later that Nicolas learnt that the officers he had left at the card table rock only minutes earlier had been killed by a stray bomb from the first wave of aircraft.

As the bombing continued, patients, hospital facilities and staff were rapidly transferred from the exposure of flimsy tents to the better shelter of caves at the beach edge, where dealing with the carnage they struggled on in limited space. Casualties just evacuated from Greece were being killed on their way to hospital, together with their stretcher-bearers, and the caves were soon not big enough to hold all that streamed in.

By May 26th, after six days of conditions that became worse than primitive, the hospital held more than 250 serious casualties, with sand everywhere, hardly any water, darkness and very scant food for everyone. Records of the devastatingly high numbers of casualties could not be kept accurately, and could not be verified until four distressingly long months later.

PRISONERS OF WAR

Though the battle raged on for two more valiant days, on May 28th defeat had to be conceded, everyone in the hospital became prisoners of war. Their unceremonious removal was soon started by airlift in Junkers 88 transport planes. The first destination proved to be a German military prison in Athens where, demoralised by hunger and defeat, troubles started between prisoners of different nationalities who snapped and snarled at each other. Severely wounded men had to endure a further transfer to the captured No 5 Australian General Hospital.

After six days of incredible privation and neglect—and with only what the medical team of Max Wallis, Padre Hopkins, Corporal Kelly and Nicolas could improvise to try to ease their plight—the less seriously wounded casualties, men and officers alike, stripped of whatever personal possessions anyone had, and treated with inhuman brutality, were trundled off to Corinth, to a German base camp.

On June 6th, the tenth unending day into their hideous transit, 500 injured men; lame, sick and in need of treatment but dubbed 'convalescent', were dispatched to a so-called convalescent camp where, irrespective of physical condition, their German masters put them through two routine daily parades. Two inadequate meals were the only distraction they had from the fleas, flies, bugs and rats that tormented them continuously in the all-pervading sand.

For six long weeks the team ran sick parades, supervised cooking and did what they could to try to bolster the men's sagging morale when, on August 20th, 552 Allied and Greek men were crowded into the airless conditions of four holds of a banana ship bound for Salonica. All the men were ill; not just seasick, but as infected unhealed wounds festered in the heat of a Mediterranean summer, the already weakened men's devastating conditions worsened throughout the nightmare four-day journey.

They had hardly any water, little air and only two days' supply of the grossly inadequate food. Men so sick that they were barely able to stand had to hang perilously to the rungs of rope ladders dangling over the vessel's side for latrine purposes. Arrival at Salonica was no easier, and the single day they had to spend there, was nearly beyond endurance. The Greeks among them did their best to be helpful, but there was little anyone could do. The mosquitoes, bugs and rats gave them no respite, and the Germans' attitude towards them was despicable.

The next day, August 25th, more than 1,000 men, locked into windowless trucks and grimly overseen by German guards, were launched on a seemingly endless northbound train in the swelter of a mid-European summer. At occasional halts the doors were briefly flung open only to be locked again the moment food, accompanied by loud commands, had been pushed in along the wagon floors.

The medical team battled with the guards, trying—as best they could—to ease the men's hardships, checking that food and water supplies were as nearly adequate as it was possible to achieve, but nothing could be done about non-existent latrines.

The men, so crowded that they were more or less propped up against each other in the stench-laden sultry heat, were able to do little else than doze most of the time. Food became progressively more scarce with each of the nine agonising days of the nightmare journey.

The medics devised a sick bay truck into which they took newly sick men when possible, but the conditions there were no better than elsewhere. At Niz, Belgrade and Zagreb, Red Cross hospitals detained men who were too sick to continue on, others being squeezed into their space and yet more were added at Graz and Regensburg.

After those nine grim, unending, cooped-up days in the airless, dark, goods wagons, the battered men were glad to stand up in open air when on September 2nd 1941, they reached *Stalag* VIIIB, a German prison transit camp at Teschen in Upper Silesia.

Red Cross parcels were gladly accepted by the crushed and demoralised men; each eagerly seeking for letters, and long-depleted medical supplies were replenished. 'Old stagers' drew compatriot newcomers into their huts, anxiously enquiring for news from outside, and welcoming them with pooled Red Cross provisions. These, except for such occasions, were carefully hoarded as reserves for any escape. Although four months had passed since their capture, at last the International Red Cross could notify grieving relatives of the missing men's survival as POWs, or sadly that it was otherwise.

The *Stalag* system assembled the prisoners into camp units of 500 men. These were dispatched to one of the many mining centres in the area and allocated to work coal mines where long, weary and heartbreaking days dragged on. The mine receiving a unit either accommodated the men in existing hutments, or gave them space where they set up huts for themselves. Discipline was strict; keen-eyed overseers were everywhere and very severe.

To a great extent *Stalag* VIIIB acted as HQ for the area; its well-equipped hospital, sturdily built by early prisoners, served as a base hospital for the district from where the medical needs of newly arrived men, and those in the camps, were dealt with. By October 14th the men and the duties of the intake from Crete were sorted out, each man's ability being put to Germany's greatest advantage.

Nicolas, with his language knowledge, was to act as liaison officer between the British MOs (Medical Officers) and their German commanders. Nicolas soon found that it was essential to supervise camp food and its cooking, as dysentery was rife and enteric fever threatened. Actual ill-health was frequently disregarded by the German medical staff as they tended to regard many men's illnesses as 'repatriation fever,' men hoping to get repatriated as being of 'no further military value to their country.'

A great part of the *Stalag* hospital's work was taken up with casualties from coal mine camps. The nature of these casualties soon made it obvious to Nicolas that the men in outlying situations needed moral support. He felt sympathetic routine medical inspections at their camps could provide this, and eventually got authority to set up such a system. There were, however not enough Allied medics to run the scheme adequately. Even so, the relatively rare visits he and the few others managed to put in were helpful. The grim work the men were forced to carry out in long, unbroken shifts in harsh mine conditions, was monotonous and totally without incentive. Though paid a minimal wage for their work, prisoners' pay was in token money, only to be used in the mine canteens. With no opportunity for any uplift or variety of any kind in their lives, the rarely-received cigarettes from home, distributed by the Red Cross, were the only negotiable currency they had.

Nicolas soon saw that, in its present form, his scheme of visits from the main camp was not really effective. As *Stalag* VIIIB was largely regarded as HQ, the sympathy and moral support offered by officers from there could not be fully acceptable to men in their widely different circumstances. Nicolas realised that an MO should join one of the units in the midst of the main group of mines. As no other officer was interested in the project, he decided to take the step himself and by mid-1942 joined Camp E535 at Milwitz.

He chose this camp from among the many he had long been visiting because it had space in which to set up a Lazaret—a cottage hospital—which, besides all the other considerations, was a sorely-needed general facility for the area.

This camp held a New Zealand unit, with many Maoris, a sprinkling of Tommies (British), Spaniards and Cypriots—who called themselves the Kiwis—and was greatly heartened by the presence and activities of the Lazaret. Although fully engrossed in his new project Nicolas continued to minister to other camps. There were still few Allied MOs in the *Stalag,* but most had proceeded to *Offlags,* officers' camps. In the new improved atmosphere, Camp E535 went on to do a brilliant, unexpected job of producing a weekly newspaper, *The Tiki Times.*

Contrary to all regulations, which strictly forbade newspapers of any kind, *Tiki Times* was produced regularly and was routinely posted up on the camp notice board each week for all to read on its twelve sheets of foolscap paper. Happily the renownedly thorough Gestapo failed to notice that the censor's stamp the *Tiki Times* carried was camp-improvised. This fortunate lapse was thankfully attributed to the protective powers of the brightly painted red and green Maori god Tiki who was shown standing menacingly at the head of his *Mere* (a short war club) on each of the twenty four issues they produced.

The weary men, encouraged by the enthusiasm of the editorial staff, gladly contributed material for the paper. This was unfailingly hand-printed in pen and ink each week at the end of long, weary days' work in the mine, from its first issue on August 1ˢᵗ 1944 until the events of January 1945. It was indeed a mammoth achievement. Nicolas's presentation copy of the post-war New Zealand Memorial Publication of that unique, valiantly produced and salvaged document acknowledges his prison-time activities and is now in the care of the Liddle Collection of Personal War Records at Leeds University Library.

The Lazaret went on developing, and by mid-1943 had become a much-appreciated minor general hospital serving its surrounding area, and even came to be used by German service personnel. The camp *Kommandant*, while strictly maintaining his correct interrelationship with enemy prisoners, appreciated the advantages of the new importance of his camp.

This allowed a degree of give-and-take to develop between himself and Nicolas, and enabled some mutually agreed conventions to be established. One such new decree allowed for a specified number of individuals to be regarded as unfit for work on any one day, the men agreeing to their own rotas. This did much towards restoring a little of the men's belief that some degree of justice still existed, and abolished the need for scrimshanking—goldbricking, as the Americans would say—and the self-inflicting of wounds formerly resorted to for that purpose.

Germany's strict general regime required POWs *en route* to their work posts to be marched in the roadway, and that they should stop and salute any German officer encountered. One day Nicolas was surprised to learn that the authorities had awarded him the 'privilege' of being excused the salute, and that he was allowed to walk on the pavement. As Nicolas's many inspection trips were made either on foot or by public transport, the new concession enabled him to assimilate local information much in demand by the POW Escape Committees.

As Nicolas spoke German, Russian and some Polish, and in the new state of affairs had access to shops, he gradually became aware of the existence of a Polish resistance movement somewhere in the vicinity, whereupon a discreet and tentative request for a wireless receiving set was dispatched on a cautiously filtered journey to the group. As materials essential for such an undertaking could only be obtained from German vehicles, the process was slow and risky, but eventually a set was completed. Getting the set into the camp was the next problem, as every person going through the camp gates was minutely searched, and especially thoroughly 'gone over' on re-entry.

One day it was noticed that security lapsed when an injured German soldier went through the gate on his way to the Lazaret, so a detailed conspiracy was thought up. It was decided that if a pit prop should 'happen' to fall awkwardly during a mine inspection a guard might suddenly need to be taken to hospital.

Nicholas' official German POW photograph taken in 1942

Before long such a charade was accomplished, and the longed-for receiving set was welcomed warmly and promptly christened 'The Canary,' who's every chirp lifted the men's hearts. Knowing full well that it was a virtual time bomb, Nicolas took complete charge and responsibility for the set. Gestapo-operated wireless detection vans were very active, and any pinpointed set had to be found and destroyed in the presence of the camp's *Kommandant,* whose duty it then became to trace and execute the keeper of the instrument.

In the event of a detected set not being found, the leader of the offending search team would be regarded as a traitor, and as such would be executed.

As soon as there had been hope of getting a wireless set, knowing the severity of German penalties, the men of Camp E535 devised a safe in-camp hiding place for the instrument, and built a dummy receiver as a decoy, with lights and switches. They hoped that, if detected, any search party leader seeking their set might choose to regard the fake machine as a find, rather than face the consequences of failure.

On Christmas Day 1944, a Gestapo search party, intent on finding a set that had unfortunately been detected at Camp E535, approached relentlessly. Every inch of the camp was minutely combed, with no nook or crevice being overlooked. Fortunately, carefully co-ordinated forewarning gave Nicolas a few minutes' grace in which to set up a well-rehearsed plan.

Though repelled by the malodour, the search party penetrated into the Lazaret latrines, and could not help but recoil from the sight of a nearly fainting man bent double with pain, sweat welling from every pore of his body as the contents of his bowels exploded noisily into his thunder box. The MO regretfully explained the distressing and infectious nature of the case he had on hand.

The searchers were not to know that the man, who really was going through excruciating pain, was the brave volunteer who had just had an enema following a good dose of Croton oil. As a result of this very potent and instantaneous medication, the man fully presented a very realistic picture of a victim in the throes of a recurrence of a very contagious fever, supposed to have been contracted during a tour of duty in the tropics. Thus the search party was diverted from their quarry.

At the end of the most exhaustive search, the leader could do no better than confiscate and dutifully destroy the only set they had found; the providentially constructed dummy the men had so wisely improvised, and to which two lives were owed that day.

From their early association a respectful camaraderie had developed between Nicolas and the camp *Kommandant* who visited Nicolas in his room on occasional evenings. Placing his revolver on the table, the *Kommandant* would produce a bottle of Schnapps from his pocket and share a welcome drink with Nicolas, while chatting idly and enjoying one of his host's English cigarettes. That Christmas evening they shared the Schnapps, and though no words could be exchanged on the subject, Nicolas silently acknowledged the *Kommandant*'s grace who, on leaving, observed that he was glad that they were still together and that he had not had an unavoidable, abhorrent duty to perform.

With each passing day, though news was suppressed, a feeling of anxiety pervaded the area. Tension rose as letters, underground whispers, translated snatches from glimpsed German papers and their radio all warned that the Soviet forces, referred to as the 'Red Roller,' held back some time earlier at the approaches to Cracow, only seventy-eight miles away, were threatening to be on the move again.

THE LONG MARCH

Every prisoner had long-known that if the war became unfavourable for Germany, POWs would be used as a reserve weapon for the protection of the *Fuhrer* from Allied air attack on his hideout in the Bavarian Alps.

Although this was many hundreds of miles away, they knew that their feet would have to convey them. Conscious of the prospect of an inevitable move—and knowing that their receiving set would need to be inconspicuously mobile—the Kiwis somehow devised an attaché case to fit the receiving set and Nicolas, who dealt with dental troubles, filled this with an over-generous supply of dental instruments to the exact weight of the receiver.

He carried the case with him constantly, and, to ensure that it became a well-known essential item of his medical equipment that should accompany him on his every move, he frequently 'forgot' to pick it up at the end of camp visits.

Before long Russia's threatened advance proved to be unstoppable and, without preparation for the exceptionably fierce cold of early January 1945, all troops and prisoners in the area had to retreat.

Initially their destination was said to have been the Sudetenland (now the Czech and Slovak Republics), but actually they marched south. Camp E535's sub-officer 'Bull', so named by the Kiwis because of his big voice who—though severe was more fair-minded than many another—led the column as it trailed out from its quarters at Milwitz. Nicolas, keeping in touch with the medical state of the marching men, brought up the rear. A well-known carrying case of equipment most precious to them all was obligingly accommodated on a horse-drawn sleigh which, for some time, accompanied them for emergency use in the likely case of roadside casualties.

Launched on a forced march of unknown duration and destination, without prospect of rest or shelter in the winds and blizzards and frosts at 25° below zero, the men tramped on. Their very sparse food became ever scarcer as days passed. Each man's backpack carried his 'everything', together with whatever he could muster to fight the bitter cold. *Tiki Times'* editor Private Gallichan's pack was heavier than most, it held the tightly rolled-up *Tiki Times* pages. Though his weary frame often longed to jettison the extra weight into some convenient gully, he valiantly bore the precious burden that held the words of so many tortured hearts.

Men from camps and mines at Sosnovitz and Katovitz joined the Milwitz stream and were soon added to by others from *Stalag* VIIIB near Teschen. At Beuthen retreating German troops lengthened the trailing POW column tramping in an ever-hungry plod to the never-ending rhythm of boots on cobblestones, driven onwards by their guards. Any POW who attempted to escape was simply gunned down by the vigilant *posten*. One man—too hungry to think of escape, but starved enough to bend down to pick up a trodden crust of bread—was shot while his cold-stiffened hand was still trying to reach for the soiled delicacy.

Gleiwitz, Ratibor, Neustadt, Nysa, Goerlitz and Melnik all added to the trials of the empty-bellied marchers as they now began to drag themselves through dense forests. They slept in the snow. As they clambered up to cross the craggy high Carpathian Mountains the blinding blizzards grew more fierce as they gained altitude.

"Any chirps from that blessed bird, Sir?" would be anxiously whispered to Nicolas when chance permitted them to listen, but transmissions were rare.

The long, unnumbered, *posten*-driven column continued to lengthen as disheartened, weary men in remnants of strange uniforms—'other nationals'—joined the trail of several thousand frost-bitten plodding men, of whom well over 1,200 were Allied POWs.

Occasionally kind farmers offered night shelter in chance barns, pigsties and cowsheds, where the warmth-starved men welcomed the body heat of the animals. Guest houses were sometimes ordered to shelter sick marchers, and factories, if operating by day only, were forced to give night shelter to as many men as could be squeezed in. As local purchase for so many was difficult to find without forewarning, the only food they sometimes had was what the Red Cross could muster; the men sharing the food parcels as fairly as they could.

Air raids along the route were unpredictable, frequent and disastrous. Any compacted column that sustained a hit resulted in the maximum number of casualties and if scattered, the guards were forced to regard any out- of-column men as fugitives and gun them down. The loss of life either way was absolute carnage.

As they were nearing Regensburg, Nicolas and his guard, detailed to go on an advance foray to buy food for the column, set off along the proposed route on the rickety bicycles they had chanced to pick up. They were going about their business in the town when an air raid warning sounded and they got hustled into a shelter. After a tense, trapped time they both felt an overwhelming need to get out. Feeling that some semblance of officialdom would enable them to move through the tightly packed crowd, they donned their Red Cross armbands and slipped out. They emerged into a rapidly intensifying heavy raid, through which they hastened back towards the column wisely crossing the river by an inconspicuous footbridge. They later heard that their shelter had sustained a direct hit.

The American air force continued its methodical and intensive raids on the various aircraft and heavy-industry installations in the area, and scored a hit on the bridge over the Danube just as the weary foot-slogging column was crossing on its way to Regensburg.

Part of the column managed to cross over while the bridge was still intact, but many of the POWs and their guards, caught on the bridge, still lie in primrose-covered graves in the valley, a sombre reminder of that lurid past. The remaining part of the column had to scramble through the debris of the partially demolished bridge as best it could between onslaughts.

Glad eventually to distance itself from Regensburg, the column moved on towards its next point, the men taking stealthy creeps towards Nicolas and the 'Canary.' When there was a chance during night bivouacs, late arrivals whispered anxiously: "Any songs I've missed, Sir?" but nothing of value or cheer came over.

As they neared Landshut am Isar the radio began to chirp out whispers of hope to the exhausted and dispirited men. They listened to the canary's midnight twitters with growing interest and intensity, but needed to indulge their wish for encouraging news with increased stealth and circumspection. The *posten's* snatched fragments of information told them too that the American forces were advancing northwards: this made their supervision more strict than ever. Longing to know what the changed news might mean, but not daring to build their hopes too high, they dragged on many more weary miles when, to their unbelieving joy, General Patton's army met them at the river Leitha on May 10th 1945. At last they were all sheltered and the Allied POW's *posten* were now prisoners instead of them.

The 800-mile march had lasted four and a half cruel months, and had taken an inordinate number of lives. Of the 12,000 or more POWs who had set off together to trek through the bitter winter frosts and slushy thaws, one man out of every nine was not there to see the sunshine of that Bavarian spring, and of the 500 Kiwis, nearly half had gone.

In the colossal sorting task undertaken by the American headquarters, Nicolas's interpreting abilities added greatly to his medical functions. Besides the several thousand Allied forces, nearly 3,000 Russians, large numbers of men of various other nationalities as well as vast numbers of German POWs needed to be interrogated and when rested and patched up, directed to their appropriate destinations.

In late June 1945, surprisingly kitted out as a smart American officer, Nicolas reached England and ultimately found his wife Kathleen in Windermere, where she was visiting their schoolboy son John. Nicolas was very proud to meet the brown-eyed, copper-headed, thoughtful little boy he had only seen as a very new baby in September 1939, and knew that father and son would soon be good friends.

One day, shortly after his return, Nicolas was taken aback to learn that he was appointed a Member of the British Empire (MBE) and felt very humble. It was to the men with whom he had shared those years that he owed this honour. Throughout the time their comradeship had been reward enough, they were one big team and each had done his best.

A WOMAN'S WAR

Called up in January 1941 and posted to Reading, I was glad to escape from London's heavily bombed southeast, where I had patrolled hospital grounds studded with naval anti-aircraft guns and dealt with air-raid casualties in the then-London County Council hospitals.

Smart in my RAMC officer uniform, complete with maroon forage cap and a well-polished shoulder brace issuing from its trim Sam Browne, I reported to the Reading Military Hospital. This proved to be a small unit housed in a ramshackle, disused school building fairly near the town's Battle Hospital. My military duties proved to be mainly FFIs (Free From Infection inspections), though a Grecian slipper that I had devised for a soldier's broken foot was actually very commendable.

I was billeted with a very respectable well-to-do family that appeared to be composed of an accumulation of cantankerous elderly aunts and uncles to whom my presence was disconcerting, and ultimately other arrangements were made.

In off-duty time I did some eye work at the Royal Berkshire Hospital where I discovered that a course for the Oxford Diploma in Ophthalmology (DO) was available at the Oxford Eye Hospital. I applied for a transfer and on being posted to the No. 8 Military Hospital at Oxford did the DO course in my free time.

George Brammer's mother and sister welcomed and arranged for me to be billeted with a friend of theirs, a Mrs. Rathbone. This charming lady lived in what she called her "little villa" in Bellbroughton Road just beyond the University Parks, and was a delightful hostess. Though widowed and living alone, the house was always full of visiting family and other interesting guests including the late Quentin Hogg, who had relinquished his inherited title of Lord Hailsham in order to enter Parliament.

The Rathbone family—of whom one or more were MPs—were all Conservative, whereas the lady's aunt by marriage, one Eleanor Rathbone, was Liverpool's celebrated Labour MP of that time. On the occasions when Aunt Eleanor, as she was called, visited the house her left-wing politics and outspoken comments tended to lead to very spirited exchanges.

In my very trim battle dress, I rode my jaunty second-hand bike through the parks and quaint alleyways to the Examination Schools that housed the Military hospital. After the morning's duties and a quick snack lunch at the Copper Kettle across the road from the schools, I went on to the Eye Hospital. Spending my mornings doing FFIs, I missed the vital clinical work at the eye hospital, and with only the lectures to go by, I failed to get the DO. I had, however, enjoyed and benefited from everything I did, including being wined and dined by Professor Samuel Ernest Whitnall, the author of the early main textbook of ophthalmology, *Anatomy of the Human Orbit* of 1921.

I did my textbook reading mainly in the Science Library reading room where I met Jim Moffet, the unit's ENT (Ear, Nose and Throat) surgeon who was writing a thesis. Jim was a tall, spare, Irishman who spoke of *kelpies* (fairies) and the like, and I soon made friends with him. We were able to spend time together in many social and academic ways, and were very content to go on innocent off-duty jaunts together. Quite often my little car would run us up to Boar's Hill where we walked and chattered in the clear air, and enjoying the distant views of Oxford's 'dreamy towers.'

Jim was recovering from the shattering effects of involvement in a ghastly accident, and was glad of the peace and harmony in which he could talk about it. The back wheel of the slowly moving jeep in which he was riding crushed a toddler to death in one of Oxfords one-car-wide side streets.

Oxford's happy period sadly came to sudden end. One distressing day I learned that the No. 8 Hospital was being posted overseas and, as a woman MO who had not specifically applied for overseas service, I knew that I would not be going with the hospital. The prospect of Jim's going caused me deep distress.

Jim too, it seemed, had been taken aback by the posting but realised a sudden personal warning. In a resigned way he gently hinted that perhaps it was as well that the unit had to go, or he would have been hurting someone who did not deserve to be hurt. The question as to whether Jim was married or not had never needed to be raised, but now I knew he was, and that we were playing with fire.

Though my dismay was overwhelming and I longed to let him know how I felt, I knew I must not, and when the time came it was all said in a look, a handshake and just the words: "Goodbye."

"Goodbye." But the endless, tormented circling of Christ Church Meadows' pathways did not heal my breaking heart.

Many years later we met again and found that the enchanted bond still stretched between us. A fragmented correspondence maintained it for many more years until a sudden uninvited pang suggested Jim had died.

I started looking for an obituary to confirm my feeling, and when it appeared in 1996, though saddened, I was proud to learn that it had been Jim's ENT skill that had enabled transport mules to be silenced, essential for the vital element of surprise on which the top-secret *Chindit* operation of the Burma campaign in 1943 had depended.

At the last pre-departure inspection when the No. 8 Field Hospital was leaving Oxford in 1941, I had two unofficial chances to say where I would have liked to be posted but as I had, on both occasions, unwisely asked to go with the hospital—an impossible request—I was posted to Blandford, a hutted camp where I found snow-blown camp life very trying.

Fortunately that posting did not last long and was followed by Aldermaston, an Auxiliary Territorial Service (ATS) intake unit housed in the lovely Aldermaston Hall with its Minstrel Gallery, in the centre of what then was still just a lovely village. I was the only medical officer and non-ATS. My duty was to scrutinise girls recruited by the army from London's East End, searching for lice in their hair, and scabies on their bodies.

After a short period there I found myself in Bristol where its Southmead Hospital housed the Army's blood transfusion headquarters. I found a flat at the top of a very tall and narrow house overlooking the beautiful Clifton Bridge, and enjoyed walking through the park to my hospital duties, but was distressed to find how quickly the charming flat got covered in tufts of dust and the like.

Trained in blood transfusion, I was posted to the charge of a blood-collecting unit in Bournemouth. This proved to be an army hut situated in the Talbot Chine, on the Poole side of Bournemouth, whereas I was billeted in the Suncliff Hotel on the Overcliff Drive leading to Boscombe, a mile east of the town. After the buffetings of Blandford, Aldermaston and Bristol, the Suncliff Hotel, by then an ATS-run officers' mess, was bliss. It overlooked the gleaming cliffs of the Isle of Wight, and I had plenty of time to gaze out of my picture window and dream.

During a brief stay in London to re-take an ophthalmology exam, I met and was charmed by a South African naval ophthalmic surgeon commander who was taking the opportunity of adding the London Diploma in Ophthalmic Medicine and Surgery (DOMS) degree to his other qualifications. We had chatted over cups of coffee and gazed at the full moon, admiring the complete frost-ring around it, and romance had seemed to be in the air when, tantalisingly, I learned he was stationed at Southampton.

Following soon after the London episode, a letter from my mother told me that Roger Jackson, the former fellow student and friend of medical school days, resplendent in Royal Naval Voluntary Reserve (RNVR) uniform and accompanied by his mother, had paid Vera an unexpected visit at her Studio in Manchester, and that Roger was on leave from the naval hospital at Southampton.

Both Roger and his mother appeared to be glad to hear that I was in nearby Bournemouth, and both seemed to want to reopen contact with me. It soon transpired that an older, married woman, who was having difficulties with her alcohol-inclined husband, was pursuing Roger.

Amused by this story, I quickly visualised a pantomime-like elderly dame with long skirts hitched over one arm, running full tilt after Roger, intent on clutching him to her ample bosom. As I was interested in the chance of contact with Southampton and the South African ophthalmologist, I wrote to Roger enquiring politely how life had been treating him and, amongst other suitable comments, hinted at hopes of getting an invitation to at least a dance at his hospital. A letter soon came from him and was promptly followed by a visit, thus reviving the friendship of our student days.

Roger was very heartened to learn that I had changed my surname, and told me that he had officially changed his first name long ago. He had not liked being Roland, a name so similar to his father's Rowland, and had changed to Roger, and that he also wanted to change his surname to one which would honour Shakespeare, whom he regarded as a kindred spirit.

We spent time discussing his projected choices and admired the pleasant views from the mess windows and after one of the many empty silences with which his visit was liberally sprinkled, he remarked: "You are nicely set up here," continuing with: "This is nicer than our hospital quarters," to which I eagerly put in "But don't you have Mess Nights and dances, and other functions?"

"Yes, we do," came from him grudgingly, but no invitations or suggestions followed, and as my enquiries about the South African officer had received very off-hand and belittling replies, from my point of view, the visit had been a waste of time. Not so, however, it seemed, had it been for Roger. His next words: "We've known each other quite a time now, we'll have to keep up the record," suggested an interest in continuing the friendship.

As I was kept busy by studying for more ophthalmic exams, my Southampton interest faded, but Roger who was feeling generally disappointed with life, continued to be interested in Bournemouth.

He felt his life was blighted in many ways. Naval life did not really appeal to him. The war generally was preventing him from making any real progress in his profession. He hadn't had time to choose a definite interest, and felt hampered by the fact that he had made it impossible for him to claim the high university honours he had earned.

He had been a brilliant medical student who was likely to have qualified with high honours, and had meant to do so, but feeling despondent when the 1937 finals were coming up, he decided to postpone taking the exams. He had not realised that as honours are only awarded at the time of the first taking of degree-carrying examinations—and though he had gained higher marks than anyone had done before—he could not claim the honours these marks deserved when he took the exam at a later date. As time had gone by he vaguely blamed losing my companionship for the loss.

The hitch in Roger's career was doubtless a big disappointment to him as well as for his parents who, though sympathising with his chagrin, were proud of his abilities and the fact that he—the only son of the only son of a long-established family—was now a doctor.

Roger's father, Rowland Jackson, was the oldest of five children and the only boy in a well-respected Cheshire family who lived in Altrincham, one of Manchester's satellite towns on the borders of Lancashire and Cheshire. He had been a handsome young man with a friendly rosy face who, in the usual custom of his time had started as an office boy in an engineering establishment in the Broadheath area of their town, had soon became a traveller for the firm, and many years later became a director. He met Trudi, an office girl, on one of his youthful business trips to Birmingham in the early 1900s. He had barely graduated from his office-boy status when he and Trudi, just launched on her office-girl career, became friends and, one way or another, they eventually married.

Though he was loyally devoted to Trudi all his life, Rowland's four duly married sisters did not approve of the young girl he had chosen, and ignored the pair of them; the rift continuing even when, in due time, they had three children; Roger, Tony and Joyce. Tragedy, however, led to a friendship with one of the sisters.

When Rowland and Trudi's middle child, ten-year-old Tony, was in hospital for some minor condition, to everybody's horror, an epidemic of meningitis swept through the ward, killing him and eight other children including

Tony's cousin Alan Williamson the elder of the two sons of one of the disapproving Jackson sisters. United by the calamity, the stricken mothers became friends.

Though bright and gifted, Roger, the remaining son, grew up with the feeling that he was never quite as good, or as clever, as the dead brother who, having died young, had not had time to fail in any way. Nor could Roger compete with his sister who, besides being younger, was a girl and as such was treated as very special. He had either to fail or to excel, a difficult dilemma for a child to grow up in, and one that resulted in life-long discord between the siblings.

Stephen Williamson, the brother of the other dead boy, left solitary and deeply upset, was eventually glad to make friends with his stricken cousins Roger and Joyce, the three spending a great part of the rest of their growing years together. The friendship, however, was often marred for Stephen by the perpetual squabbles between the brother and sister.

Joyce, a talented young person who insisted on being called Jan, had considerable acting talent and had held vague ideas of going in for a theatrical career, but these ideas evaporated. She was an attractive young woman whose dislike of study precluded her from taking up any serious career. Her wartime radiography—which she enjoyed and did ably as a VAD (Voluntary Aid Detachment, a wartime medical assistant)—was cut short by lack of qualifications and left her disappointed and dissatisfied only ultimately to become her mother's reluctant caregiver. In later life she did some producing of children's plays for the BBC, but this, like her other undertakings, led nowhere and did not last long.

Trudi, whose real name was Gertrude, was considerably younger than her husband and seemed never to have quite outgrown the attitudes of an aggrieved adolescent. She insisted on her children calling her by her chosen name from their early teenage years, and preferred to ally herself more with her children than with their father, right up to his early death in the mid 1940s.

ROYAL NAVAL VOLUNTARY RESERVE

Roger had tried his hand at various branches of medicine in the period between completing his finals and being called-up for the RNVR by taking successive house-jobs at the Manchester Royal Infirmary, but none appealed enough to lighten his customary gloom which had been deepened by missing high honours on qualifying.

Trying to enliven her frustrated and unhappy brother, Jan tried to persuade him to go with her when she visited her ballerina friend Dorothy, one of the three Addis children with whom they had all played tennis in their growing-up days. As Dorothy's brother Campbell, a former fellow medical student, was often there Roger eventually agreed to visit the family home where he soon met Caroline, the married eldest sister, who occasionally happened to be there with her two children. She came to Dorothy for moral support in her distress about her husband's increasing interest in alcohol and the three young women did their best to try to cheer Roger up.

Sonny, Caroline's husband who collected his wife and family on his way home from work on these occasions, was a red-haired, well-developed Manxman with a hot temper who disliked Roger from their first encounter, and was a man who did not hide his sentiments. Incompatible with Sonny's personality, Roger soon enjoyed the annoyance his presence caused Sonny and, on that account, was sorry when his call-up for the RNVR came.

Jan, however, knew about the difficulties between Caroline and Sonny as well as the latter's hot-blooded nature, and feared that Roger's provoking behaviour might trigger Sonny's quick-tempered nature into violence. Jan and her mother were glad that the call-up came, and were happy to see Roger launched into his naval life, which, before long took him to Southampton.

From the earliest wartime days, and throughout my Reading and Oxford times, my long-standing easy friendship with former fellow student Bill Parker, also a naval doctor, had been flourishing contentedly. Bill's open-topped Vauxhall touring car had taken the two of us on sunny jaunts over many parts of 'Ox and Bucks' (Oxfordshire and Buckinghamshire), the friendship continuing comfortably into my Bournemouth era.

Bill, a big, warm-hearted, generous-natured, fair-haired young man, with a round, friendly face, who looked older than his years, was indeed a good and genuine friend. He was the devoted and affectionate only son of a long-widowed lady who applied herself nobly to giving her son the best opportunities she could. She supported him whole-heartedly in his ambition of becoming a doctor. This, in time he achieved, qualifying at much the same time as Nicolas.

When, however, Bill's friendship grew more serious and he began to press for an engagement and marriage—since I had not yet visualised myself in any marrying situation—I felt I could not accept his proposal, but was very distressed by the break-up to which this inevitably led. I missed the comfort and the reliability of his companionship, but—full of thoughts of duties and obligations to my family—my mind rushed on in an immature way to an unknown somewhere.

Had Bill overcome his own insecurity and returned to show his sincerity more boldly, I might have grown more mature and realised the value of what I was throwing away. But Bill, deeply hurt by being rejected, decided that he would leave the country, engage his wounded heart in other people's troubles and volunteered for immediate active service.

Quite early in my Bournemouth time I had begun to find life in the officers' mess limiting, and was being tempted by the reasonable wartime rental of a charming ground floor modern studio-type flat in an enchanting purpose-built block called San Remo Towers at the foot of Boscombe Pier. This was just a mile from the centre of Bournemouth, from where 'the Towers' looked like Switzerland's Chateau de Chillon.

The flat consisted of one huge room with a bathroom and kitchen, was on the garden level, and offered guest rooms on request.

The fact that my mother was not well, and badly in need of a break, helped me decide to take the flat and, having enjoyed getting it furnished, I was happy to be able to invite Vera to stay.

Vera, in fact, proved to be quite seriously ill and was in urgent need of rest. She had been running evening temperatures with night sweats for quite a long time at home and, at the end of her long and complicated train journey from Manchester, was barely able to walk the few yards to my car at the station entrance. Fortunately with care and several months of bed-rest in the comfortable little flat, and convalescence in the balmy seaside conditions of Bournemouth, the recurrence of her early 'doubtful patch' settled and she was eventually able to return home.

After Vera had gone home I began feeling very alone and in low spirits, and was quite glad when Roger reappeared, having come over to Bournemouth for a concert. Roger's occasional escort to concerts made his visits an asset; a neighbour's unwelcome attention in the communal garage and corridors of the flats was becoming a nuisance, and had made me send off for information about overseas service.

On finding that he could rent a guest flat in my block, Roger began to come to the Bournemouth concerts quite often, and a casual concert-going association developed. When Roger decided to extend a more-than-usually strained visit by accompanying me to work, and hovering around there, rocking himself on a patients' bench and staring into space, I was exasperated and felt it was time to wind up these visitations.

I did not know that he had been posted to Scapa Flow in the Orkney Islands off the northeast coast of Scotland. This was a transit station from where he was to proceed to a seagoing posting, something Roger had no wish for, and had not mentioned.

As he was still there by lunchtime, we spent it in Talbot Woods, which lay behind my Nissen-hutted unit. I decided to broach the subject of breaking up this routine, which had grown tedious, and launched into the matter by saying: "You seem very 'down' these days, are you unhappy in your job?"

"No, it's all right—it's not exciting, but what do you expect? Do you enjoy life?"

"I quite like this job. The VADs are a nice bunch and we certainly have a constant variety of people to deal with." As there was another silence I continued: "All the donors are volunteers. It's a blessing that they keep on coming; because it's vital that the Army Blood Bank is kept up."

"You're luckier than I am," he said, but did not explain why he thought so, and continued to examine the pine needles at his feet. After a long while he ponderously conceded in his deep voice: "I need to express my sexual urge" and then added: "Don't you find you need that too?"

Glad to have at least that side of the problem open I replied with all honesty: "I don't know anything about sex, but have no intention of experimenting with it" going on after a short moment: "You know—I think it's time we called off this association of ours," continuing in a relieved way as there was no comment from Roger: "You did say there was a train for you at half past two? You go off and get it and Godspeed. It's been nice knowing you, but, its best if we say goodbye." and was glad to have, as I thought, dealt with the matter.

With possibly a slightly rueful smile and little more than a nodded head and a muttered: "I'll be off then" he departed.

Back at the centre where the girls had, of course, taken great interest in the progress of the 'association' I told them that it was finished.

They concurred that I'd been wise, laughingly confirming my own view that my friend was too gloomy for me, and we all set off contentedly on the afternoon session which was due to take place at Christchurch. On our return journey, as we were about to pass Boscombe, I invited the girls to come in to see the flat and to drink to the dispatch of the dismal visitor.

To everyone's surprise, as we filed into the flat we found Roger dead to the world on the settee at the far end of the room. The VADs, as taken aback as I was, turned about on their heels and filed out silently, and returned to their jeep in amused astonishment, leaving me, very nonplussed, to deal with the unexpected situation.

Roger, whom I had sent packing so definitely that lunchtime, had, he said, "suddenly seen things in a new light". He said that he had never before realised that he had long wanted to marry me and—whether unmindful or not of the likelihood of wedding leave possibly deflecting the unwelcome posting—proceeded to ask me to marry him.

Knowing nothing of Roger's life between 1937 and 1942, I was surprised to be faced by a suddenly totally different, softened and friendly young man who professed to have loved me since our student days, and who now managed to smile and even laugh! Pressed by the many various accumulated wartime events and feelings, I easily persuaded my warm-hearted self that I loved this misjudged young man and agreed to marry him.

Suddenly full of warm affection—which I had long needed to pour on someone—I was confident that all Roger needed to change his morose nature was the abundant love of my out-going nature. He certainly appeared to be a happy man as he hurried off for a train.

The situation having arisen so suddenly, the character of the relationship having changed so unexpectedly and radically, I now attributed Roger's former gloom to unhappiness, and was full of contrition at not having understood him before. Curiously I did not wonder why I was not bursting with the wish to tell my news to the world. Nor did it strike me as strange that I was reluctant to speak even to my parents; there was no reason why they should not know, nor was there any reason why the two of us should not marry, but what I did not know was that when truly happy in such circumstances, the news just cannot be kept in!

On reaching Scapa Flow Roger put in an urgent application for wedding leave and fixed the date for December 16th 1942. He chose the date as, besides deflecting the posting he was eager to avoid, complied as nearly as possible with his numerology superstitions. He explained the precipitous choice of the date to me on the grounds that it was the only available time and that it was likely to be run-in with Christmas leave. The real explanation slipped out many sad years later. In the heat of the torrid letters that flowed busily between us, though conscious that the early date in barely three weeks' time gave us no chance of meeting as prospective partners before the actual wedding, I let myself be persuaded to agree to the speedy arrangement.

To my relief, little more than two weeks later, Roger's affectionate and caring ways on his late arrival on the pre-wedding evening dispelled all anxieties and appeared to endorse the seeming rightness of the proposed sharing of our lives.

A WAR WEDDING

With Roger in his smart RNVR naval uniform and me as an elegant RAMC captain, the marriage was solitarily solemnised in the Boscombe registrar's office after which we went on to a guestless lunch at Branksome Towers Hotel, a smart-looking establishment in Poole at the west end of Bournemouth Bay, which Roger had been glad to find open for the occasion.

To our discomfort we found ourselves in a cold, deserted dining room in the mid-week, mid-December emptiness of a seaside holiday resort hotel in wartime 1942 where the 'just married' self-consciousness, together with the fact that Roger had never before taken me out for a meal, made us very ill at ease with each other. Snacks at my flat had been convenient on his recurring visits.

After lunch, idly walking towards the centre of the town with no plans for the afternoon, we caught sight of a fortune-teller's nameplate on the door of a terrace house and went in at my suggestion that it would be something nonsensical to do, for fun.

The Groom: Roger Jackson Warwick

We were shown into a gloomy old-fashioned dining room where an aged gas fire spluttered in its hearth above a shabby tiger-headed hearth rug. Before long an elderly Pekinese dog tottered into the room through the partly open door, voided its bladder on the tiger's head and waddled out again, amusing Roger greatly. After a little while a small nondescript lady of considerable age sidled in around the edge of the heavily curtained door, and beckoned me away for consultation.

My amused protestations and explanations on hearing that both crystal ball gazings and palm readings foretold that I was not likely to be married for a

The bride in her RAMC uniform

long time yet, were countered by the lady's long and serious: "No, that young man out there does not enter your life. A real, true man is waiting for you, but you must cross water to reach him."

Laughing at the whole incident, I returned to the waiting room and Roger was led away. His only comment, hissed out between clenched teeth on his thunder-faced return after a long absence was: "That woman had the cheek to charge me for two consultations."

At first I had assumed he had not expected to have to pay for my part of the proceedings, but it transpired that his resentment had been towards the whole consultation. The lady, having told him things he apparently did not want to hear, had taken extra time in which to do so, and had charged accordingly.

Though I had laughingly started telling Roger what I had been told, his un-changing glower quickly silenced me, the grim atmosphere growing all the more tense as we walked along. Drenched by a sudden December sleet storm as we approached the end of the mile-long Undercliff Drive, we reached San Remo Towers looking like drowned rats.

To my delight we were greeted with a surprise party arranged for me by the kind VAD supervisor and the girls from my unit, but Roger's thundercloud state ruined everything. The kind ladies politely withdrew, glad to be away from the smoulder of Roger's fuming mood.

He was either angered beyond endurance, or perhaps the psychic influences and inflammatory atmosphere of that chance session had stirred some long forgotten semi-formed notion which made him regret that—having that very day ensnared himself by this sudden wedding—he was no longer free to follow a will-o'-the-wisp idea from his past, and that he and Caroline probably did care for each other

In time, however, he simmered down and must have come to terms with events as they were, and the brief honeymoon continued.

Just as he was about to set off to return to duty, my overseas posting details arrived. In the rush of the events so suddenly crowding in upon me, I had thought no more about my application, and was surprised at being posted to the School of Tropical Medicine in London for pre-overseas training. Roger's comment on seeing the papers was an immediate and terse: "If you take up that posting it finishes this marriage!"

Was my volunteering too 'near the bone' for him, as he had just evaded his own overseas posting, or was this the straw he was snatching for after the recent psychic jolt?

By this time, however, I thought I was in love, and love is blind; my un-complaining, loving nature assumed my husband's incredible ultimatum to be a deserved rebuke uttered because he loved me. Any thought that it might have been his suppressed wish did not enter my trusting mind: no thought of Caroline had entered my thoughts since I had laughingly dismissed from my mind the amused mental caricature of the pursuing older married woman chasing after Roger in pantomime mode.

As a serving officer in wartime, who had volunteered, the posting had to be complied with. Irrespective of Roger's reaction, the posting that spelt 'tropics,' dismayed me, as I could never stand hot climates.

Roger, however, who did not as much as ask how I felt about the matter, set off for Scapa Flow to be instructed regarding his next posting.

Four days later we met again at Oban, where I arrived full of happy anticipation on Roger's Boxing Day birthday and looked eagerly for my young husband. Considerably disappointed when he failed to meet me off the only train of that day, I eventually found him sitting idly in the lounge of our hotel adjoining the station. As he was generally undemonstrative, though full of loving words, I had not expected a great show of welcome, but would have at least preferred better manners.

Full of tenderness and overflowing with all-forgiving love, however, I quickly imagined him to have missed the time amongst his daydreams and his professed perpetual poetry composing with which, he had often said, his mind was constantly occupied. Perhaps it was this perpetual romantic preoccupation that gave him his dour and disapproving look; or was the poor man just hankering after a phantom?

After a very short stay in Oban we went on to London where I had to start my training and Roger went on to Plymouth's naval hospital to take up his posting.

As the pre-overseas tropical medicine course progressed, my distaste for any tropical situation grew in intensity. Nor did I want to break up the marriage that had barely started. As pregnancy entitled a woman to a 'release from service on family grounds,' and as my married state permitted such a situation, I negotiated that solution by borrowing a pregnant friend's urine sample.

Demobbed, I joined Roger in Plymouth and quickly took up the post of Assistant Medical Officer of Health for the City of Plymouth with tuberculosis duties, my LCC hospital experience standing me in good stead.

Roger had been appointed medical officer in charge of the Genito-Urinary (GU) department of the naval hospital and was considerably overwhelmed. In his early days he had shown some interest in gynaecology, but of the lower end of the sailor he knew nothing!

Any medical specialty—especially one involving so much invasive surgical work as GU—needed extensive training and experience, and as Roger lacked both, it was no wonder that he was having difficulties. He largely bluffed his way through without thought for the men he was supposed to be helping. Had he been honest, he would have pointed out his inexperience to the authorities straight away, but for reasons of his own he didn't.

Unlike most medical officers in Plymouth who had flats on the Hoe, Roger arranged to take a woodsman's tiny unfurnished bungalow called Dashel, at Bickham in the romantic-sounding parish of Buckland Monachoram, some ten miles out on Dartmoor near Yelverton. When Dashel was ultimately furnished, mainly with the contents of my Boscombe flat, we drove along a rough winding field track in an old five-cylinder Ford car Roger had just bought, to start our married life in very gypsy-style surroundings.

Bickham being on the opposite side of the moor from my sanatorium, which was at South Brent, I had to travel twenty miles or more to my work each day after the ten-mile run to drop Roger off in town.

There had been a very suitable and even more romantic and isolated chalet to let conveniently near the sanatorium, but to my disappointment, Roger refused to consider taking it instead of the Bickham bungalow. In South Brent

I could have walked to work, going into town with Roger on the occasional days when I did Child Welfare clinics in the city, the car being at his disposal the rest of the time. Perhaps he anticipated that his tour of duty might not be long, in which case the bother of a removal would not be worthwhile.

In actual fact the GU posting dragged on in increasing gloom for nearly a year, throughout which he could not find enough means of venting his frustration. One channel he chose was to start on yet another deed poll.

He had taken the name of Warwick by deed poll very soon after we had married and as he now could not see why a man should give his name to his wife without taking hers, a further deed poll was set in motion. He now became Seaford Warwick.

Roger's main home occupation, however, had soon become the felling of trees in the woods near the cottage. These were in no way his to cut. Perhaps because he realised he was trespassing, he often said his life's ambition was to own an island where he could sulk to his heart's content! I could not see that anything was preventing him from doing that where he was, but treated the statement as an intended joke. Pending the ownership of such an island, his unaccountable refusal to either try to grasp more of the elusive GU subject, or face his difficulty, drove him deeper and deeper into gloom.

Before long the Naval Director of Medical Services conducted an alarmed formal inspection of the department in Roger's charge. The fact that Roger chose to be absent from the inspection earned him a punishment posting to Basra, in southern Iraq, the wartime equivalent of being court-martialled.

Remembering how, in their early student days Roger had lyricised about the sounds of children's voices coming from the open windows of the nursery of a charming house near his family home—and trying to ease the hurt of the ignominious posting—I suggested that a pregnancy might be one way of making the best of our separation.

PENELOPE

During my routine weekly overnight sanatorium duty at South Brent, I was billeted in a nearby house, but shared the sanatorium matron's sitting room during the day. This led to a good friendship developing with the tall, slightly stooped Alice Willison whose main preoccupation was her longing for retirement, about which she and I often chatted. Miss Willison aimed at getting one of the flats being built especially for retired nurses near her sister's house in Hull.

Before long, delighted that I had conceived, I was also glad to realise that I was thus free to resume my eye work and studies. I resigned from my post and Miss Willison and I exchanged good wishes and home addresses on parting. Besides everything else I was glad to be able to move away from that bleak and isolated bungalow. American troops had suddenly appeared in dense encampments on Dartmoor right up to the edge of my field, and dark faces with white teeth gleaming out of broad grins had begun to stare in through my windows!

As Vera and Sergei had wisely kept some accommodation in their house for family use, I was able to pack up all the Boscombe possessions that had furnished the cottage and dispatch them to Manchester. Resuming 'bed-sit' life in London, I filled my days with ophthalmic clinics and eagerly applied myself to reading diligently for the essential exams.

Roger's emotional letters, the ideal vehicle for his self-expression, flowed endlessly. They were written on flimsy blue Air Mail Letter Cards (AMLCs) closely covered in a minute version of his usually bold handwriting, addressing me as: 'My most precious beloved darling', or 'Dearest of adored hearts', and the like. The progress of the 'so-beloved' child I carried was referred to chronologically—in all the anatomically named stages of development as they evolved according to the calendar—and was said to be loved deeply. Every letter was poetically agonised by love and anguished by the frustration of his exile in which he felt he was defiled by the conditions surrounding him.

Soon these letters began to show an element of growing anger at what he regarded as the injustice of woman's unfair advantage, which was giving me the opportunity of furthering my career, the anger and the envy steadily increasing as time went on.

In reply to his unending effusions, I poured out long, loving letters, reassuring him of my love and devotion, and my distress at being helpless over his exile. Nothing had any soothing effect on him, though he said he longed for the daily arrival of letters, and insisted that no day should end without one being sent off. He had a special cedar wood, partitioned chest built to hold the letters, and stressed how much he treasured the ones he received, and that they were what kept him going. He felt that life was wronging him, his anger and indignation growing in intensity and rancour with each passing day.

When the German V1 'doodlebug' missiles arrived in London, followed by V2s with all their devastation, I decided it was unwise to stay on there in my pregnant condition. Resigning from all my various posts, I went to Manchester where, furnished by my possessions, part of the recently vacated flat—which had originally been made for Nicholas—made a very comfortable small married home for me and the expected child, and was ready for Roger whenever he should return. I secured a post at the nearby Manchester Eye Hospital, and in due time and to everyone's delight—especially so to Sergei's loving heart—little Penelope arrived and was warmly welcomed and adored.

The happy maternity weeks went by much too quickly and though the new business of mother-craft had its difficulties, it was a great wrench for me to have to resume work after the contented weeks of full-time maternal life. Though my post was only part-time I was very reluctant to go back at the regulation time, so—to lessen my feeling that I was abandoning my baby—my father delightedly arranged to do more of his office work at home so as to keep an eye on the various nannies who, in the stressed employment conditions of the time, were difficult to find.

He thoroughly enjoyed playing with Penelope, and lavished his warmest devotion on her whenever the nanny would let him. He and Penelope would eagerly watch from the nursery window for my lunchtime return from the hospital, when he would unwillingly hand over his treasured burden to me and set off to his workshop, or to school or the Studio.

Marie, known as Granny—who had come to Manchester early in 1939 when World War II threatened, was still elegant and beautiful and still dressed her now white hair in a becoming way—became Penelope's proud great-grandmother. She gladly took part in what she could of the new life in the house, and affectionately watched nursery procedures. Sergei, by now a little greyed and be-

Penelope and I enjoy a happy moment while her father was at war

spectacled, was in his element adoring little Penelope at every possible moment, and enjoyed many chats with his mother-in-law and relived with her much of her latter story. She had lived in France since 1923, but reluctantly came to Victoria Park on Sergei and Vera's insistence some little time before the September outbreak of war as otherwise she would have been marooned in France.

The family had parted in mid-Bosphorus in December 1920 at the end of the Russian Revolution when the Shcheyteenins had had the unique opportunity of setting off for England, whilst Marie and Shoura had gone on with the rest of the refugees. Marie and her youngest and only surviving son Shoura—the slim, hazel-eyed and very French-looking young ex-naval officer who shared Vera's impish sense of humour—had chosen to be among the refugees France was accepting. Thus they continued on from Constantinople to Bizerta in Tunisia, from where they were conveyed further south down the African coast to Sfax to be housed in a Legionnaires' camp at the edge of the Sahara Desert.

Shoura's early naval training had left him very able, but with no preparation for civilian life. He had, however, been fortunate in finding a training post in Sfax, and eventually became a surveyor. As soon as it was possible, he and his mother moved from the camp into humble lodgings in the little town.

When trained, Shoura did a term of service in what was then the Belgian Congo. The salary from this post enabled him to finance his mother's modest transfer to France, away from the difficult conditions of life in North Africa.

Marie got a room in the *Maison Russe*, a charity rest home in Menton on the French Riviera, formerly maintained by Russian ladies of means and now housing its former patrons. She was pleasantly surprised to find her daughter-in-law Lyda there with her mother. Lyda was the olive-skinned and bewitching widow of Marie's late middle son Paul, the submariner whom Lyda had married soon after she had become the very youthful widow of Russia's world-renowned marine artist Ayevazovsky. Lyda had been in Venice dancing with her ballerina sister Ileana Leonidova, so had fortunately been out of Russia during the Revolution.

Lyda was indeed a *femme fatale*; twice widowed and now a ballerina like her sister—both of whom had at one time been members of the famous *Chauve Souris* Russian Ballet Company in post-Revolution Paris and had shared in all its sordid and fantastic complications. In a later third, brief, marriage she had found herself in Edgbaston in England with a gentleman of Russo-German extraction, a Mr. Baumann whose romantic picture as 'the war hero on crutches with an absent leg' was soon dispelled when it transpired that the leg had been lost when he fell off a Berlin tram! That marriage having soon disintegrated, Lyda and her sister accompanied by Ileana's Italian husband Massera, all eventually went to Lima in Peru, where they started a ballet school.

Marie did not stay long at the *Maison Russe* as she preferred to rent various little shacks in neglected, overgrown gardens, sometimes in Menton, at others in San Remo, where, amidst exotic plants and abundant native shrubbery, she gently thrived in solitary contentment. When she had accepted my father's urgent invitation to come to England in 1939 with war imminent, she had not expected her exile from France to last long and had left her main possessions with the landlord of her latest shack.

She hated Manchester because of its poor climate. As she did not speak English and refused to try to learn it, she did little else than yearn for Mediterranean sunshine, but as the war years went by she gradually had to accept the permanency of her stay. She confined herself more and more to the little back bedroom of the Victoria Park house, where she busied herself with her houseplants and in trying to catch the sound of her favourite French and Italian programmes on the radio. The fact these stations had been her local ones and now, as distant overseas ones, came over badly, caused her great frustration.

As time passed and took its toll, Marie refused treatment for her teeth when they deteriorated, and though her cataracts were advancing she would only consider intervention if she were to be sent to Switzerland. The cumulative effect of the inability to potter in a garden in Manchester's inclement climate, the absence of the solace of handiwork because of poor eyesight, together with nearly five years of distaste for the unavoidably pressure-cooked monotonous family meals, led Marie to undisguised discontent. Vera, undermined by her mother's attitude together with various staff difficulties at the Studio in the 1943 pre-Christmas rush, had eventually to admit that she needed help at home.

Fortunately just at that time Mrs. Luckhurst, the friendly tenant who had shared their house for many years, had been considering moving to be nearer to her family and willingly vacated the flat. This made it possible for my parents to accommodate a resident helper and still have some vacant space for family use. Though sorry to be parting with their house-sharing good friend they were glad to be able to employ a kindly Russian lady, a Mrs. Androsova, as companion-housekeeper to care for the ageing lady and relieve Vera of domestic chores

HOMECOMING

Living contentedly and busily with little Penelope in the happy atmosphere of the welcoming and suitably adapted Victoria Park home, my only distress was the interminable unhappiness which was so stressed in Roger's frantic letters. These now included the child in his outpourings of devotion, and continued to arrive in anguished profusion to which I strove to reply as supportively as I could.

One day I was delighted to learn that he was due to come back to England and, with very little actual forewarning, he arrived in the early days of Janu-

ary 1945. He had apparently got himself so over-frustrated that he was in-
valided out of the RNVR.

His return, however, did not seem to lift the cloud of his discontent.
Though I had waited hours at the station until well after midnight to welcome
him, he seemed so busy with his luggage and railway passes that he barely
acknowledged my presence. Neither did finding himself eventually in the
contented little home, or meeting his daughter, do much to improve his frame
of mind, nor did the gloom lift when he was rested. It was many years later
that I learnt the explanation for his abstraction.

During his time in Basra, having envied my progress, he had found his way
to the nearby hospital at Abadan to try his hand at eye work. As he continued
to show interest in the subject on return, it was decided that he would join the
first available intensive ophthalmology course at Moorfields like the one I
had taken years earlier.

To enable him to set himself up in the career which seemed to appeal to him,
I was delighted to be able to help finance his training with a sizeable 'nest-egg'
made up from the £400 paid by Sergei for our petrol-less car which I had sold
to him for Nicolas's return from Germany, together with the untouched navy
family allowance saved as I had lived with my parents, and most of my hospital earnings. Leaving Penelope in Sergei's and Vera's loving care and a
nanny, Roger and I set off for London and Moorfields' Spring 1945 course.

Roger, though proving to be a crusty academic (and in spite of the fact that
he found people generally, and patients especially, bothersome—not to say a
nuisance—) grudgingly struggled on trying to be a clinician. We sometimes
happened to be at the same clinic and occasionally, when working at adjoining desks, I had been embarrassed to hear Roger's deep voice counter some
meek patient's complaint with unsympathetic comments such as: "I don't see
what you find wrong with your eyes; mine are much worse than yours!"

As Roger did not hold with conventional contraceptives, it was not surprising that I should be pregnant shortly after his return from overseas.

Towards the end of the six-month eye course, as my confinement had to be
faced, I suggested that if he took a London-based wartime general practice
locum post. Since such posts usually offered family accommodation; he could
still continue his ophthalmic work part-time.

His terse reply to the suggestion was: "I have no wish to breed." a somewhat belated realisation in the circumstances. This he followed with: "I'm
not going to interfere with my career by wasting time doing general practice!" These statements should have warned me of the events that had to be
lived through in the incredible ensuing weeks; one of which was his an-
nouncement that he now wanted to take up anatomy and physiology as a
career.

As Roger was to attend an interview for a research post with Professor LeGros Clarke of Oxford's anatomy department on a day when I did one of my clinics at the Oxford Eye Hospital, I accompanied him to the University. Although the two of us were very pleasantly welcomed by the professor in his office, Roger sat silent and looked resentful throughout the introductory exchanges. To break an awkward and prolonged silence, I looked at Roger and tentatively raised the point that there were various ideas he wished to discuss with the professor, and offered to withdraw. In response to these observations Professor Clarke, who was an open-faced, alert man with a twinkle in his eyes, looked enquiringly at Roger who glumly said: "Yes".

Little more was said by either the professor or Roger, but he was not invited to continue with his application, and after polite leave-takings we returned to London with Roger's mood not improved. He grudgingly fumbled on in ophthalmology.

The darkness of that period is best not worded. Days eventually just followed one another and added up to months and more; time limping on, during which my career slowly funnelled me into becoming a senior house surgeon at the Ear and Eye Hospital at Maidstone. Roger, who had been offered the junior of two posts at the same hospital, refused to take it.

As the situation between the two of us grew more strained Roger's miserly inclinations surfaced more markedly and worried me. Though Roger neither earned nor paid Penelope's nanny's salary in Manchester, his resentment of the need of such a salary frightened me. I suddenly worried lest Roger decreed that Penelope be looked after by his sister Jan in Bowdon, rather than the child's grandparent and a nanny in Manchester.

Though legally both situations were equally justifiable I knew which I preferred. In actual fact neither Jan nor her mother were the kind of people who would consider any such undertaking, nor had Roger had any such thought, and even if he had wished it, he knew the ladies well enough not to entertain any such suggestion. Ignorant of the unlikelihood of losing my baby in this way, I hastened to get Penelope into my own care in Maidstone as quickly as the resident nature of my post could permit.

Having found a nearby flat, and got Penelope and the nanny down, I was aghast to find on close observation how unsuitable this woman was. With a cigarette perpetually drooping from her mouth, she playfully dangled Penelope by the wrists and had other slovenly and unsavoury ways about her, and needed to be replaced. By good fortune a surprisingly suitable nanny happened to be available just when my need was crucial.

Ruby Rose, one of whose sisters proved to be living in the house next door to my flat, happened to be looking for just the kind of post I was offering and, when all details were dealt with and references exchanged, Ruby was happy to take Penelope to her warm and capable heart.

Nanny, the name by which Ruby Rose wished to be addressed, was the youngest of thirteen girls, all of whom lived in various parts of Kent and were the daughters of a Kentish fruit farmer. Ruby regarded her eldest sister's home in Bromley as her base and was a nursery-trained children's nurse who had joined the ATS early in the war, and had become the ATS staff sergeant in charge of the highest-ranking staff officers' mess at Luton Hoo.

Having just been demobbed, she was eager to be back in the work she loved, and gladly took up her new post in September 1945, just when Penelope's first birthday was approaching. She quickly made the little flat into a well-run and comfortable little home where she and I were content to watch the sunny little girl's happy progress. Roger, who was still bluffing his way through eye clinics in London, leafing through patients as if they were inconveniences to be pushed out of the way, occasionally joined the three of us at the Maidstone flat. One such occasion was on the day when the first news of the splitting of the atom was flashed across the world.

On his next visit Roger announced he had the option of two Anatomy Demonstratorships, one at Cambridge and the other at Manchester Medical School. Having long hoped that he might be more contented if his work was more to his liking, I welcomed the news and expressed my pleasure at it. I indicated that if Roger chose to go to Cambridge where it would be a new start, I would resign my post and go with him as soon as arrangements could be made. If, however, he chose to go to Manchester, where he could live either at his mother's house or at Victoria Park, I would finish my work contract before joining him. He made no comment on anything I said.

Some days later we set off for what I imagined to be Roger's interview for the Manchester post and to return the car we had borrowed from Sergei. As we approached Bowdon I asked whether, whilst passing, Roger might like to look in to see his mother and sister.

To my shattering astonishment his cool reply was: "I've got the Manchester job," continuing after a brief pause: "I'm staying in Bowdon 'til I make other arrangements but I'll drop you in Manchester."

No thought of Penelope or me had as much as entered his mind in the making of his plans. My uncomprehending expostulation that it would be easier if I were to drop him in Bowdon and then go on to return Sergei his car, was grimly countered by Roger's words: "It's my car, I bought it in Plymouth and I'm keeping it."

I was dumbfounded; that was indeed the very last straw. The money from that car had been the greater part of what had enabled Roger to take the Moorfields ophthalmic course.

The fact that he had calmly arranged for, and walked out of, our marriage had not as much as struck me, but the vile meanness of his dastardly action over the car finally confirmed my long-formed opinion of him. Taking the wedding ring from my finger I placed it in the breast-pocket of his jacket with the words: "I wish never to set eyes on the despicable creature that you are."

Never before had a marriage been ended so simply! It was only the ring I ever regretted, especially as it had been one I had had to buy for myself. My concern had long been to protect Penelope from involvement in the gloomy scenes and tense atmospheres Roger always created. Now, with all vestiges of the loyalty to Roger that had struggled to survive in me finally stamped out by him, I was glad that the genuine warm love which had surrounded Penelope from her earliest days in Manchester and Maidstone no longer needed to be disturbed by his morose periodic presences.

As Roger was a man who did not honour obligations and had never actually supported me or Penelope—nor even ever paid his own way—it would have been useless to try to extract any due financial responsibility from him. There was indeed a chance—the divorce solicitor advised me when matters reached that stage—that Roger, as still a trainee in his newly chosen career, might claim maintenance from me, as I was further advanced in my profession, thus only adding to the pain of the proceedings.

Grateful to my parents for having equipped me with the independence of my career, I wished only for a simple end to the situation. Even so it proved to be a long cold wait of seven years during which my career took on another pioneer role: I became a professional woman and single mother.

Both were unusual circumstances at that time. There were none of the special concessions or allowances single mothers receive today; it was your own affair and you were expected to keep quiet about it and "soldier on." Being a professional woman was not an asset either, especially in the field of medicine. Women were not really welcome in the profession. In my years at university there were about seven female students to about 100 males.

When I became a consultant I was only paid for seven half-days out of a possible eleven half-days, though my turnover records far-exceeded anyone else. The seven half-days' restriction was imposed because I saw National Health Service (NHS) patients in my rooms for the Supplementary Ophthalmic Service, which was the first branch of the NHS to be established. This required me to supply accommodation, staff, and stationary, and pay travel costs to and from hospital out of a capitation fee that was, in turn, subject to heavy income taxes.

As it was, however, although my visit to Victoria Park on the day when I had been so grimly and finally deposited there had not been a happy one, no-one could have foretold the incredible nature of my next presence there some few months later.

Chapter Four

Post-War Years

BLOOD TRAIL IN THE SNOW

On February 27th 1946, the telephone at 38 Park Range, Victoria Park rang repeatedly throughout the day, and went dead each time Mrs. Androsova, the housekeeper, picked up the receiver. Annoyed by the repeated disturbance, she told Sergei and Vera on their return about the calls. They wondered whether it might have been me, unsuccessfully trying to ring through about the new post in Sheffield I was due to take up.

When the doorbell rang early into the snowy small hours of the following morning, thinking it would be me at the door and hurrying to let me in, my father tumbled out of bed and sped across the wide entrance hall clasping his pyjama collar to his neck.

Unable to unfasten the rusted old anodized-copper safety-chain that had come with the house, but eager to welcome his daughter, he unlatched the lock to be faced by a masked man.

The intruder promptly wedged his foot into the gap, and breaking the frail safety chain by thrusting his bulk against the partly open door, burst into the hall. The noise of the sudden banging and raised voices brought Vera from the bedroom, just in time to see the horror of the door flying open with the intruder cascading into the hall, and the two men falling into an immediate fighting tangle. Rushing to the phone, she started dialling for the police, but was almost immediately punched in the mouth, and knocked to the floor by the man, who continued to struggle with Sergei.

Though not a big man, my father was wiry and muscular, and was just about managing to manhandle the brute out through the door when the exasperated villain whipped out a revolver from his breast pocket and, holding

97

Sergei by the front of his pyjama jacket, shot him point blank through the chest. As his victim sank to the ground the assassin fled.

The whole event had been so quick that Mrs. Androsova had barely stirred, Marie had heard nothing, and the old spaniel had not uttered a single sound, but Vera's desperate anguished cries soon rallied everyone. Supported only by the dismayed housekeeper and a bewildered Marie, poor bruised and battered Vera faced the ghastly realisation of the murder, and understandably collapsed while the housekeeper eventually got through to the police.

Hurrying away from the scene of his crime, the murderer may not have realised that the shot had gone straight through between the two bones of his own forearm, and that he was leaving a trail of blood in the snow before he fainted.

He next found himself in the casualty department of the Manchester Royal Infirmary in the hands of the police, who had picked him up some distance from the house, unconscious from loss of blood.

Radio news of the tragedy soon brought Roger from Bowdon. Nicolas, just repatriated, came as quickly as he could from Harrow, and aghast and unbelieving, I hurried from Maidstone. With Penelope safely in Nanny's capable care and promptly taken to the Bromley sister's house, dealing with Victoria Park's immense problems fell to me.

My mother's deeply shattered state grew worse with each passing day. It became necessary for her to be sedated on account of her grief and mental shock, and in bed because of her physical injuries. When the matters of reporters, inquest, commiserations, the funeral, responses to sympathy and all the other turmoil had been dealt with, the question of day-to-day existence and how it was to be continued had to be faced.

Three devastated elderly ladies could not be left to their own devices; not that I was much of a protector, but at least I was not elderly and although Vera needed me, I could not stay long. To add to the family's distress on top of so serious a crime, some mean-minded scoundrels carried off nearly all the carefully economised precious coal ration from an insecurely locked coal shed behind the scullery.

As soon as Vera began to recover she was further exhausted by the realisation that, besides all her personal and home problems, the staff at the Studio needed guidance.. Though their combined efforts were splendid, there were various matters only Vera could handle.

The police, who were very helpful, soon unravelled what they could of the sad story. It seemed that a twenty-six-year-old army reject called Swallow had been temporarily living in a lodging house in Victoria Park, from where he felt he might carry on his last-resort 'trade' of burglary. A pupil from Sergei's Russian language class, who, I later discovered to have been Henry Best, was a long-term resident at this lodging house, and while cooking a

Sergei, Vera, and Liza (rear) in the year before his murder

modest supper for himself, frequently recounted the stories of Imperial Russia's splendours he had heard from his teacher.

Hearing one of these accounts, Swallow visualised vast hoards of imagined 'crown jewels' to be in Sergei's nearby house, and determined to appropriate them. Having also heard mention of the Russian gentleman's association with the Studio—which, to Swallow, sounded like a flourishing business—he decided to visit the place to size-up his quarry before taking action.

In retrospect, my mother was able to realise that Swallow had actually visited the Studio on a pretext of offering goods for sale, and had thus seen both her and Sergei. As Swallow's various needs had become very pressing and, as the daytime approach to the house had been foiled by the answered telephone, bolstering his courage by the possession of a gun, he decided on a night entry.

The Crown was bound to defend even its undoubted criminals, presumably to avert the death sentence that was still in effect in 1946, and appointed Harold Laski to defend Swallow. He was the celebrated left-wing trade unionist lawyer whose pro-proletariat views may possibly have given him pleasure in exonerating the man as best he could. Adding to all the other sadness, the long wait for the court case was a further torment for Vera to face in her shattered condition. Eventually a disgusting charade of a trial took place.

Swallow, wearing the face of an imbecile, sat slobbering and gibbering at the parapet of the gallery of Manchester's Crown Court, where the dock had been strategically positioned. Laski, standing in the main body of the courtroom, his arm pointing up towards Swallow in the raised accused box declaimed dramatically: "Look at this man! Is that a sane man? Can the sorry creature that you see there, know what he was doing? This is a man to be pitied—helped!"

Found to be 'guilty, but insane', Swallow was sentenced to a term in Broadmoor where he instantly recovered from his feigned imbecility. Supported by good behaviour together with the fact that Vera's grievous bodily harm caused by his assault had been overlooked, the sentence, doubtless would have soon been remitted to a minimum and Laski's exorbitant fee discretely pocketed long ago, whereas the victim's injured and shattered widow and family received no consideration.

Different human beings react to the injustice of violence and sudden killing in various ways, and though neither Vera, nor Nicolas, nor I had any wish to have Swallow put to death, the charade devised by Laski has remained offensive to all of us; the conduct and tone of the trial adding to the feeling of distrust of the rest of humanity which the murder had engendered. The overall lack of thought for the victims of the aftermath of crimes is something that governments are at last beginning to examine.

Many years later, I was working for a short time as an eye surgeon in Coleford in the Forest of Dean when a patient named Swallow came to see me. A quick check showed that this man had been 26 years old in 1946, the age of his namesake of that time. I was tempted to make superficial probes, but as the innocuous-looking middle-aged man before me might—or might not—have had a past of which he was not proud, I decided it was not worth re-opening old scores. (I had no cause to examine the man's left forearm for evidence of an old gun wound.)

For Sergei to have died battling to defend his all; his beloved wife, his home and all the dear ones in it, was the way the valiant warrior that he was would have chosen to go. To be so pointlessly murdered—just when he and Vera had begun to feel that they could at last relax and start taking part in the longed-for cultural activities from which they had been debarred so long by their demanding work—was tragedy indeed. That gentle, stout-hearted Sergei, who had been faithfully devoted to his family, and had loved my mother deeply and uncomplainingly throughout his life, should be prevented from enjoying the rewards he deserved so well, made the tragedy the more poignant.

Vera, whose clear-minded personality had steered the family through many of its troubles, had tended not to appreciate the steady back-up her husband gave to their combined battles against the hardships with which life was continually facing them. She quickly built on his wise forethought and suggestions, but often criticised his cautiousness.

The calamity of his murder had suddenly made her realise she had not been fair to him. This realisation was the scar that served to cripple her for so long. She could, in time have accepted his loss, but what tore at her soul was that in all their long years together she had not told him how much she really loved him, nor acknowledged to what an extent she depended on his wisdom in all their ventures.

As Sergei had occasionally shared with me his faithful but often hurt feelings, so bruised by Vera's recurrent hasty rebukes, I could well understand my mother's anguish. Vera needed to tell someone of her love for her 'Seriozjha,' and be reassured she was not just persuading herself she had not meant to be as harsh as she may have sounded. She longed to tell Sergei so, but he was not there to hear her.

Trying to bolster Vera's spirits, I encouraged her to get on with odd bits of unfinished handwork. We would sit quietly doing something of that kind when Vera, whose mind had obviously been circling painfully around her torment, would suddenly say: "Ninoosia dear, I always relied on Seriozjha. You know that, dear, don't you? I always listened to what he said."

"Of course you did, dear," I replied. "You couldn't have managed otherwise, could you? You were always such a wonderful team! Just think of all that the two of you have achieved together!"

Another time she would say: "I didn't sound brusque really, did I? I didn't mean to, you do know that?"

"Yes, dear," I assured her. "I knew, and so did Papa, if he ever noticed. But you weren't sharp, you were just overtired."

Conversations of such a nature crept in most days, but grew fewer as, with time; Vera began to come to terms with her distress. Her recovery was slow and unwilling, and she was not ready to be left alone.

I had been due to report to my new post in Sheffield early in March that year but had been given leave to delay this in the circumstances. After a further two weeks' deferment had been granted, I racked my brains searching for a solution to the problem, knowing that if I delayed any longer the posting would be lost.

The situation needed a friendly relative or a long-standing friend; not an employee, but someone who would support Vera even when she had recovered enough to resume the double task of the care of her mother and that of running the Studio without Sergei's help, but no such person seemed to be available.

My mind, which still had the knack of retaining addresses, suddenly brought 46 Lomond Road, Hull to my attention; the address of Miss Willison, the Plymouth matron with whom we had exchanged addresses in those far-off days in the peace of the shared Didworthy Sanatorium sitting room, and of whom I had not thought consciously. I quickly began to hope that perhaps Miss Willison, who by that time would have retired, might come for a while.

A letter soon sped off to Lomond Road, telling the lady of the circumstances and difficulties, and of the hope that perhaps she might be able to help out for a short time just to enable me to take up my post, if only to allow me to see how matters progressed. To my immense delight Miss Willison agreed to come for a fortnight.

In happy fact she stayed for many years! She was, indeed, one of my guardian angels, as so too, in his way, became a little Cairn terrier, Jolly.

GUARDIAN ANGELS

Soon after Sergei had gone, the old spaniel breathed his last and, in view of everything, the ladies decided they should have another dog. The consensus of opinion was that little yappy dogs made better guard dogs than placid spaniels. On taking up the Sheffield post I found pleasant temporary digs in a vicarage near Penistone, where my hostess, a Mrs. Gerber, bred Blencathra Cairns and happened to have a puppy for sale.

Although I had not been convinced about the preference for small dogs, but having met the puppy, I could not have resisted him even if the household had been clamouring for a St. Bernard.

Little Jolly, as the puppy was called, at once knew he was meant for me and Manchester, and though with nothing of the vicious guard dog about him, he served and protected his new family for many years, not as a noisy brute but as a gentle and understanding companion, and before long became the love of Miss Willison's life.

She herself soon became virtually a member of the family, and in Miss Willison's meticulous and affectionate care, my mother gradually recovered. The fact that the Studio needed her attention was indeed a splendid spur to her recovery.

Miss Willison had not been expected to keep house or look after Marie, whom she addressed as "Madame Matousseyevitch," so, some years later when Mrs. Androsova needed to leave, another housekeeper had to be found. After much searching a Mrs. Cartledge; a pleasant and elegant white-haired lady from Lincoln was interviewed and, regarded as suitable, was engaged.

Why such a seemingly cultured lady should need a housekeeper's post was not considered to be relevant. Marie welcomed Mrs Cartledge's cultured manner, and was glad of the more varied meals she served and, as Miss Willison and the new lady appeared to be companionably at ease with each other, life flowed amicably along.

Needing to have my family with me in Sheffield, I bought a little house conveniently near the hospital.

This was a small, detached villa, in a pleasant modern cul-de-sac on the south edge of the town, which Nanny Ruby Rose ran happily whilst looking lovingly after her blossoming charge with delightful white-overalled expertise. Each afternoon, dressed elegantly in her neat outdoor suit and trim velour hat, she took Penelope out in a Victorian pram in which the two-year-old sat upright and resembled a miniature Regency lady in a sedan chair.

Enabled by this smooth-running life, I slipped over to Victoria Park quite regularly and was able to keep an eye on matters there, and was glad to see that they seemed to be settling happily. After a time, however, Mrs. Cartledge's occasional bouts of unconsciousness without any other signs of ill health puzzled Miss Willison.

Eventually, on discovering Mrs. Cartledge's great interest in greyhound racing at the nearby Belle Vue greyhound stadium, she decided that the strange interludes were the results of either excessive drowning of sorrows, or celebrating of successful betting days. Some time later, to my mother's and my surprise, Miss Willison began to accompany Mrs. Cartledge to the racecourse and their friendship seemed to deepen.

In the early days my mother had not had occasion to observe any financial inaccuracies in Mrs. Cartledge's domestic accounts, but in time errors appeared and gradually got more complicated; money given to buy insurance stamps was going astray and when questioned, Mrs. Cartledge's apologies were profuse and, accompanied by promises to refund the missing sums by cheque, sounded genuine.

On checking bank statements, Vera was surprised to find that Mrs. Cartledge's repayment cheques were not being honoured. At the next payday again, profuse apologies and a replacement cheque would first be promised, and eventually flashed about dramatically before being handed over. This again would curiously happen to get cancelled by some inexplicable mischance. Fortunately, when Mrs. Cartledge wrote out her next cheque in payment for her now quite considerable debt, I was able to drive my mother to the bank where she cashed the cheque before it could be cancelled.

As my mother and I emerged from the bank, we were met by the obviously surprised and annoyed Mrs. Cartledge at whom we both smiled benignly, but with raised eyebrows in feigned surprise at the lady's presence in the establishment.

After a short lapse of time, repeated threats of violence against the occupants of 38 Park Range appeared scrawled overnight on the approaches to the house. These harped vaguely on the subject of past murders. Then similar messages, written on paper and wrapped around pieces of coal, said to have been thrown through smashed windows, began to appear during the day.

As all the breakages were in the small coloured windowpanes of the front bedroom, my hunch was to suspect Mrs. Cartledge, but I could not imagine any explanation. Before Vera and I considered any other action I arranged to watch the house from a friendly neighbour's well-positioned villa across the road where, prepared to watch all night if need be, I settled down in a convenient bedroom window, having arrived disguised as a very official looking nurse.

After a long wait the faint glow of a lit cigarette appeared in Mrs. Cartledge's un-curtained bedroom window, and moved from the depth of the room towards the window where; lit more clearly by the street lamp outside, I was able to see the lady open the window, seat herself on the wide out-jutting sill of the Oriel window and, carefully leaning out backwards through the opening and crooking her arm round its edge, she smashed a hole inwards through one of its small coloured upper window panes using a high-heeled shoe as a hammer.

The reason for the intricate manoeuvre was doubtless to make the break look as if, like the earlier ones, it had been caused by a prepared threat-wrapped missile thrown from outside.

Vera and I immediately called the police who came quickly and were very helpful. They found the relevant evidence, and promptly asked what charges they were to lay. With their advice, and Miss Willison's knowledge, it was agreed that if the lady removed herself instantly, no charge would be made against her.

To our utter amazement, later that morning, a haughty Mrs. Cartledge left accompanied by a wordless, stony-faced Miss Willison.

It was many years before the strange events of that period could be understood in all their complexities.

Without the two ladies my mother again faced the problem of the care of her mother. She felt that having stopped her evening teaching after Sergei's death, she would be able to cope with the needs of the Studio and the care of her mother with non-resident help at home.

She found a Russian lady, a Mrs. Karpenko, who came on a daily basis even though she lived a long way away. On the weekends when Vera was with us in Buxton, Mrs. Karpenko stayed overnight. Though this arrangement had its advantages, it did not give Vera enough help. During the couple of years that it dragged on, Vera overworked and neglected herself so much that she developed diabetes, which soon began to damage her eyesight.

Casting about frantically in my mind as to how to deal with the new problem, my longing thoughts turned to Miss Willison's meticulous, trained and devoted care. I wished desperately that Miss Willison could be available, but wasn't sure if I dared approach her again. I considered the matter very seriously and discussed it with little Cairn-dog Jolly and, as he looked into my eyes so earnestly and wagged his tail so happily, I decided to go to Hull (with Jolly) to ask her.

Jolly's innocent devotion had been quite right to encourage me; Miss Willison, who still loved Jolly dearly, was glad to come, and it was then that the saga of the bogus attacks on the Victoria Park house unfolded fully.

During her years in Manchester Mrs. Cartledge had persuaded Miss Willison either to invest her savings, or to loan her the greater part of them for some dubious, supposedly cast-iron, secure investment scheme. Unbeknown to Miss Willison, Mrs. Cartledge, having gradually lost the lot on the greyhounds, had cleverly kept in the lady's good books by giving her little flattering gifts and a show of affection which, although vaguely suspicious and totally unnecessary, had not warned Miss Willison!

But when my mother discovered Mrs. Cartledge's financial inaccuracies, Miss Willison began to question the lady regarding the security of her money and, not fully reassured by the great show of simulated confidence, had asked for its return.

Mrs. Cartledge, knowing that she was unable to repay the debt, needed to escape. The excuse she devised for a sudden untraceable departure was the bogus threats dodge when, pretending to be in fear for her life, she would insist on leaving hurriedly without any forwarding address.

Miss Willison—who was actually an astute lady—was feeling very annoyed with herself for having entered Mrs. Cartledge's rosy-sounding scheme, and having asked for the arrangement to be cancelled, needed to allow the woman time in which to arrange the return of the money.

When the situation came to its sudden crisis overnight, needing to have a hold over Mrs. Cartledge, Miss Willison offered the lady hospitality in her former home at her sister's house in Hull, but in the speed of events she could not explain matters to my mother. Fortunately her scheme, persistence, and brother-in-law's help enabled her to recoup some of her savings, but in the process, besides the monetary loss, Miss Willison also lost her turn for the longed-for flat.

With time the situation at Lomond Road had grown more difficult for various reasons, and to my delight Miss Willison again agreed to come to Victoria Park.

Though Vera resented the strict routine, the sight- and life-saving regime which Miss Willison promptly instituted was essential in her worsening diabetic state. It had been a mercy that the kind lady had been able to come so quickly.

Vera in her later years

She eventually saw Vera through the cataract operation that in time became necessary and, to everyone's relief, the diabetes gradually receded. It was many years later, and only when the coveted flat became available for her, that Miss Willison ultimately set off for Hull.

MIGHTY MANXMAN SONNY

With no interest in my former husband Roger, and no wish to know anything about him, I was very surprised when, shortly before my move from Sheffield to Buxton, in Derbyshire, I had a visit from Sonny Rigby, Caroline's husband. Sonny had come because he felt that I should know that he resented Roger's friendship with his wife.

He regarded Roger's unwelcome visits to be too frequent and intrusive and even though Roger was supposed to be a long-standing family friend, Sonny wanted to make it fully understood that he wanted Roger's association with Caroline to cease. Sonny had hoped to find an ally in me, and was very disappointed to find that I was of no help to him, and was not willing to join him in employing a private detective to shadow Roger's misdeeds.

On learning of the Caroline situation, I was glad to find that it did not affect or concern me. Roger was of no interest to me, but I began to understand much of our past. I had long forgotten the early Bournemouth reference to a link between Roger and an 'older married lady' whom Roger's mother had disliked, and no thought of that lady or anyone else of her kind had as much as entered my trusting heart. Not even on Roger's phenomenal reaction to the fortune teller's disclosures, or his wordless dumping of me in Victoria Park on the day he took up his post at the medical school, had the thought of that association come to my mind.

Sonny Rigby had met Caroline Addis in the late 1920s. He was then a medical student who attended various local medical society dances and receptions with his father, an eye specialist, where Caroline was often there with her father, a gynaecologist. Before long, an ardent affair developed and Sonny and Caroline married. As good Catholics they soon had two children.

By the later 1940s they were living in Didsbury, a suburb near town and the university. As they were finding Sonny's Manchester Assistant Medical Officer of Health's meagre salary inadequate, they thought that it would be wise for Caroline to go in for medicine. In view of Sonny's increasing dependence on alcohol, Caroline herself welcomed the thought of the advantages a medical qualification would give her if her husband's problem became acute. Bravely starting at the medical school, it was very natural that Roger, a family friend who by then was in the anatomy department, should offer to help Caroline with anatomy that, as a mature student, she was finding difficult.

The Rigbys soon asked Roger to give Caroline tutorials at their house, something Roger was eager to take on, as his demonstratorship salary was small. Roger and Sonny's mutual dislike of each other had bristled instantly on renewal of contact, and the fact that Sonny regarded the tutoring arrangement to be on the 'old school tie' basis, annoyed Roger intensely.

Sonny, who was deeply and possessively in love with his wife, soon came to dislike the close association these tutorials gave Caroline and Roger. He possibly saw more in the developing relationship than there may have been at the beginning, but his violently expressed resentment antagonised the two of them against him and heightened Caroline's maternal protectiveness towards her welcome young tutor and protégé.

In the time spent together over tutorials, Roger and Caroline got to know more about each other. Caroline was sorry to learn of his marriage difficulties. Not knowing how heartlessly uninterested he was in his daughter, nor of any of his other unnatural actions and pronouncements, she was distressed for him to be deprived of his child, and doubtless wanted to pour balm on what she imagined to be his injured soul.

Roger's frequent presence at the Rigby's house had to be tolerated on account of the lessons, but when one day Sonny, a tall, well-developed powerful man with a hot temper found the house doors locked on his return from work, his intense anger, fanned by rightful male jealousy, exploded at what he imagined to be going on.

With his anger at white heat, he decided to leave them be, as he felt that the situation needed serious action. Intent on teaching Roger a lesson, he retraced his steps; strode into a pub where he drank himself silly, and spent the night in his car. Next morning he found his way to the top floor of the medical school which housed the anatomy department, stalked up to Roger, grasped him by his receding forelock and dragged him, head first, down eight or more flights of the building's stone stairs.

He sent me the hair which had remained in his fist when Yoxall, the porter, managed to restrain him with the help of students and staff, who rallied round and dusted down the bruised and dishevelled anatomist. This sordid but understandable episode got Sonny 'warned off' the university premises and grounds, and thrust the two culprits, Roger and Caroline, more closely to each other.

Sonny now unceremoniously turned Roger out of the house if he found him there, but the greater his protests became, and the more outrageous his behaviour and accusations grew, the closer Roger and Caroline drew together.

Sonny's frequently repeated reminders that he had no intention of giving Caroline her freedom just irritated her and Roger, who both found these statements laughable. Roger's introvert nature, which from early childhood had been made to feel outshone by his dead brother's celestial perfection, flourished in Caroline's motherly benevolence which, combined with her readiness to be taught, gave the two of them a very good interrelationship and was very satisfactory. It was, however, not until after Sonny's 1962 death that they were able to marry.

From my point of view Roger was a total stranger. Our marriage had been a mistake and was finished. But I was deeply scarred by the immeasurable damage his inhuman attitude had done to Penelope, for whom her father's rejection had been increasingly hurtful as she grew older. Penelope had sought nothing more than occasional social contact with a nebulous father, knowledge of whom she needed so as to be able to relate him to herself, a cognisance which was essential for her own self-assessment.

BUXTON

Penelope's first fifteen or so months were spent in Manchester and Maidstone. Her second and third years were in Sheffield, from where, in May 1948, I was appointed Honorary Ophthalmic Surgeon to the Macclesfield Royal Infirmary and the Buxton Hospital. The three of us—Penelope, Nanny Ruby and I—moved to Buxton, where I took over Dr. T. S. Harrison's practice and house on his retirement. Though the National Health Service (NHS) had been scheduled to start in July of that year, and as no one knew what would be happening, things continued much as before.

Little Penelope and I settled into the small house in Hartington Road overlooking the Pavilion Gardens and Buxton's celebrated Broad Walk. Though most of the ground floor of the complicated house was given over to a consulting and a reception/waiting room, Nanny Ruby Rose ably managed the housekeeping for the whole house while caring lovingly for her little lady. Penelope by this time was a smiling curly-headed feminine version of Sergei, her late grandfather, and was a growing joy to everyone.

On being engaged as Penelope's nanny in Maidstone, Ruby Rose had asked if she might bring along her much-loved cat Billy, a neutered tom, and although the request was happily granted it took surprisingly long for him to arrive. The delay had ultimately to be explained: the 'neutering' and the 'tom' had been misnomers as, on Penelope's first birthday, five ginger kittens and a couple of black ones with white markings arrived, firmly founding the child's love of cats.

Billy and the smallest black-and-white kitten, called Blackie (who ultimately and indubitably lived to be 21), started the family's animal department, soon joined by Lassie a stray Border Collie and later by a pale blue budgie, who all combined in the making of a happy home.

The Supplementary Ophthalmic Service (SOS) for the care of peoples' eyes was the first part of the NHS to be put into operation, and everybody clamoured for the new free eye tests and spectacles. The Buxton rooms worked at full capacity, and as rooms were needed in Macclesfield, I bought a house there and appointed a very pleasant and efficient Miss Wadsworth as secretary to take charge of that section. I loved the scenic drive over the Pennines in all the changing phases of the year, and tended to welcome unheralded holidays caused by snow blocking the perilous roads.

Before I had gone as far as looking for a secretary for Buxton, a Miss Gaertner offered herself for the post. As she was an established local resident, and a member of the golf club besides her secretarial skills, I employed her but was soon surprised by the lady's undue interest in the my domestic and family affairs. She assumed for herself a kind of over-liberal social secretary's role. Missing from the office much too often, I would find her in the upstairs family sitting-room where she would promptly suggest that I too should "sit down, have a sherry" and join her in the cigarette she was enjoying.

She refused to accept correction and, as she soon suggested that the day's dictation could be more comfortably done at her home rather than in the office, I realised it was necessary to find someone else for the post.

In the meantime my divorce was proceeding apace in the hands of a young Manchester solicitor, a smallish, pale, sad-faced young man called Gerald who had been involved with the Spanish Civil War, and was a great sportsman and hockey enthusiast. After some minor social undertakings he had invited me to join him on a Grindelwald skiing trip. To his great disappointment my main delight had been Switzerland's snow—which evoked long forgotten memories of St. Petersburg—even the nursery skiing slopes terrified me. The trip proved to be a total fiasco, but the friendship continued.

Gerald's cousin Alan—who ran the Littler family's law stationery business in town—came to see me one day about his mother's aged Pekingese dog's troublesome protuberant eyes. He lived very near me in Buxton with his elderly mother and their housekeeper, and soon became a firm friend and good adviser. Blue-eyed Alan was a trim, well-built, light-footed man with a quiet sense of humour who only uttered words when they were essential. This may have been because the pipe he generally held between his widely upward arched short teeth interfered with speaking. A subtle moustache classed him with the Territorials, whose activities he enjoyed and before long he invited me to regimental dinners and dances.

As an established Buxtonian, and long-time member of the golf club, he was surprised to find that I had taken Miss Gaertner as a secretary and very soon said meaningfully and insistently, in his laconic way: "Shed that load!"

In response to my uncomprehending look he very simply repeated: "Shed that load!" This time I understood, and began to see what lay behind the surprising manifestations that had been developing in my house and office: a problem personality situation.

That evening, looking for a reason to sack Miss Gaertner, I made some critical annotations on the day's notes and typing, intending to have a difficult encounter in the office next morning when, mysteriously, the lady failed to arrive for duty. Neither she nor I telephoned and, as uninvited as she had come, just as wordlessly she went! It didn't take long to replace her by a delightful young girl called Jean who worked capably and happily for many years.

Amongst the many good friendships made in the Buxton days there had been a quaint one in the later years when Penelope was a young teenager. A prosperous stockbroker's surprisingly complimentary attention for quite a time, to both me and Penelope, suddenly stopped one day when, presumably having discovered I was his senior by a couple of years, he enquired anxiously: "Have I committed myself?"

Though not sure what he was alluding to, but assuming that he had been mulling over a proposal, I assured him that he had not committed himself and was glad that he hadn't tried to put words to a proposal. After a short silence he confirmed my deduction by going on to muse: "I suppose Penelope is really too young to get engaged?"

Fortunately, as the question didn't require much of an answer, the whole episode faded into the past and a friendly Christmas card correspondence continued to his death.

From the earliest days in Buxton a friendship with Colonel Harry Sowler was outstanding and heartfelt. He was a military man, and a true countryman who had owned by that time the long-defunct *Manchester Courier*, and now lived in very reduced circumstances in the country at King Sterndale, a minute village near Buxton. His house, now in sad need of repair, had doubtless been delightful and was still hung with untended and damp-damaged wall-size family portraits in the reception rooms.

In spite of the evident penury, he still behaved in the socially approved mode befitting a gentleman of rank. He arranged parties to the local Hunt Balls, and was a staunch Conservative and Unionist. No longer having horses, he followed the hunt on foot, and although his thin shaky legs in their old cavalry breeches betrayed his age, his enthusiasm and energy were phenomenal.

Doreen, his kindly, unmarried younger daughter was his unfailing helpmate who faithfully supported him and fluttered in his wake as, doubtless, his honoured beautiful late wife would have done in years gone by.

Years later, when looking for someone to replace Jean, the young secretary who was about to be married, I considered Doreen as a candidate but first offered the post to a patient, a Miss Parkin, whose main advantage for the post was that she lived conveniently nearby. Though obviously enjoying her remarkably recovered and improved eyesight following my recent operation on her cataract, she was not interested, so Doreen was next on the list.

Though Alice Parkin refused the post, I gratefully accepted the willing offer of her modest minor services in any other required capacity on a strictly unpaid basis. She very soon became an indispensable and much-loved associate member of the family affectionately known as 'Parky' and became another of my guardian angels for nearly twenty-five years to the sad end of her days.

Parky was the victim of an old law precluding a man from marrying his deceased wife's sister. As the youngest of a worthy Buxton man's family of five children, Alice had helped her widowed mother to educate the older brothers and sisters of whom incidentally, the eldest son was eventually the City of Portsmouth's civil engineer throughout World War II. In the early 1940s, after having lovingly tended her mother's final years, she went to live in Edgware with her sister, and started to enjoy the independence of wartime employment.

To her chagrin she was soon recalled to Buxton to care for family uncles and aunts, whom she went on to nurse unfailingly through their successive terminal illnesses. According to the laws current at the time, when Parky's father unlawfully married the sister of his late young wife, who died bearing his first child, the four following children of his family of five were held to be 'born out-of-wedlock'.

Although the Legitimacy (retrospective) Act of 1926 legitimised the children involved, the local people — including the uncles and aunts — still considered only Bertha, the first daughter, to be legitimate. Excluded by this outdated premise from the well-deserved substantial legacy rightly hers, Parky only received the aunts' little house and a small pension in thanks for her years of devoted service. Even so, she was proud of her hard-earned independence.

After many years of enjoying Parky's unfailing helpfulness, I eventually met her sister Mabel who had been a teacher in Blackpool. To all our combined astonishment, it gradually transpired that Mabel proved to be the wife of the friendly Blackpool chemist John Dodd who had, on that windy, dog-troubled, locum-serving day in early 1939, so fortuitously directed my steps to Moorfields and thence on into 'eyes'.

When the actual time came for Jean, the little secretary, to leave in the early 1950s, Doreen Sowler became my devoted amateur secretary. As typing had not been included in her upbringing, to my professional disadvantage, a *pro forma* system of reports to doctors was soon devised, but as the Sowler family was badly in need of an income it didn't have to matter. Doreen, however, did not keep her post for long.

One evening in the powder-room at one of the Colonel's Hunt Ball parties a very apologetic Doreen said: "There's something I have been meaning to ask you to look at for me if you would." and drawing her low-cut evening gown to one side, she exposed a raw and weeping, fungating growth. Apparently, although this breast lesion had been developing for some time, Doreen did not seek medical advice because she could see that she would need hospital treatment, and felt unable to leave her father unattended.

With the Colonel incorporated into my all-accommodating home, Doreen was immediately hustled off to hospital, but it was too late for her to have any effective treatment and she soon died.

Shortly before leaving Buxton many years later, while chatting one day with my good friend and medical adviser Moya Applebee, and reminiscing about the twenty-five years spent there happily, though so many loved ones had had to go; on mention of the Sowlers I had gently chided Moya for not warning me of Miss Gaertner's locally well-known lesbian propensities.

My friend's amused reply was a shock: "We weren't to know that you weren't one too!" she proclaimed with a laugh, the 'we' denoting the Buxton medical fraternity: I had not known how wise Alan Littler's urgent "Shed that load" advice had been.

In Manchester during those long Buxton years, time had seen my grandmother Marie's eyesight deteriorate so much that she was virtually blind and confined to her room. As the Victoria Park house badly needed to be decorated, and the old lady could not tolerate the smell of paint, she had agreed to go to stay with me in Buxton during the decorating. Whilst sitting snugly in the passenger seat of the little purring car on our way over to Buxton, Marie put a confiding hand on my arm and said, "If I was to ask you, Ninachka dear, to operate on my eyes, would you?"

"Why, yes of course, dear," I happily replied. As Vera had wisely forewarned me of the possible request and making sure there would be no time for my grandmother to change her mind I added: "In fact, you know dear, you can come into hospital on Tuesday".

Contrary to the custom of not operating on a relative; in view of the otherwise insuperable language situation, and together with the fact the operation was long overdue, I was fully prepared to operate without delay, and had made provisional arrangements. A French-speaking nurse had been located, and was engaged for the days in hospital, and happily the operation was a success.

Having enjoyed her stay in Buxton, and now able to see, Marie agreed to try living in a private nursing home near to my house. This was a long-needed arrangement that ought really to have been contrived much earlier, as it greatly eased my mother's life in Manchester. Vera who, though fond of her mother, had found it increasingly taxing on top of her very full-time work, to have to face Marie's constant discontent.

Fortunately a nursing home in the Broad Walk had a vacancy, and Marie settled in. As 'Great-Granny,' she enjoyed visits from Penelope and was surprisingly relaxed. A happy arrangement was arrived at in which a half-French lady, a Miss Dickie, spent a companionable daily hour or so with the old lady on a pseudo-lesson basis, thus sharing my care of my grandmother who, with endearing naiveté one day, delightedly half-whispered to me: "You know, dear, I think this nice Miss Dickie must like me, she comes so often!"

It was a joy to both Vera and me that the old lady was content in her new setting. She was surrounded by her beloved house-plants and took pleasure in being taken for walks along the Broad Walk; a pleasure she was able to enjoy right up to her death in 1955 in her ninety-fifth year.

HOME LIFE

In 1949 little curly headed Penelope, brim-full of smiles, enjoyed the preparatory school she started, and though my domestic arrangements had been running smoothly in Nanny's capable hands, as time went on an unexpected disquiet crept into our contented midst. Ruby and I had naturally become good friends from our early days together but, like most long-term nannies, Ruby could not help but grow possessive of her charge. Her growing, though doubtless unintentional, 'Mother excluding' attitude began to alarm me.

Though in many ways Nanny kept the child to unnecessarily baby ways, she showed a degree of harshness towards the little girl as she grew older, and an unexpectedly severe discipline seemed to keep Penelope in fear of her displeasure.

Sunday lunches, which had become established as 'guest-occasions' ran relatively smoothly as the child had been well schooled for them, but on the rare occasions when I was able to take part in odd mid-week family meals Penelope's natural chance naughtiness would result in Nanny bursting out with an angry: "Why can't you behave yourself? You always do when we are by ourselves!" as she swooped on the miscreant, adding: "Just sit down and get on with your meal!"—Penelope obeying meekly and doing her best not to burst into tears as plates or table napkins would be brusquely resettled.

This would be followed by: "The minute that mother of yours appears you start being silly, she'll think I don't teach you how to behave!" thus turning the welling tears into torrents and the meal into an unpleasant scene on every such occasion.

The repeated association of my presence being the cause of disgrace, tears and unhappiness is not a suitable basic psychological foundation for any child to grow up with. Besides this, Nanny's persistent currying of favour with the child by 'bettering' whatever presents or pleasures anyone gave her, probably a subconscious countering of her severe ways, was a further unsuitable principle for a child to assimilate.

I would have gladly kept Ruby as my major-domo forever and a day, but as Penelope's happiness and mental make-up was at stake, regretfully I had to tell Nanny that she must look for another post. Penelope, though not apparently upset by Nanny's going, certainly played-up very cleverly for subsequent helpers without the strict domination she was used to.

Having given a lot of thought to the question of Penelope's growing up and education, I could see that I needed to spend more time with my daughter. Paradoxically with the child at boarding school, I felt I could programme my work round school terms and then be freer in school holidays to spend with Penelope. All told, it began to appear wise to consider the idea of a good boarding school with a preparatory department.

As Malvern Girls College appeared to have the necessary qualities, I set off with Penelope and Vera, now the proud and doting granny, to consider its suitability.

Malvern's headmistress, Miss Brookes, was a very friendly, mature lady whose cultured care, I felt, was preferable for Penelope to that which would surround her if she were to stay on as a day pupil at the pleasant little school in Buxton, and live at home where she would be in the midst of part-time office staff and probably mostly in the company of a kindly housekeeper.

Miss Temperley, the headmistress of Parkfield, the preparatory department of the school where we went from the very impressive main school, was another cultured lady whose caring approach to her charges was reassuring. Parkfield was a large appropriately and comfortably adapted home-like Victorian house surrounded by delightful grounds.

Penelope showed great interest in all she saw, and expressed delight at the prospect of being a member of the happy and congenial group of pretty little girls, all in their similar frocks. I was touched by the evidence of long experience with little bodies, who tend to grow homesick as the first term progresses, when I was told by the gentle Miss Temperley that parents were usually asked to arrange for the child to have a pet to bring back to school for the second term.

Charmed by the school and the whole occasion, we returned home heartened and full of enthusiasm for Penelope's proposed new life. The idea of going to the new school appealed to Penelope, but when it came to the actual departure she was somewhat subdued, but full of questions and seemed happy. For me, the heartbreak of having to leave my baby was very hard and I had to persuade myself repeatedly that it was the right step to take.

Penelope seemed to take to being away at school very contentedly, and I was very grateful to the boarding school Exeat system for the close contact that it enabled us to establish over the years. In fact I had the feeling that boarding actually proved to be more of a joint experience for us than the separateness which tends to develop in a child's school life in a nearby day school. Our two lives would have run their very separate parallel courses without the happy sharing of interests and points of view we were able to enjoy together in our Malvern days.

THE HOLIDAYS

Throughout her time with me, Nanny Ruby Rose spent her holidays with other members of her family and their various children, and from her early days had asked whether she could take Penelope on holiday with her.

As the sisters all went to Cliftonville the "Nannies and Children's Paradise," I gladly agreed to the arrangement. I regarded holidays as times for catching-up, and was delighted for Penelope to have appropriate holidays where all the little people contentedly built sandcastles, and had duly supervised donkey rides and the like. For the summer holiday after Ruby left, Penelope and I went away together very happily to a country house with wide rural attractions at Great Milton, near Oxford where Penelope—in jodhpurs concertinaed on her short little legs—sat on her first pony like a little soldier and lost her heart to the soft-eyed creatures.

There being no riding facilities in Buxton, a stumpy black-and-white first pony called Patch was found, and a nearby Buxton farmer was prevailed upon to rent some grazing and stabling. Saddles, bridles, grooming brushes and hard hats were acquired and the lure of the horse took hold.

As the years went by outgrown Patch was followed, in their turns, by Pye, Topsy, Flick, and later by Gretty and Rory, who all gave years of happiness and helped to found Penelope's deep love of all nature's beings. Stable duties; shared by many friends in school holidays, and maintained by me during term, contributed very largely to the enjoyment of those fresh-air-filled pony days and happy friendships.

Penelope's closest friend at home was Elisabeth Lees who, though a few years Penelope's senior, was as youthful in spirit and, much as an elder sister, provided the happiest of companionships. They were both too young to be unaccompanied with the ponies, and as I enjoyed the unaccustomed freedom and out-door life of the holiday periods, and loved the ponies as much as the girls did, we made a carefree trio who giggled happily together through many idyllic days.

Middle school that followed on from junior school for which Miss Temperley's care had been preparing the little people, ultimately led the girls into senior school where academic inclinations needed to be defined.

As Penelope certainly had a good brain, I—who was generally attracted to Oxford since my wartime days and enjoyed yearly Oxford Ophthalmic Congresses there—wanted to kindle Penelope's interest in that city of dreaming towers, with all it offered. Hoping that Penelope might want to go to Oxford as an undergraduate one day, I sometimes arranged for the two of us to spend time there during occasional school exeats.

Eventually we went on a weekend Commonwealth course at Worcester College sponsored by the Royal Commonwealth Society. This proved to be attended largely by dark-skinned Africans in splendid flowing robes, who all seemed to find youthful golden-haired Penelope very attractive. Though the lectures were more detailed than either of us needed, the course gave us considerable insight into the might of the Commonwealth, and the experience of staying the three days in college surroundings gave Penelope the 'feel' of Oxford life.

Miss Burgess, the new Malvern headmistress who succeeded Miss Brookes, monitored her girls' progress carefully and closely and felt that Penelope had potential for the classics, but needed encouragement. The wise lady suggested a cruise of the Greek Isles might stimulate the required interest.

Though financing a cruise frightened me, Swann's Hellenic Tours brochures and the prospect of a Mediterranean April were very tempting, and we duly set off on a lovely expedition. Air travel having not yet then quite taken over, ours was one of the last of the cruises which started from a special platform at Victoria Station by Pullman train in first-class splendour. The Channel crossing, however, had its usual drawbacks and Penelope soon began to whisper that she was definitely dying, as her poor little face grew green. But as Calais fortunately soon came into sight, matters eased.

An exciting luxurious train journey across France brought us to a slow and long-protracted arrival at Marseille. Carriage wheels squeaked as the long snake of the curving train waited and crept in turns. People hung from lowered corridor windows; some looking about impatiently, others enjoying the anticipation of what was to follow. Eventually the cruise ship was boarded, and with the cabin found and settled into, cruise life started in earnest. Well-known accompanying Oxford professors chatted volubly with Cambridge colleagues, and greeted old friends and acquaintances.

A restful cruise took us gently through a sunny Mediterranean Sea, and as evening darkened we watched Mount Etna's volcanic grumbles finger light patterns in the sky. Having rounded the foot of Italy, we sailed smoothly into the enchanting harbour of Dubrovnik, the lovely fortress city that was then still only slightly damaged. After the next days' exciting slither through the Corinth canal and a number of brief calls at successive islands, we paused at Troy, after which the smooth waters of the Hellespont took us to Bursa with its Blue Mosques.

As the following morning dawned, the beauty of Istanbul's fantastic skyline of domes and minarets gleaming in the early sunshine came into view. This was a very different view of that enchanting city from that of my 1920 approach to it from the east in a rough tub of a rowing boat and its two villainous Turks all those years ago.

Early next morning, driving in the comfort of cruise-arranged coaches along the European shore of the Bosphorus to the ancient round-towered fortress of Rumili Hissar, we watched delightedly as rainbow-coloured mists rose slowly from the treacherous but deceptively mirror-smooth sun-lit waters and gradually evaporated into the blue of the Mediterranean sky.

After a short time in Istanbul our spectacularly lovely and luxurious return journey brought us home bewitched. The whole holiday had been an incredibly lovely experience and, as it had convinced Penelope that it was worth taking classics, she happily joined three other budding classicists the next term.

Just about when term was due to start, the girls' college classics mistress had a bad car accident, and had to be away for the next few terms. Fortunately it was possible to arrange for the four girls to cycle across the town to the boys' college to join its pupils, where Mr. Kennedy's well-practised and inspiring methods of kindling classics interest in his students launched the girls into the subject very satisfactorily.

By the next spring, as several of the various young boys' college masters were said to be enlisting as couriers on a Greek cruise run by the smaller firm of Fairways and Swinford, I felt that another cruise among young people Penelope knew, would be a well-deserved and pleasant reward for her interest in classics. As she was delighted at the idea I booked to go on that year's spring cruise, during which Canada became more than just a name in an atlas.

THE CANADIAN CONNECTION

The Canadian province of Nova Scotia prides itself on being peopled by the descendants of the surviving hardy immigrants from Scotland who had miraculously withstood the rigours of the highland clearances and the perilous Atlantic crossing in the good ship *Hector* which left Loch Broom in Ross-shire in1773.

One such handsome, sturdy Scots descendant was Simon Murray, who in the trying mid-1800s often gazed out across the ocean from Nova Scotia's northeastern coast and pondered on those distant Scottish highlands of his forebears' days.

Among other staunch Scots descendants, Simon met Jane Falconer, who was as tall, determined and industrious as he, and they soon fell in love. Well-accustomed to the harsh ways of their surroundings, they started married life as small farmers at Granton, inland in Nova Scotia's Middle River region of Pictou County, where life was primitive and made the more difficult by the often severe climate of both winter and summer. With good honest hard work and, in time with the help of their four bright children, they thrived modestly.

Simon was an intelligent man with energy and enterprise, who saw opportunity in the coaling business, and established a wharf near the shire town of Pictou.

The family moved there, and what became known as the Company House was soon built at the riverside. The three boys grew up 'messing about' in boats, barges and coaling trucks and the girl, whilst keeping up keenly with her brothers, helped her mother.

Though Simon ran his wharf and was the local constable, he had enterprise and ability to spare and soon organised and built an ice rink in nearby New Glasgow, and ran both enterprises successfully.

Of their four children Cliff, the eldest, on finishing his education moved to Truro, Nova Scotia's railway hub, where he went into the coach and truck building industry. Kathleen, the third child, became an efficient secretary and took part in the ice rink business and Fred, the youngest son, went into the rapidly expanding developments in textiles and moved to the United States. Their second son Leonard, lured by the sea, was happy to go to Canada's embryonic naval college that was established in Halifax, Nova Scotia in 1911, from where he graduated as one of its earliest founding cadets and joined HMS *Berwick* in January 1913.

Though Scotland has peopled much of Canada, Britain had lured back many Canadians including Elizabeth Scott, the widow of a member of a long established and prominent Ontario family and who had been a minister in the federal government at some time around the turn of the century.

Elizabeth was an ardent Anglophile who, deeply distressed by her husband's death some little time before the First World War, was soon persuaded to join her English friends, the Whistlers, in England. As her four girls were Florrie Whistler's contemporaries, Elizabeth was happy to be near her friends and soon settled in Eaton Square.

Florrie's father Edward Whistler, who had at one time been Lord Mayor of the City of London, died in 1899 leaving his wife and daughter many obligatory social duties. On her mother's death in 1911 Florrie tried to fulfil all the outstanding obligations and was glad of Elizabeth's help. As these mushroomed with the declaration of the Great War, all the Scott ladies' services were welcomed. VADs were being recruited, service clubs needed hostesses and soup kitchens needed to be organised.

Well on into the 1914-18 war, very honoured to find himself at the Admiralty in London, Leonard Murray, the Nova Scotian early graduate of the Canadian Naval College—a tall, fair, well set-up handsome young officer of considerable standing who had been seconded to the Royal Navy from the Royal Canadian Navy—was, one day, pleasantly surprised to meet the welcoming Canadian Mrs. Scott, who was busily providing hospitality for Naval officers in London.

Glad to make friends with the lady he soon also enjoyed the company of her daughters. Of the four daughters Rita and Marjorie had become naval wives early in the war and before long Leonard found the third daughter, Jean, to be very charming.

Unlike her sisters who all enjoyed social activities, Jean had joined Florrie Whistler in her ultimately chosen way of contributing to the war effort by supplying fresh vegetables to service clubs. The market garden business they started at Crondle, in Hampshire, was so successful that they soon needed to employ a considerable force of workers. Feeling that one of those new-fangled motorcars would be useful, Florrie popped into Harrods one day and bought one. Having been told what to do to make it go, and relying on finger points for direction, she happily sped off for home in an elegant machine.

Having captivated Leonard Murray's heart, Jean could soon see herself as another naval wife, though a Canadian one this time. Young Betty, the fourth Scott sister, was not married. She had always liked being different; was a keen sportswoman and enjoyed independent life.

Leonard and Jean married at the end of 1921, and went on to spend many happy years together. Their two handsome sons, though born in Canada, were both at Stubbington in England before going on to Dartmouth from where both graduated with considerable distinction. They both gave the Navy loyal service before proceeding into scientific careers in England on the early retirement imposed on them by the Senior Service.

The Second World War was gallantly served by the Canadian Navy and by Leonard who, as Admiral L.W.Murray, RCN CB CBE, was Commander-in-Chief, Royal Canadian Navy, Canadian North West Atlantic. With the unfailing collaboration of Admiral Percy Noble RN, Admiral Roger Bidwell RN, and Captain Eric Brand RN, who together started up Canada's elementary War Office at the outbreak of war in a small room over a grocer's shop in Halifax (the capital city of Nova Scotia), Leonard master-minded the Canadian half of the Battle of the Atlantic from April 1943 to the end of hostilities.

Though the losses to the merchant navy and the royal British and Canadian navies and air forces were devastating, the fierce unending battle against the German *Luftwaffe* and U-boats did manage to protect the greater portion of

Admiral Leonard Warren Murray, the Pictou County, Nova Scotia sailor who became the love of my life

the convoys that were Britain's lifeline, maintaining food and supplies throughout the war.

Convoys sent off from Halifax's Bedford Basin were under Canada's control, but on reaching the mid-Atlantic half-way line between the continents, Britain took over the care of the rest of each convoy's run; the command of the operation transferring from Leonard to that of Admiral Nelles, who was subsequently followed by Admiral Max Horton at the battle's corresponding British HQ at Derby House in Liverpool.

On VE Day, May 8th 1945 the long striven-for day of victory, to everyone's justifiable disgust, the mayor of Halifax's incomprehensible order to shut all liquor stores, tea-rooms and other places of relaxation and entertainment as well as the town's lavatories resulted in the notorious 'Halifax Riots.' Jubilant servicemen of all forces, as well as rejoicing civilians, unable to find venues for their well-deserved celebrations, rioted and tore the town to pieces.

At the first eruption of disorder Admiral Murray—who was the senior officer of the port—tried to establish some measure of order by loud-hailing a call to all service personnel to return to their units. He stood on the roof of a Jeep repeating his urgent command as the cautiously moving vehicle carried him round all the town's streets. Gratified to find how compliantly most of the sailors obeyed his command and went back to their ships, Admiral Murray was distressed to see how the other services and vast hordes of outraged civilians; incensed by the inhuman restrictions on that day of all days, persisted in breaking up and looting the town's liquor-stores and shops.

Their rampage was assisted by the manager of the local Oland's brewery giving away ample supplies of beer to feed the frenzy.

After protracted reviews of the events of the day the armed forces were regarded as culpable, and Leonard, as the senior officer on duty, was held responsible, disregarding his personal undertakings on the day. Bearing the injustice with noble dignity he eventually resigned from the navy, to which he had given his total devotion throughout his life and, foregoing the highest rank to which he was entitled, he and Jean moved to England in 1946.

In actual fact Leonard continued to be held in high esteem by the navy, and was highly honoured in Halifax in the later years of his life. Posthumously, following meticulous research started shortly after the end of the war into the local history of the time, he was totally exonerated in the late 1970s. The investigations which went into the minutiae of the local history of the time, together with detailed enquiries into actual events on the disastrous day, proved the civic authorities to have been at fault, and that the services had been wrongly held responsible.

Leonard has been honoured by having buildings, like the Murray Building (S-15) at Canadian Forces Base Stadacona, the Navy's headquarters in Halifax, sea cadet units, and streets in various parts of Canada named after him, and a memorial erected in his honour at his birthplace.

To this day, however, there are those in Halifax who persist in their wish to hold Leonard accountable referring, in hushed tones, to his 'obstinate pride' as the cause of the fracas.

This is indeed a very untrue and a totally inaccurate assumption, and an impossible assessment of the valiant man, broad-minded and caring personality. Leonard was a very wise and considerate man who may have been too proud to stick up for himself when wrongly blamed, but his pride was in all the men who made up the Canadian Navy.

Some of this lingering reluctance to lay blame where blame is due—with Mayor Allan MacDougall Butler and his council—still exists among Halifax's social establishment. The city has long been described as the most British of the British North American communities.

This was certainly true of its social structure, which was so closed that for the longest time, in order to satisfy convention, the mayor's position was alternately given to a Protestant then a Catholic for one-year terms. The 1955 election of Leonard Kitz, a Jew, greatly disturbed the accepted order of things.

In England in those early post-war years Admiral Murray took up law in London, became a barrister—partly to qualify himself to extract as much information about his discommendation from the Royal Canadian Navy—and proceeded to practise marine law while his wife Jean was very glad to rejoin her sisters whose early RN marriages had proved to be successful. Rita and her husband Ricky—Sir Lewis Ritchie, one-time Paymaster Admiral of the Royal Yacht—were living near Oxford, and Marjorie, the widow of naval architect Admiral Ricardo was living in Pirbright in Surrey. Tall tomboy sister Betty flourished in St John's Wood in London, but lived mostly in Switzerland.

Fairly soon after their return to England, having tired of central London flat-life, Leonard and Jean bought The Baskings, a lovely country house at Selsfield in Sussex. This proved to be a happy home where Leonard soon became engrossed in wide voluntary activities in politics and local government.

Florrie Whistler, Jean's faithful friend who had mothered the two young Murray boys throughout their growing years in England, joined the family at The Baskings, where she was eventually happy to see both Hugh and Sandy launched on their married lives.

To everyone's distress Jean developed cancer in 1960 whereupon Leonard retired from his law practice to be with her, but, as at that time treatment had little effect, she died in November 1962.

Having dealt with probate, Leonard found a suitable flat in a nearby beautifully converted country house near East Grinstead. The removal to the flat—and all the business of settling in—was ably undertaken by Betty, the late Jean's jaunty youngest sister from St John's Wood.

As present-day law no longer precluded a widower from marrying his deceased wife's sister, Betty, though a confirmed 'bachelor-girl', could not help but ponder whether she too might become a "naval' lady. But for the moment, having made quite a job of Leonard's flat, she set off for Switzerland to pay attention to the chalet she was having built for herself near Chateau d'Oex.

Leonard, anxious not to burden his sons and their young families with his sudden solitude in the approach of Eastertide, catching sight of a travel brochure with pictures of sunny Mediterranean seas, decided to go on a spring cruise of the Greek Isles.

A GREEK ROMANCE

As Easter holidays started, Penelope and I launched on our Spring cruise on the Greek steam ship *Moladet*. Having chosen the first meal sitting, we were not aware of the excited flutterings amongst a group of ex-Wrens around a genial retired Canadian admiral who happened to be in their midst at the second sitting.

Actually we had both been conscious of a pleasant gentleman on several of our day expeditions, whom we had found to be very friendly. He was a big, rosy-faced and blue-eyed, contented-looking energetic man who walked with a spring in his step and was polite and considerate towards all the various members of the cruise parties, and whose warm greeting Penelope and I welcomed whenever we chanced to be together on expeditions.

On one of the later trips I happened to stumble at the top of a steep climb at Epidaurus and, starting to slip down the slope, gladly grasped the admiral's timely offered helping hand.

To be held by that hand gave me the immediate unexpected and never previously experienced sensation of having 'come home;' of having suddenly found where I belonged. I did not want to let go of that hand, nor did he seem to hasten to draw his away. We just happily drew close for a long moment before the group all moved on, but an accord had been struck in that instant. It surprised us both and quickly coloured the whole situation.

The warm-hearted admiral was Leonard Murray, CB, CBE, RCN Rtd., whose pleasant and unexpected easy friendship was further advanced when we found that Penelope, while at school in Malvern, had met his scientist elder son Sandy, and as they all joined the Hellenic Society in London, the friendship continued. Leonard and I arranged to meet when I was due to be in London seeing Penelope off at Heathrow on her way to do a stint of Red Cross relief work in France.

Having stayed overnight with my brother Nicolas and his family in Pinner, Penelope and I met Leonard at the Royal Commonwealth Society, from where he drove us to Heathrow and, with Penelope safely seen to her plane, he and I returned to London. Following a very happy lunch at the Senior Service Club, we drove out to Greenwich where Leonard proudly showed me around the Queen's House and the Naval Academy with its beautiful painted ceilings.

As I had planned to drive to Buxton that evening we returned to the Ladies' Room at the Senior Club for a restful tea, after which we went along to get the car, but found the temporary parking enclosure (the site of what is now the Clore National Gallery Extension) securely locked. In my haste on arrival I had not seen the big sign stating that the car park was closed from 4 p.m. on Saturdays, and would only reopen on the following Monday morning!

Undaunted, Leonard quickly made suggestions for spending the next day together and, with me booked into the Royal Commonwealth Society and he into his Senior Service Club, we settled ourselves into the comfortable lounges of the Commonwealth, where, in time, we enjoyed a leisurely dinner and the evening slipped by much too quickly.

Early next morning a message was delivered to my room from Leonard saying that he would like to meet me for breakfast in the Society's dining room. This was indeed a very delightful opening to what proved to be a very happy day.

After breakfast we again went to Greenwich to see the historic ship *Cutty Sark*, which we hadn't had time to see the previous day. From there we went to Leonard's late wife's sister Marjorie's lovely thatch-roofed house at Pirbright near Guildford. There, after pleasant chatter and a walk round her beautiful garden, the progress of her sister Betty's chalet in Switzerland was discussed over a so-called 'scratch' meal in a warm and welcoming atmosphere.

When we returned to London I had an urgent wish to have my brother meet Leonard, and suggested that I would like the two of them to be my guests to dinner that evening, and was glad that Nicolas was pleased to come. The contentment-filled day continued into a happy evening during which many common interests were discovered. Leonard, as a sailor, was interested to hear about Nicolas's army experiences and was anxious to know how he had found the attitude of Germans to prisoners whilst Nicolas questioned Leonard about matters Canadian.

Between the more serious topics there was plenty of light-hearted chatter with laughs and anecdotes, and everyone was sorry when it was time to part.

The next morning, with Leonard's supervision making sure that my car was in order, I set off for Buxton with a very happy heart.

Years later, widowed and living in Kew in Surrey, I met a neighbouring friend, a Moira Jordison whose name had a vaguely familiar ring about it, causing me to wonder whether we had met in Greece. So, one day when we again chanced to meet in the street, I broached the subject and had been right: Moira proved to be one of the several ex-Wrens who had hovered so eagerly around Leonard on the *Moladet*. On hearing the ship's name Moira shot out an accusing finger at me and uttered a shrill realisation. "You . . . married the admiral!"

In those early days of 1963—years before that Kew meeting—when the simple wedding plans were being made and Leonard was due to be moving to Buxton, during some unimportant chatter but apropos of something, Len had laughingly said: "Those Wrens will be disappointed when they hear our news!"

HISTORIC BUXTON

From my 1948 arrival in Buxton, the more I saw of the town and its surroundings the more I loved it in spite of its severe climate. Its historic centre consists of a beautiful Georgian crescent which lies to the south of the town's High Street shopping area, and separated from it by The Grove, the town's main through road. The Crescent faces a moderately steeply rising grass-covered mound called The Slopes, at the top of which lies Higher Buxton with its market place. At the bottom of The Slopes, a centrally placed decorative building contains Buxton's ancient and therapeutic Sulphur Springs.

Beautiful Assembly Rooms with their superb painted ceilings form the central part of the Crescent, which continues southwards to join the long established Thermal Baths with their imposing frontage. This in its turn adjoins the famous Old Hall Hotel where Mary, Queen of Scots used to be kept when she came for treatment for her rheumatism during the time she was imprisoned by Queen Elizabeth I at nearby Hardwick Hall.

A much overgrown and secluded path in the Pavilion Gardens just opposite the entrance to the Old Hall is known as Queen Mary's Walk, and is said to have been the lady's exercise ground during these visits.

In 1772 John Carr, a contemporary of the architect Robert Adam, was commissioned by the Duke of Devonshire to build six houses in Buxton for his land agent, lawyer, vicar, physician and other officials in what is known as The Square.

Unlike the usual residential square—where houses surround an open area—this, not unlike the Elizabethan country house which was built around a courtyard, is formed by a terrace of six houses angled in pairs around a cen-

The Square in historic Buxton, my happy home in the early 1960s

tral service area forming a cube whose outer facades are formed by continuous arcades. The south face of the building overlooks the Pavilion Gardens.

In 1958, when one of the south facing houses alongside the Old Hotel came vacant, I was glad to be able to buy it.

After the outdated interior of this delightfully spacious and stately dwelling had been radically repaired and modernised, its generous proportions provided appropriate accommodation for my busy ophthalmic practice. Besides making a comfortable family home for me, the renovations extended onto the second floor and offered a self-contained home for my mother, who eventually occupied it. Servants' quarters on the third floor provided welcome overflow accommodation.

It was to this stately house at 6, The Square, Buxton that Leonard came to join me when we married in 1963.

As Leonard was not a wealthy man, and was not able to bestow financial independence on his wife, I needed to continue with my professional work to maintain my multiple commitments. We had thought of transferring my hospital appointments to Sussex when we were planning to marry, but this would not have been plausible; Vera was living in the upstairs flat, the ophthalmic practice was established, and we were both content for Leonard to transfer to Buxton. He found people to whom to entrust his many voluntary activities and resigned from the deputy chairmanship of Cuckfield Rural District Council.

Leonard put his modest means into my household 'kitty' and was very distressed that his means were so small. As all his family's former financial advantages had come from his late wife Jean, and her money had reverted to the two sons, besides his very small Canadian Navy pension, there was little else. He was later further dismayed to learn that as his marriage to me was contracted after retirement, his pension would not be continued for me after his death.

None of this troubled me, for although a little extra cash would have been an advantage, I was not marrying Leonard for money or status, but for the warm loving human relationship which he offered so generously, and which both Penelope and I had so long lacked. His genuine affection and warmhearted personality were riches enough!

We chose to marry on Leonard's eldest grandson Julian's seventh birthday on August 23rd 1963 when I—the new grandmother—would be regarded as a birthday present for the boy. The wedding proved to be a happy family event, except for the fact that Penelope was still away in France.

The big house, built to be full of people, blossomed. Leonard's two handsome sons with families of all ages big and small; his nieces and nephews with their families and parents mingled with my family and many friends. The catering was contentedly carried out by Maud, my part-time cook, who had also found great joy in baking the superb wedding cake.

As my leave quota for the year had been fully used up, our honeymoon was a weekend spent at Leonard's East Grinstead flat, after which we were very glad to take up our happy married life together in Buxton.

In his earlier days Leonard would have liked to have a girl to join his boys, and now he gladly and warmly welcomed Penelope as a daughter. He offered her the paternal love and care which she had so sorely missed in all her earlier growing years and,, addressed as 'Pappy,' he soon became the affectionate adviser she needed in her awkward, confusing, late-teenage years. Besides his warmth towards Penelope, his genial presence immediately enriched all aspects of the complicated household that he entered.

Leonard himself faced all that lay before him with affectionate pleasure; a new mother-in-law Vera, addressed as "Mrs Shcheyteenin" in the upper floor apartment, a hubbub of patients and receptionists on the ground floor, and our family living-quarters somewhat publicly exposed on the elegant main first floor. Leonard and Vera were good friends immediately; she would have wished him to have been younger, nearer my age, but in every other way she was very happy for the two of us, and for herself.

As none of the current receptionists were typists, Len took on the practice typing duties as well as the total administration of family affairs. He also undertook a considerable part of the household shopping, on which he was accompanied by Lassie, the family's Border Collie who was soon his inseparable companion.

Breakfasts and Scotch-broth lunches were his undertaking, but the main housekeeping, catering and cooking, continued to be done by Maud the devoted and much loved part-time cook. Maud conveniently used the kitchen and dining room in Vera's quarters on the second floor, where she put on the main evening meal for the whole family. Sunny, smiling, singing days followed one another happily; Leonard contentedly whistling or humming little tunes under his breath as he went about his many undertakings.

Having saved up the next year's hospital leave, we spent all the six weeks in Canada, where Len introduced me to his many friends on Vancouver Island and in Ontario, and ultimately in New Glasgow in Nova Scotia, where I was glad to meet my new mother-in-law — generally known as Granny Jane — who was in her late nineties.

As Granny Jane was outliving all her friends in Nova Scotia it was decided that she should come to Buxton. Having lived in a nursing home in Canada following a slight stroke some ten or more years earlier, similar arrangements were made for her in Buxton where her new life gave her great happiness. Besides spending many Sundays with Len and me, she thoroughly enjoyed visiting her great-grandchildren; Sandy's in Malvern, and Hugh's in Hayling Island. In between, in her nursing home room, she got through nearly the whole of a large-print book in a day.

In her third year in Buxton she revelled in the celebrations of her 100th birthday and was delighted to receive the Queen's telegram. Fred, her youngest son

Leonard with his mother, Granny Jane, during her last days in Buxton

and his wife Lucy came over from the United States for the birthday, and followed it by a trip to the Continent, after which they again visited to say goodbye to Granny Jane.

During the night following the farewells the old lady had a minor cerebral episode, which affected her eyesight. When she realised that she could no longer read, she decided she did not want to 'stay' any longer and firmly refused to get out of bed, insisting that it was time to die.

A couple of days later, after a poor night, she told me that she had been over to the 'other side' where it was so beautiful that she had not wanted to come back. The following night she did not have to come back; she died peacefully and having been an honest and devout woman all her life she deserved to go to that beautiful place, wherever it might be.

"Madame" in retirement

Although my mother moved into her flat at the top of the house at The Square in 1960 she did not retire until a couple of years later. After her tragic bereavement in 1945 the fact that the Studio needed her had stimulated her recovery, and once on her feet the creative nature of her work was her prime interest throughout the years that followed and, helped by her devoted "girls" at the Studio, and Miss Willison at home, she continued her very personal art business splendidly.

When after many years of mutual friendship and care Miss Willison got her long-awaited Hull flat and left, Vera employed a Miss Cross who looked after her very maternally; somewhat brusquely, though warm-heartedly nonetheless. This lady had been eagerly saving up her earnings over the years for a long-planned holiday to visit her brother in South Africa and eventually went off happily on this wonderful trip. To everyone's surprise on arrival there she became ill and quickly died of some unsuspected internal growth.

Rather than start looking for another housekeeper, Vera wisely decided to sell the Victoria Park house and go to live in the flat at The Square and commute daily to the Studio. Though the Studio had largely been the whole family's salvation from its early days and throughout Vera's solo years, it was time to encourage her to ease up; especially so in view of the long distances she had to travel since she had come to Buxton.

After a considerable length of time and much persuasion, she eventually managed to pass the business on to an artistic young entrepreneur, and actually retired. To her surprise she found she enjoyed her unaccustomed leisure, and was glad, amongst other themes, to be able to visit her much-loved brother Shoura and his wife Irene who, by that time, lived in Paris. There she learnt more about their earlier lives.

After the 1920 Sevastopol evacuation Shoura and his mother Marie were among the small number of refugees from defeated Imperial Russia whom France had accommodated in Tunisia. From there Shoura eventually went to the Belgian Congo later going on to a surveying post on the eastern frontier of Iran. As he was a French subject and a reservist—the equivalent of a Territorial—he was called up when war threatened in the late 1930s and posted to Metz for work as a surveyor for the building of the projected Maginot Line. While in Paris, being briefed for the undertaking, he had met and fallen in love with Irene Trifanoff, a Russian émigré doctor. There were, however, many obstacles to their romance.

Though Irene's girlhood marriage had promptly been ended when her young husband had been killed in the early attempts on the life of Rasputin—the Russian monk who had so influenced the Tzar and his family—there was no legally acceptable proof of her widowhood. Searches that had been going on for years for evidence of the young man's death, without success, now urgently needed to be intensified.

Just when Shoura and Irene were getting desperate, a friend happened to look at an old browned newspaper that had long lined a cupboard drawer, and noticed part of an article which mentioned that particular young man's heroic death.

This find, when substantiated, at last enabled them to marry. They were able to incorporate Irene's mother into their new life very happily, and as Shoura had to be away in Metz a great deal of the time, he lovingly thought it would be an advantage all round if Marie too was near them in Paris.

Not knowing how discontented his mother could be away from her beloved Mediterranean sunshine, he rented a small flat for her in their block but the arrangement was a catastrophic error. Having nearly broken up Shoura's marriage and created an irrevocable rift between herself and her son, Marie returned defiantly to Menton. Before long, when war became inevitable, she was compelled to move to Manchester.

As Irene's Parisian medical qualifications were attained unsupported by the French school-leaving *baccalaureate*, she was not able to practise medicine in France so, when her mother died, she gladly took an appointment as doctor to the French legation in Teheran, and left Paris. After the war Shoura, happy to resume his Iranian surveying post, joined Irene in Teheran where they were at last able to enjoy the easy and comfortable life of that country as it was at that time.

Many happy Iranian years later, Shoura's health began to fail, obliging him and Irene to return to Paris even though their financial prospects there were nil. Very fortunately some friends from Irene's early days, the Jouberts—who had great difficulty in obtaining a certain very popular brandy-snap type of biscuit for their well-established select grocery business in Paris—suggested Shoura and Irene might start baking such biscuits and promised to market their product.

Taking up the challenge Shoura and Irene bought a little two-roomed shack in a run-down industrial area at Colombes on the outskirts of Paris, installed a biscuit-baking oven in the cellar of their tiny home and started producing French brandy snaps.

Though Shoura and Irene lived many years in Colombes they were on little more than nodding terms with their neighbours, with whom they had little in common. Nor was their popularity enhanced by Irene's Iranian habit of throwing coffee grounds straight from her coffee-making saucepan out through their only door onto the road outside. In her Iranian days this coffee was welcome compost for the extensive gardens that surrounded their house, whereas in Colombes only a flimsy paling some two feet away separated the open door from passers by.

Shoura's failing health and the unaccustomed strain of many biscuit-baking years eventually defeated him and he died.

By then a widow, my dear Leonard having died some five years earlier in 1971, I went over to Paris to support Irene in her grief. Arriving at Colombes for the funeral I was surprised to find the house deserted, Irene doubtless having left early for the church in central Paris, where I needed to follow her.

Having luggage and wearing too many clothes for the unexpectedly hot day, I asked the near neighbours, who had been steadily watching my arrival, if I might leave my small grip with them. I explained who I was and the circumstances, but they would not accept the case; a disdainful hand-wave in the direction of the Matousseyvitch's house was scornfully accompanied by: "They're foreigners! How do we know that the case doesn't contain a bomb?"

When, however, I topped the case with the suede coat I had been eagerly taking off, the lady conceded, saying: "It's not likely that the English lady would want to blow up such a nice coat!" and took the things in.

I visited Colombes frequently in Irene's last years, but did not manage to cure her of her habit of throwing out coffee-grounds, nor could any rains wash away the dark brown stain stretching across the road opposite that door.

Chapter Five

Kaleidoscope

LEONARD'S BRIEF BUXTON LIFE

From our first enchanted 1963 days, life in Buxton ran in its happy vein; Leonard casting his beneficent spell all around. He welcomed Parky's irreplaceable help, and enchanted the relays of girls who ran the office on the ground floor that, to his surprise, besides being an office, was a hive for a soft toy industry.

This sideline business had unexpectedly been launched one day when one of the office staff, who had been taking soft toy-making evening classes, complained that she had difficulty with getting a face on to a rabbit she was making.

I saw no problem, and quickly did as asked, but felt sorry that the poor lady had been called upon to make such a grotesquely shaped so-called toy, and was convinced I could produce animals of recognisable species and breed. I promptly designed and made prototypes, and got the office staff to take part in repeating the prototypes between making appointments. One of the girls would cut out the material for the toy, the next day's receptionist machined the prepared material into shape; a third stuffed it, but the finishing and the animals' faces came back to me to make.

This new industry soon got Design Centre approval, was called Admiral Toys and I became an award-winning member of the British Toy Makers Guild. As a result of being on display and sale at the Design Centre in the Haymarket, marketing grew and Leonard and I quite enjoyed supplying local gift shops on our various off-duty country trips with the life-like little dogs and other animals.

When in London for Leonard's stately naval occasions, we bought necessary materials and one day our car, packed full of huge plastic sacks of materials, was parked in formal splendour outside Buckingham Palace whilst we attended a royal garden party!

Leonard takes the salute at Buxton's Trafalgar Day celebration in 1971

The modest amateur business grew, but when in 1969 an order came in for three gross polar bears to be delivered within two months to Fenwick's in Newcastle, the enterprise had to be wound down, and not before time. Ridiculous tax demands were being made on me, who did not know that as the owner of the concern I could not claim for the time I devoted to the making of the product, nor to the running of the business. The only way I could have claimed for my part in the time consuming undertaking would have been for me to appoint Leonard and myself as directors, and claimed directors' fees.

It was, however, just as well that 'the industry' was phased out, as Len had become unwell. His condition was gradually diagnosed as an infection of a long-existing but unsuspected kidney cyst that needed urgent treatment. In its congested state it was causing pressure on his heart. After a long and painful convalescence following a successful excision of the cyst from the kidney, Leonard recovered well and was again striding about energetically, humming or whistling a tune under his breath in his usual happy way, and was in sunny contact with what seemed a contented world around him.

One day, to his great distress, he learned that his elder son, Sandy, was having trouble with his marriage; Shirley his vivacious wife was getting herself entangled in someone else's life. Devastated by the prospect of divorce, Sandy came to Buxton to share his trouble with his father who was deeply disturbed by the tragedy. The unaccustomed atmosphere of unhappiness seemed to undermine Leonard's health, making him listless and subdued.

Leonard happily making his shopping rounds in Buxton

Before long he caught a chill and was poorly enough to stay in bed for a week. Tests were started in view of the possibility of an infection of a suspected cyst on his other kidney. Because he did not like to admit how unwell he felt, Leonard pushed himself and wrote a detailed outline of his life at the request of the Canadian Readers' Digest. As he was over the acute stage of that undiagnosed illness, he was contemplating getting up and dressing to attend hospital for X-rays, and even suggested that he would do his usual self-imposed stint of getting breakfast, but agreed to have it in bed.

Enchanted by the view from the tall windows of the room he had come to love, he stood gazing out across at the waterfall opposite the house with the Pavilion Gardens beyond. Savouring the beauty of morning sunshine glistening on the hoar frost of that November morning he gave word to the thoughts that flowed through his mind.

He mused, saying what a fortunate man he had been; that he was grateful for all the interests his life had given him, for his two sons and their mother, and for me, to whom he gave a verbal bouquet which cannot be matched and, smiling lovingly towards me, he got into bed. He put his head on the pillow, drew up the bed-covers and in the next moment he was dead.

Just about to fetch his breakfast tray, I could not believe what I saw. Though without any real hope, every means of resuscitation was tried but was of no avail. For all who were left it was overwhelming, but for Len, though much too soon, it was a blessed way to go, and one which he well deserved when the inevitable time came.

In the latter weeks before his death Leonard had been telling me that he kept having persistently recurring dreams in which he was sailing away over wide seas, and that I was not going with him. We had talked softly about this but had not attached much significance to the dream.

In those bereft, incredible and incredulous days after Len had gone, the strange words uttered twenty nine years earlier by the quaint little fortune-telling woman in Bournemouth in 1942—that not then but much later, I would cross water to reach my 'real man'—kept coming back to me. Doubtless the day will come when I too will be sailing over the wide seas that Len had been telling me about. Though sustained by many happy memories and the knowledge that Len's all-loving spirit was unclouded to the last, no words, thoughts or actions could dull the pain.

PINNER TROUBLES

In all this time Nicolas's strained home situation had continued to worsen. Returning in 1945 from his POW years, he had purchased a lovely Victorian house in Pinner. It was set in a charming garden, and was big enough to house a small branch surgery besides being delightful to live in, but sadly it did not make a happy home.

Nicolas's genuine and wholehearted interest in people endeared him to his patients, whose demands on him grew rapidly and engulfed him. As the success of a solo practice is so much a personal matter, enlisting help is not easy and Nicolas found he could devote less and less time to his home life.

Between the happy times when he and Kathleen visited their son John, who by this time was at school at Radley, Kathleen was left in ever growing solitude in which her resentment deepened. Had she considered taking some small part in the running of the practice or some minor paid or voluntary post, their estrangement might not have grown quite so wide, but no such idea was within her scheme of life.

Foreign holidays, formerly enjoyed together, no longer mended the strained relations between them even temporarily; in fact they accentuated matters by contrasting Nicholas' restrained behaviour with the easy flattery of Latin hoteliers and gigolos.

On returning from their latest holiday, Kathleen resumed her desolate views on the monotony of home life and, missing the facile continental admiration she had naively considered to be genuine, she decided to go back alone, only to return even more distressed than before.

In Nicolas and Kathleen's early days their common interest had been their love of beautiful furnishings and antiques. Combining searching for that kind of thing with finding pleasant eating places had become their foremost occupation and recreation. Kathleen had busily studied books on antiques, and the latest *Home Culture* magazines.

Besides regarding every new gadget advertised as essential to be possessed, she had soon begun to crave the most perfect of items in their antique acquisitions. This resulted in Nicolas being spurred into taking on more work in order to afford the high prices they now had to consider and, before long, young John's first question on coming home at the end of term had become: "What's new this time?"

Eventually the house could hold no more treasures, and their searching expeditions had to stop. As they had no other shared activities to replace their only common interest, Kathleen grew to feel more and more unappreciated. She began to regard herself as overweight, and determined to regain allure by slimming. She was, in fact, a very normally proportioned, attractive classical brunette, much in the mould of Nicolas's deservedly admired mother, and had no cause for discontent.

As Kathleen's mother had grown heavy in her later years, Kathleen feared she too might lose her figure, and launched on multiple slimming treatments.

Debilitated by the rigours of weight-reducing regimes and medications, her customary pep pills now just depressed her. As she spent the greater part of the day in bed, and didn't cater for her and Nicolas's simple needs, he had to pick up a daily hot meal from a nearby hotel. As Kathleen chose to eat her share of the food upstairs, probably throwing away most of it; by the time she came downstairs Nicolas would be just about ready to get back to work.

He hated having to leave her, because he understood that the emptiness of the deserted house would again thrust her into deep gloom, but he was obliged to go. For a long time he tried to soften the impact of his going by tender little loving actions, but his considerate acts were soon regarded as inappropriate. In time he grew taciturn when at home, and gladly escaped to his work.

On leaving Radley young John found it difficult to live in the strained atmosphere at home, and on failing his exams in the mechanical engineering course at Imperial College in London, he abandoned his university training and took up a post as an untrained schoolmaster in a small preparatory school in Hampshire.

Remembering his own early years, he had great sympathy with small boys away at school, and was heartened if he saw a small homesick boy appear to be comforted by his friendly attitude. Before long he was glad to recognise a kindred spirit in the school's young matron Helen, a tall, intelligent blossoming brunette who came from Warminster, with whom a good friendship soon started. Helen's family's warm welcoming hospitality and the comradeship they gave him in their nearby home supported John greatly.

A WORLD CRUISE

Hoping to dispel her depression Kathleen—who had inherited some money from her late father—decided to spend the money on an extended world cruise. Though doubtful of a cure being attainable, Nicolas encouraged Kathleen to go as there were friends in various distant places.

In Kathleen's absence Nicolas was able to lead a less abnormal life. Without home obligations he devoted himself to his work at his own discretion, and was content to relish his many evening visits, which by that time were really socio-medical calls, enjoyed by both visitor and hosts. He felt free and unrestrained and was even able to enjoy a stay in Buxton at the time of my 1963 wedding of which—having liked Leonard from that first Commonwealth Society evening—he approved whole-heartedly.

Over the years Nicolas had come to use the friendly local family-run chemist's shop as a convenient haven where, besides hot coffees for himself, his prescriptions were efficiently dispensed and his various home difficulties were no secret as the owner was a near neighbour. On learning of Kathleen's absence Ethel, the tall assertive cosmetics assistant who liked the look of the handsome doctor, quickly undertook to make life easy and comfortable for him in his new lone state.

Charmed by Nicolas's lovely home—a sub-conscious re-creation of the background of his heritage, which he had assembled so lovingly with Kathleen's able help—Ethel soon regarded herself as in love with the well mannered dapper man who, when not oppressed, was genial, warm-hearted and good fun. Nicolas, on his side, was glad to see the pleasure Ethel derived from being in the beautiful surroundings and her approval of everything, added to which he found the free and easy tomboy rough and tumble of her uncultured life-style to be an unexpected breath of fresh air.

Though of a physique and appearance totally unlike that of anyone he knew, occasional contented glimpses in Ethel's basic face with its forceful under-slung jaw surprised him by seeming vaguely familiar to him, as if somehow belonging to a neonatal memory deeply buried long ago.

In his becalmed state of bemused relief from customary difficulties, these vague questing touches, though confusing, added to his surprise at Ethel's common-sense presence, and made his unprecedented ease very pleasing. Ethel, though she doubtless could not help but be influenced by the lure of all the many tempting possibilities that lay before her, probably did begin to care genuinely.

A perplexed and disturbed Nicolas soon began to wish that Kathleen would not hurry to return, and visualised the carefree comfort of her absence as long-term or even permanent by mutual arrangement.

He began to wonder whether perhaps Kathleen might be hankering after a divorce. He did not think that her wartime fling with Philip Rawson had really been serious, but began to wish that it had been, and wondered whether Kathleen might have planned to meet Philip when her trip took her to Canada. In his perturbed state of mind Nicolas was easily persuaded to put the suggestion to Kathleen; that if she was contemplating a divorce she might prefer to avoid facing it on home ground by staying on with her good friends in Australia, where she was offered long-term hospitality. Kathleen's response was to take the first available flight home.

Whatever her thoughts and unhappiness may have been, Kathleen had not thought of considering throwing away her married status, unless some tempting romance offered preferable advantages and cast-iron alternative arrangements. Without any such securities she had no intention of letting herself be walked over, even if Nicolas did think that he preferred someone else. What business had he to think that she might be prepared to be cast off? Fully intending to stand up for her rights, she returned intent on winning whatever battle she had to face, whereas Nicolas did not really know what he wanted; he just liked being alone.

He had loved Kathleen deeply, and was still an honourable and devoted man, but they had long been drifting apart. That he regarded Kathleen as still the family's focus, and that all he wanted was a peaceful and friendly existence, he probably had no chance to say so, since, regarding herself as wronged, Kathleen was too incensed and aggrieved to let him speak. Kathleen might have understood had Nicolas suddenly been captivated by an attractive and alluring younger woman, but that Ethel — whom she knew and regarded as grotesque — should be claiming her husband's affection, she could not accept.

On some later occasion when Len and I were visiting Pinner and past matters chanced to crop up, Ethel had, somewhat defensively, put in that if Kathleen had shown one flicker of love for Nicolas on the day they had tried to talk, she would have "stood down."

Was choosing St. Valentine's Day the day on which to take sleeping tablets proof that Kathleen's love was great enough to give Nicolas the freedom he appeared to be seeking, or was she just trying to get to sleep and took tablets which were stronger than she knew? Had the nature of the news in a recent Canadian letter from Philip been the last straw? The inquest left the whole matter open.

Tragically alone, Nicolas ached to take his tormented soul far away into some totally absorbing overseas service, either humanitarian or military. But he could not abandon his deeply distressed young son, who probably needed him more at that time than ever, both emotionally and financially. John, uncertain with regard to a career and trying to weigh up whether he was dedicated enough to launch on a theological training, needed both anchor and support.

As Nicolas's troubled thoughts searched frantically for a guide as to what he should do, his mind drew him a picture of Ariadne, the little sister who had lived and died before he was born. His longing saw her as a handsome, mature lady, either widowed or accompanied by a kindly, retired husband, but free and able to guard his home and succour distraught young John.

That picture faded and his thoughts; circling like swallows in a summer sky, next visualised the little mite who would have been John's elder sister but had failed to live some thirty years earlier. He now saw her as a capable young woman; loving, willing and available to be there to care for his home and for her brother: and why not then for him too? He would, in that case come home from that overseas post, and what's more, he would be glad to be back in his practice; its people were such friends and into which he had put so much of himself and which had indeed shaped his life.

While all these phantom dreams and fantasies contested with reality in his tormented mind, a real, live young woman, anxious to please and very willing to fill the void was there and being helpful and considerate in those numb, stunned days. Well used to alcohol, Nicolas found it a great stand by and Ethel, an insidious brand of intoxicant in her self—hormones in full flood— also stood by. What looked so temptingly like rescue was too easily available for him to withstand!

In the intoxicating months starting with Kathleen's cruise, Ethel, whose marriage had been hum-drum, had given little consideration to her husband. The father of their two daughters, who had cared devotedly for her and the girls for many long years, was indeed not a happy man. Ethel moved in to Nicolas's house immediately after Kathleen's death, and would not accept any offers of a more culturally acceptable approach to the situation.

Eventually Ethel's marriage was annulled—probably on basic religious grounds—but with what heartache will not be known, and ultimately Ethel and Nicolas married.

Ethel cannot be denied the credit she deserved for easing Nicolas's life in many ways. In her own way she had given him a chance to recover when he was very nearly at breaking point, and then went on to share what she could of his responsibilities; if perhaps in a somewhat domineering way, but in ways which had not been eased before.

Nicolas availed himself of the services of the new West London Central Locum Service that supplied locums on a pre-arranged basis for night calls and off-duty days, and set up a new appointments system for both the Harrow and Pinner surgeries. This was run from the Pinner house by Peggy, Ethel's recently retired ex-civil servant elder sister, who was glad of the job

Needing to improve on her elementary housekeeping standards, Ethel took a cookery course, and tried to tempt Nicolas to return home earlier than his usual custom by putting on sumptuous evening dinners. She did not, however, manage to wean him from his evening visits, as he still needed the respite of the peace and undemanding companionship of long-standing patients who had become real friends, and who had long sustained him.

Ethel's two daughters, both brash young BBC employees, enjoyed living in the Pinner house. The elder one, Lesley, who had joyfully gone on holiday to South Africa, to everyone's horror, was killed out there in a terrific car crash. Ethel's ageing, sick mother soon joined the busy household, and before long her sister Peggy virtually moved into the house. Maggie, Ethel's younger daughter, whose early marriage soon broke up, returned to the Pinner home in due course with two small sons.

John, Nicolas's son, endowed with his valiant grandfather Sergei's all-pervading kind and unfailing spirit, in time came to terms with his mother's life, and with her death and all that followed. Eventually, after much thought and with the patient moral support from his true friend, Helen, decided to wind up his chequered untrained teaching career.

He was glad that he had taken time to allow his faith to strengthen, and feeling that he was making the right decision, he entered St.Chad's Theological College at Durham, and when eventually he was ordained, he and Helen were happy to marry.

Starting with a curacy at Enfield, John's career has taken him through progressively more responsible appointments until, in 1992, he had the honour of becoming Dean of Jersey, and Rector of St.Helier, a Crown appointment in the Channel Islands for whom he speaks on matters relevant to the church within debates in the House of Commons.

Nicholas has often smiled to himself remembering that in his early youth he too was said to have had thoughts of going into the church! Sergei, John's loving late grandfather would indeed have felt rewarded to have known of John's devout spirit and success, and would have been very happy for him and Helen, and for their three children, and the great-grandchildren he would have been so proud to have welcomed and known.

Throughout those years of Nicolas's trauma, my life broke too, and took me to Herefordshire.

HEREFORDSHIRE STORY

Young employees in most big establishments tend to gravitate into friendly coteries and gather in chosen pubs on Saturday nights with their respective wives and husbands. The easy convivial banter, flirtations and high spirits which flourish in the squash and push of overcrowding in the happy-go-lucky way of modern life often lead to unexpected complications, and it was one such development that resulted in me finding myself in Herefordshire's lovely Ledbury: Sandy's unexpected divorce.

It was in just this kind of situation at the end of the 1960s that Sandy, my elder stepson and his deeply loved, delightful wife Shirley sadly discovered that they faced the end of their marriage.

Deeply distressed, Sandy had gone to Buxton from where, calmed a little and having reluctantly briefed my solicitor for the unwished-for divorce, he had barely returned to Malvern when the news of Leonard's unexpected death reached him.

When it was possible to think of anything besides the sadness of Leonard's death Sandy, who was anxious to get custody of his children—for which he needed a suitable home near their schools and his work—wondered whether, in view of my unexpected widowhood I might be able to solve his problem.

I had applied for early retirement from hospital work in the early days of Leonard's illness so as to be able to spend more time with him; this however, ironically only came through after his death. No longer tied to the area, and as NHS eye work was available anywhere, I happily agreed to move what could be regarded as the family home to suit Sandy's situation. This proved to need a move to Ledbury.

Still unspoilt and undeveloped in 1972, this charming little town had hardly any property for sale, but eventually a delightful Canadian style bungalow newly built at the upper end of an old walled garden came on the market, and, in spite of the fact that the delayed sale of the Buxton house made my bridging loan grow cripplingly, it made a pleasant and suitable home available for the rearranged family in time for the hearing of the custody case.

Heavily pregnant, re-married and living in Ledbury on her solicitor's advice, Shirley was inevitably adjudged the care of the children. This was a wise decision for the children, but was very distressing for Sandy.

In time Sandy came to accept the new state of affairs, and applied for a work transfer, resulting in a long-overdue promotion. For me the outcome of the hearing was actually a relief. Had it been necessary I would have gladly gone on with the project, but combining the children's care with the professional work I was bound to continue, would have been difficult to arrange.

Without Sandy and the children the unusual and delightful house I had acquired was too big for me alone, but I was in no financial position to consider any further moves and was content to stay in the lovely new home, and did not regret my immediate willingness to help. The proposed arrangement had given Sandy peace of mind when he needed it, and had shaped for me the necessary readjustments I had to face as a result of the sudden break in my long-established life.

Though I had loved my Buxton house that had accommodated my work and complicated family commitments, it was suddenly too big in my widowhood and unduly early retirement. Besides Len, Vera too had gone by that time and Penelope lived in London. With these considerations, the cost of running consulting rooms in my home had never been advantageous monetarily, whereas in Ledbury, living privately and working at clinics had great advantages. I was able to control the dates and times of my appointments. This gave my life greater flexibility and actually proved to be more cost-effective.

Parky, my devoted Buxton helpmate, who had been very distressed to see me go, soon found she was enjoying visits to Ledbury. Sadly on one of these visits she had a mild stroke after which she had to go into what seemed to be a well-run Buxton nursing home where she was relatively content.

To everyone's horror one night she was found unconscious, lying across a still partly burning, unguarded open gas fire, where she must have lain for a considerable time as her arm and shoulder were charred and smouldering. Nursed for weeks on a waterbed in a burn unit, she survived this terrible experience and, when considered strong enough, she faced the drastic process of having the charred arm and shoulder amputated. Surprisingly what was left of her struggled to live on for another couple of years until late in 1975.

I continued to enjoy my time in the congenial surroundings of Ledbury in the uniquely pleasant modern house built in the former kitchen garden of Ledbury Hall, high up in the grounds of the centuries-old former home of the Biddulph family. I was only sorry that Len was not there to share it, and that my parents had not had the chance of spending some leisure and respite in Herefordshire's sunny climate.

Fairly soon after my arrival the other bungalow in the old kitchen garden was completed and taken by a couple said to be one of four pairs, made up of four sisters who had married four brothers, who all doubtless were diamonds, though perhaps somewhat rough-hewn.

Before long my neighbours created a stir in the neighbourhood. They were the family of a retired London police inspector. The gentleman, however, was suddenly arrested and imprisoned for his financially advantageous involvement in London's mid-1970s pornography scandals. Though no news had yet broken locally regarding the scandal or the people involved, newspapermen descended on "The Walled Garden" as the former kitchen garden was by then known and, as my neighbours were not available, went on to question me.

As I was due to be setting off to visit "step-in-laws" in San Salvador in Central America on the day following this visitation I was glad to be away from the situation.

THE YOUNG CLASSICIST

Years before those Ledbury days, while still in Buxton and towards the end of Penelope's Malvern senior-school time in the early 1960s, I had felt that it would be to Penelope's advantage to spend some of her pre-university years at home in Buxton and, as the Malvern Girls College headmistress fully agreed with this, she ensured a transfer for Penelope to Manchester High School.

Though this had meant a long train journey each day, it was sensible for her to do some commuting and sample the bustle of a bigger town from home before having to face life on her own. As things worked out it also gave Penelope the chance of being with Len and enjoy her loving stepfather's friendship.

From the sixth form of her new school she won a place to Oxford to read classics at St.Anne's College from where, after three late-teenage painful years with all their difficulties which Len's support eased greatly, she earned the M.A.(Oxon.) degree. Len's pride and pleasure in her success throughout the splendour of her 1966 Degree Day had been yet more of the happiness he bestowed on her in his brief Buxton life.

Penelope's own father, Roger, who had always said that he was drawn to poetry and literature generally, could have been proud of his daughter, but having chosen to reject her, he did not know the depth of his loss until the closing year of his life.

In her early schooldays at Malvern, encouraged by a classmate to whom fathers were fathers, Penelope had written a letter telling Roger—her unknown father—about school and herself, and had sent him a railway station automatically snapped photograph of herself, then a gawky young teenager. Not deigning to reply or even acknowledge her letter, Roger tersely notified me that he had "this letter" and commanded me to "ensure that no such occurrence was to happen again."

From Oxford Penelope went on to polish up her abilities with good secretarial training in London, and as a bright and friendly spring-fresh curly-headed blonde she was soon offered various interesting-sounding posts each of which proved to be stultifying after a promising beginning.

Feeling low and dispirited she joined the Inter-Varsity Club where after a while she met a stimulating and unconventional red-haired young man, one "Rusty," a Marshall Scholar from Rock Island, Illinois and life became more interesting.

Rusty was a young man with a brilliant mind, to whom Penelope's company and able intellect were a great joy. Their equal mental agilities gave them both great pleasure, and exploring the nooks and crannies of undiscovered London offered them many days of happy companionship.

Rusty's pleasant face had a curious construction, not obvious at first glance. When looked at more closely, the shortness of his upper lip and the paucity of his upper eyelids were an unexpected contrast to his generous, pouting mouth from which the Americanism of his speech came pleasantly unstressed.

Although he boasted quite an array of United States university degrees, as well as his UK Cambridge M.A., he was grieving that an untimely attack of appendicitis had robbed him of the St. Andrew's Philosophy Doctorate into which he had poured all his abilities, and was likely to have attained with high honours. He was a zoologist whose devoutly Lutheran Swedish parents were both professors at Augustana College, Illinois; the father a geologist, and the mother a musician and composer of church music, and where Rusty had attained some of his degrees, though he ultimately progressed to the better known universities.

Rusty's middle brother Roald was a geological scientist at a research station near Pullman in Washington State, where he was involved in the preservation of moon rocks at the time of the Apollo landings. His eldest brother, John, had been a serious minded young student who; possibly because he had been born with malformed feet, was obsessed with football, and went to every match within reach.

One sad day in the dispersal scramble at a car park at the end of a college football match, one of his disobedient feet tripped him, making him fall in front of a speeding car that ran over him.

The death of the brother, who though older had been the closest to Rusty, was very traumatic for the sensitive seven-year-old boy. He probably blamed himself for not having somehow saved John. The parents, prevented by their Lutheranism from sharing the overwhelming pain of their loss with their smallest son, did not understand his hidden distress. The suppressed torment resulted in the boy developing a deep antagonism towards his parents, which expressed itself in violent disruptiveness and revolt at any discipline, and went on to pervade all phases of life and activity as he grew.

Rusty's parents anxiously sought what they could best do for this highly-strung intelligent son of theirs as the years went by. Conscious of the threat of the draft for service in Vietnam, and knowing that Rusty's mental make-up would not stand the discipline of military service, they wisely set about arranging for him to try for a Marshall Scholarship.

Fortunately all went well and Rusty soon set off for England as a Marshall Scholar. The parents watched his progress eagerly, glad to know that he accepted the sympathetic supervision Cambridge offered, and that he enjoyed the tutorial system. When, however, news reached them that the distress over the lost St. Andrew's philosophy degree—together with the severity of the illness through which he had lost it—had precipitated a manic-depressive state, they could only be thankful that he was in England where the National Health Service (NHS) took care of such ill health.

Though he was recovering with the long, painstaking care he was receiving, his parents knew that it would be wrong for him to return to them, and were delighted to learn of the great help Penelope's friendship was giving him.

A VALIANT STRUGGLE

By the time the diagnosis of Rusty's illness had been definitely arrived at Penelope had grown to love this strange young man, and was convinced that her love would overcome everything and cure his ills.

Rusty, however, conscious of his past difficulties and knowing that he was a sick man, caused Penelope considerable heartbreak by stubbornly refusing to enter into any firm commitment. They eventually married, however, and moved from their Hampstead 'bed-sits' to a flat.

Fortunately the relative stability of the new relationship, together with the care Penelope gave him, had a good, steadying effect, added to which the guidance and warm friendship of their near-neighbours the Huxleys was a great boost to their lives.

Sir Julian Huxley had long been Rusty's inspiring doyen and as Lady Juliette, Sir Julian's charming wife, was glad to delegate her duty of accompanying her husband on his mandatory afternoon walks to Rusty and Penelope, their Hampstead ambles with the professor grew to be a great joy to them all and added greatly to their interest in, and knowledge of, natural history.

In 1974 Rusty's Cambridge tutor, who had continued to be in touch with him, arranged a minor, but prestigious, assistant librarianship with the Linnean Society, the Burlington House Society named after the Swedish biologist Carolus Linnaeus (or Karl Linné) who originated the current system of generic description and naming for plants and animals.

During Rusty's brief tenure in this post Penelope saw a chance to attempt a meeting with her father who—having done some valued research into the anatomy of the elephant's brain amongst his various undertakings as Professor of Anatomy at Guy's Hospital—was on the society's council.

Anticipating Roger's presence at a council meeting one day, Penelope took care to meet him, and after a few supercilious words and a chill: "Good afternoon," as he walked away from her. Perhaps he had not heard what she had said.

Ignoring what may or may not have been a snub at that meeting, Penelope phoned Roger at his home in St. John's Wood. She told him that she wondered whether perhaps he had not heard her say that she was his daughter, and that—as she and her husband lived in Hampstead and were relatively close neighbours of his and Caroline's—she wanted to make friends, or at least an acquaintanceship with him. Again, not unlike her school time attempt, she was turned away, but this time with far-fetched and ridiculous excuses.

These rebuffs and Roger's generally inhuman attitude towards her added greatly to the many difficulties she had to face throughout the eighteen years of her marriage with Rusty, whose mental instability continued to be devastating.

Though Rusty's mental condition appeared to be sufficiently stabilised for him to attempt the Linnean Society post, it had taken many years to regain that relative calm after a further severe relapse he had suffered as a result of a visit to his parents in Illinois

At a time when he appeared to be remarkably normal Rusty had accepted his parents' pressing invitation to come to see them, and to everyone's delight he arrived in Rock Island full of promise. Sadly, his parents' customary restraints quickly triggered off all his former turbulence so badly that, as he was breaking-up their home, they had to call in his brother Roald to help them.

Having got a sick Rusty back into England, where Penelope had to accept him in his grossly regressed state (which actually took four long years to control), Roald flew back to Spokane and set off on the two hour drive to his research station. Just as he reached his destination, one of his technicians slipped whilst securing apparatus to some scaffolding and fell, breaking an arm, amongst other injuries.

As Roald was in his car and on the spot when the technician fell, and ignoring that he had just driven quite a few hours from the airport, he immediately took the injured man for urgent treatment to the nearest hospital, many miles away. Having settled the patient into hospital, he again set off on the long drive to the research station. Anxious to get back and ignoring jet-lag, Roald pressed on and was later found dead in the tangle of his crashed car in a ravine somewhere on a straight stretch of monotonous highway.

The parents' grief can barely be imagined, nor can that of Roald's widow and their two young children.

In England, Rusty's slow recovery was made the more difficult as he was again haunted by the knowledge that, though indirectly, it had been on his account that his brother had been on that fatal journey.

Basically a kind and caring man, Rusty loved Penelope warmly and genuinely, and expressed his most tender love for her on unexpected occasions and in ingenious and deeply touching ways, but there were periods when he was not himself. Normally, when well, he was charming and a widely informed conversationalist, but even when relatively normal, his basically wise views on conservation grew progressively unbalanced.

Rusty began to regard the rubbish he could see in street waste bins, skips and at the backs of market stalls as evidence of people's iniquitous wastefulness; so much so that he felt it to be his personal duty to counter the trend. He had especial compassion for discarded vegetables and fruit, and insisted that he and Penelope should live on these. "Ratatouille" made from damaged vegetables was their staple diet for many tormented years. He would bring home his rucksack filled with all kinds of rescued discards, with which Penelope was expected to deal.

Discarded electric cookers, lamps and picture frames were brought home repeatedly, as well as cast-off clothing. On one occasion Penelope was faced with nine unmatched pairs of oddly sized and unworn lady's high boots that he regarded as a waste of footwear (and that at least their leather should be saved). Grubby rubbish had to be dealt with nearly every day, and as disapproval on her part was likely to disturb him out of all proportion, her tolerance and forbearance, coupled with a degree of necessary severity, was a difficult routine to maintain. Life was not easy for her.

Rusty's fanatic membership of every learned society he knew of, all of which willingly accepted him on the strength of the long list of his accumulated university degrees, gave him and Penelope access to various absorbing occasions, lectures, concerts and dissertations arranged by these societies. To these they quite often invited me. It was, however, somewhat disconcerting to realise that Rusty's main interest and pleasure in all these occasions seemed to be the refreshments offered at these receptions.

Perpetually hungry, Rusty was glad to scoff the generously supplied dainty sandwiches, greedily stuffing them by the handful into his mouth and pockets. Occasionally when Penelope was not with them, Rusty would lovingly explain his sandwich-filled pockets to me by saying that he was taking "these nice sandwiches home for Penelope".

Rusty was not capable of holding down any paid appointment. He went berserk soon after what might look like a sensible start, and before long it became evident that typing was what they had to make the most of. This he managed to do tidily, at home, in his own time, at his own rate and when well.

He and Penelope joined a typing agency through which they typed up people's manuscripts and theses, both of them setting about fulfilling orders if there was a rush job or if there were delays for any of the many likely health-caused reasons. As this was before the days of computers, there was quite a call for this service, but the periods when Rusty was able to do even this work grew fewer.

As time went on the recurrences of his spells of progressively more outrageous behaviour grew more frequent, and their nature and form varied more widely. Besides the repeated manic episodes requiring his urgent hospitalisation, there was an occasion when he set their flat on fire. Hospital stays were never of the length needed for effective treatment or to enable his condition to be adequately assessed, because with prompt treatment he would quickly become apparently normal and, having rationally demanded to go home, he would be released.

If not released as soon as he wanted, he would abscond; climbing out of windows if no other avenue of exit was available, turning up at home barely-clothed irrespective of the weather, and sometimes naked. Before any action could be taken on such returns, he would again present a normality that could not be disputed, and the law is such that there are no means by which cases like his can be detained against the patient's will.

Their finances were more than precarious. Though Rusty's father knew that his son was a sick man, and supported him to some extent, they did not have enough to live on. Penelope did her best to earn money, but her work was limited by having to fit in with giving Rusty the constant unobtrusive care and supervision he needed. As housework was a well-paid casual employment, and was often the only job she could fit in with her commitments, it became her main occupation.

Besides and between this, she took on as much proofreading, typing, cataloguing, indexing and any other undertakings she could pick up. Curiously, though not surprisingly, her housework contacts have led to a large number of the most interesting and lasting friendships. When she could, she poured her tormented soul into music. She had stopped studying music in her university days but was glad to resume it, as best she could in the difficulties of her current life. Finding it a great solace, she used this talent to raise money for other folks in trouble by piano recitals.

Though very often exasperated and tormented almost beyond endurance, she felt she could not jettison a man as sick as Rusty. Though the all-pervading sickness was often personally life threatening to her, she endured the eighteen years of her many hardships stoically because, between the most trying times, there were periods of tender accord and—besides his brilliant intelligence and exceptionally wide academic interests and knowledge—he had an appealing and childlike trust and dependence on her which was very endearing.

But as Rusty's demeanour ultimately showed fewer and fewer intervals of tranquillity, Penelope's patience began to wear thin. She began to realise that Rusty's condition, which showed no likelihood of amelioration, was progressively destroying their relationship, and that she was ruining her own health in his care.

She began to feel that her long repressed urge to have children, a wish that Rusty did not share, was a strong enough reason to warrant their separation. When a flat they had bought for letting purposes (with Rusty's father's help), came vacant, Penelope moved into it. As they both still had a degree of tenderness for each other, Penelope's virtual abandonment of Rusty was as distressing for her as it was hurtful to him, especially as their separate lives continued on adjoining roads. Penelope, however, felt she had done the right thing, as they just had to part.

Throughout their years together they had lived amid highly intellectual people and pursuits, interspersing their bookish days with very gypsy-like periods when they travelled 'on their wits' cadging lifts unashamedly because they genuinely had no money. Both aspects of their lives had given them great pleasure, though some of the rough trekking had been hard for Penelope to accomplish, even in her young days, in the uncivilised conditions they had to put up with.

But as time had indeed taken its toll since the days of those nostalgic memories, and nothing but distress had come to fill their now incompatible lives, though painful for them both, they agreed amicably that they would divorce.

For various emotional reasons, long, agonising months went by before the divorce proceedings began. When eventually the legal process started, it took many more years to accomplish because at several crucial stages Rusty was too mentally unfit to be able to sign any legal document. When, after a very drawn-out and exasperating process, the divorce was eventually completed, though they were glad that it was achieved, they were both very sad and conscious of their aloneness.

Rusty's kind and quixotic nature had long regarded it to be unjust that some people have homes while others are without; an understandable but barely practicable conception, which he inevitably put into effect by sharing his home with any homeless person with whom he came face-to-face.

With Penelope gone he quickly filled up their formerly shared two-and-a-half-roomed flat with five or six down-and-outs. Some of his companions were intelligent men who were just down on their luck and one or two of them were really seen through their bad patches by his help. To a great extent it was good for him not to be alone, but when he and Penelope had been together, this frequently recurring largesse had been yet another of the difficulties she had had to face.

In the years following their divorce Rusty's fluctuating condition continued to deteriorate. Although doing very poorly and in hospital on many distressing occasions, he was often well enough to be briefly in touch with some of their old friends from their early zoology-orientated Hampstead times. The friendship with the Huxleys, in which I had been considerably involved, continued into my Ledbury days.

THE HUXLEYS

Sir Julian Huxley, the well-known naturalist and former member of early radio's Brains Trust, had always been a difficult man whose awkwardness and obstinacy increased with age.

The more trying his personality became the more wearing it was for his charming Swiss wife, Lady Juliette, who, after endless years of unappreciated care, badly needed rest. She longed for her husband to be away from home for a while, but as he would not agree to go anywhere, she was growing quite desperate.

One day when at tea with the Huxleys, and knowing of Juliette's problem from Penelope (who had long been doing her best to help Juliette) I casually suggested that perhaps Julian might care to spend a few days with me in Ledbury. Unaccountably he accepted the idea, whereupon firm arrangements were promptly made.

Some very few days later Juliette drove Julian down to Ledbury, and as he appeared to enjoy the visit, and Juliette benefited by the respite, a routine soon established itself. Arranging my appointments accordingly, I was able to have Julian with me, on the average one week in each calendar month, the arrangement continuing for what proved to be little more than the last year of his life.

During this time I soon understood how difficult Juliette's life had been— and was. In Ledbury Julian behaved as a guest for the first few hours of the visit, but soon reverted to the crude and demanding style of his home habits which were incredible to observe.

The naturalist fraternity of Ledbury somehow soon learnt of the visitor's presence and, considering themselves honoured to have such a celebrity as Sir Julian Huxley in their midst, visited him with great interest. He, characteristically, was delighted to 'receive' anyone who wished to meet him and enquired demandingly each morning as to who would be coming to tea that afternoon.

The vicar and his lady, not being naturalists, sat very awkwardly upright on the edge of the sofa, only easing a little at the tea table as the talk became more general. But Julian, who did not tolerate conversation going on with anyone other than himself, insistently reclaimed the centre of attention by promptly proclaiming loudly: "I want more jam" or cake, as the case might be.

He had to be taken for sightseeing drives and walks each day, and as such expeditions were willingly accompanied by interested neighbours, his requests to be conducted round Herefordshire's old churches were complied with, where he insisted on leaving his signature in every visitors' book, wherever one was visible. As time went on his signatures became more and more illegible and his reading in the house grew more difficult. It was obvious that his eyesight was failing.

At home in Hampstead he refused to have anything done about his cataracts, but again to everyone's surprise, he agreed to have one eye operated on by one of Worcester's eye surgeons. Duly settled into the Worcester Eye Hospital by Juliette, and as all seemed to be serene, she returned to London. On the day following admission the operation was proceeding in the normal manner under local anaesthesia when Julian suddenly decided he did not want to have any more done, and vigorously did his best to sit up on the operating table. Though this is not a common operating theatre occurrence, the surgeon skilfully and diplomatically managed to bring the operation to a makeshift conclusion. Eventually the patient was resettled into his bed and, with the help of pre- and post-operative sedation, spent the rest of that day quietly and slept well through the night.

At that time, before microsurgical procedures had been as perfected as they are now, cataract operations needed to be followed by at least two days of tranquil bed rest and some two weeks in hospital to allow the cut surfaces of the eyeball to knit together. On the first morning after the operation, not heeding the many gentle requests to be still, Julian sat up in bed very briskly and announced that he was not staying in hospital any longer.

The consensus of opinion, on urgent conference, was that with the advantage of my professional knowledge and the likelihood that greater peace might be achieved if his demands were met, Julian was transferred to his bedroom at my house.

This was achieved by ambulance and with two nurses in attendance, where, it was hoped he might accept his eye nursing by my hands with less protest than he exhibited in hospital. Surprisingly the eye eventually healed, but inevitably the improvement in his eyesight was less than had been hoped for.

A few months after the eye operation his health deteriorated and, accompanied by violent protests against being taken to hospital and turbulent refusals to stay there, he died in 1975.

Juliette came to stay with me for a short time whilst coming to terms with Julian's death, and was glad to talk about many of the difficult aspects of their past shared life. These, she told me, consisted of repeated nervous breakdowns, from which he would in time emerge, and either float some brilliant new scheme or publish some previously undisclosed completed research work, and again bask in fresh limelight until the next 'furore', as she called the episodes.

Juliette's life in England had started in early 1914, just before the First World War, when she, then a very pretty, highly intelligent, severe, nineteen-year-old arrived to be governess to Julianne, Lady Ottoline Morrell's young daughter at Garsington, near Oxford.

The very prim teenage Miss Marie Juliette Baillot, the daughter of a Swiss lawyer from Auvernier who had died young leaving his family in debt, was horrified to find herself surrounded by the shocking life-style of the Bloomsbury Set.

She was amidst Virginia Woolf, Lytton Strachey, John Middleton Murry, Katherine Mansfield, Philip Hezeltine (known musically as Peter Warlock), and H.G.Wells, and met Julian Huxley and his brother Aldous. Julian, the elder of the two brothers was an outspoken young man who—knowing that great things were expected of him—was the grandson of T.H.Huxley, with Thomas Arnold (head master of Rugby) for his other grandsire.

It did not take long for Juliette to replace her strict Calvinistic views with the nudism and the open relationships of the group. Before long she married Julian Huxley and soon became the virtual pivot of the Bloomsbury Set.

In her stay with me in Ledbury after Julian's death, Juliette chatted reminiscently while admiring the lovely views from the Worcestershire Beacon. She described Julian's "fugues" and "furores;" his recurring breakdowns which were said to have been caused by his uncanny attractiveness to women. A great many of such ladies apparently fell violently in love with him, leading to unwelcome intrigues from which Julian needed to extricate himself.

When Juliette suddenly asked me whether I too had been in love with Julian, I was very considerably taken aback. More than aware of his "extraordinary" ways, of which Juliette was conscious, I assured her to the contrary and explained that it was out of consideration for her and, at Penelope's request, that I had offered the arrangement and that it had taken great restraint and good manners on my part to continue it.

Fortunately we were good enough friends to be able to laugh at the incongruous suggestion, and both guffawed when I suddenly realised that Julian must have been trying to exercise his "uncanny attractiveness" by his repeated misdirected requests for my opinion about his private parts. No wonder that the local GP could not stop laughing when I had asked him to deal with Julian's 'quaint malady.'

WORKING IN WORCESTER

As 1976 wore on I reluctantly began to admit to myself that my lovely Ledbury house with its huge garden was too big for me, and as the greater part of my work was in Worcester it would be sensible to live there.

Selling the house, however, proved difficult as Ledbury had suddenly become an attractive overflow area for Birmingham, vast housing estates having cropped up in all its former open spaces, but eventually I managed to move on.

From my early Ledbury days Worcester Cathedral's music had attracted me and I had involved myself in the cathedral's various voluntary undertakings. Even before I had moved to Worcester I had been was invited to become a so-called assistant manager of the recently enlarged cathedral bookstall where my duties were mainly ensuring the continuity of voluntary helpers and keeping the supply of cathedral guides, postcards and other sales items flowing smoothly between the stockrooms in the crypt and the sales counter.

While my busy life flowed contentedly in Worcester, Penelope's marriage—difficult from its early days—was becoming more trying and I began to feel that I should move to London, but I marked time.

I enjoyed the friendly community atmosphere and savoured the Three Choirs Festivals with their wonderful music and social activities, together with the fact that my various old friends were beginning to discover where I was. Bill Parker re-opened our old friendship when he and his Worcester-born wife Peggy visited her relatives there, thus kindling a warm and long lasting three-cornered friendship.

Some time later Bertram and Mary Miles, the entomologists of Manchester University days contacted me. Bertram had retired from his horticultural professorship at Ashford in Kent, and he and Mary were settled at Wood Broughton high above Cartmel in their beloved Lake District, and invited me to visit them.

On one of my later visits, when two of the Miles' near neighbours came in for evening coffee and were introduced as Mr. and Mrs. Roughley the name sounded vaguely familiar to me. When Mr. Roughley, a Manchester man, mentioned having lived in Eccles and then went on to reminisce about a little Russian girl with long, fair curls down her back at his school, I was able to revive many more of his memories for him. To everyone's amazement I had been that little girl and he was Charlie, to whom Vera had taught French in return for his mother's English lessons for Nicolas.

Things having worsened in Penelope's marriage, I finally decided to move to London. Warning my various voluntary and ophthalmic posts of my prospective resignation, and having put my house on the market, I started looking for work and a flat in Hampstead where Penelope was glad to welcome me. The project, however, was slow-moving as the house market in Worcester at that time was proving to be very sluggish.

I had not thought of holidays since political troubles had cancelled a planned trip to Iran, where my uncle Shoura had lived, but when some cathedral friends mentioned that they were arranging a trip to Peru and needed more members for the group, I was tempted by the thought of a holiday.

As my femme fatale aunt Lyda and her sister Ileana had had their ballet school in Lima, and as indeed a holiday would shorten the demoralising drag of time while waiting for my house to sell, I decided to go.

Suitably arranging all outstanding matters, I put the house sale totally into the hands of agents, settled my better trinkets into a safe place in the bookstall stockroom in the cathedral crypt and set off for Peru.

The heterogeneous group that collected at the assembly point at the airport soon settled into a congenial company of travellers. Our pleasant flight touched down at Kennedy Airport in New York from where, after a day in the city, we continued on to Peru, pausing briefly at Miami. During the few days in Lima we were engulfed in riots in which some members of the group had handbags slashed and wallets snatched.

From Lima we flew to Cusco for a few further days during which, after being served lashings of coca tea to help accommodate to the high altitude, we studied relics of early Inca civilisation now heavily overlaid with Spanish influence and enjoyed mingling with native market women in their many-petticoted costumes and tall hats who disdainfully dubbed all visitors as gringos, the despised American tourists.

We then took a train from Cusco which crept up into the hills, stopping at all stations on its laboured way to Machu Pichu, high in the Andes. After a few days of fantastic views and attempted climbs towards the peaks, we went to the shore of Lake Titicaca, a virtual inland sea in which extraordinarily primitive native settlements on floating matted seaweed mid-lake islands contrasted with vessels of ocean-going size plying from coast to coast.

On our further panoramic flight to Arequippa, we touched down for a short break to see yet another remarkable area of those regions. Boarding cramped ramshackle taxis direct from our plane, we trundled over rock-strewn desert land to a sudden corridor-like break between sheer mountain sides through which we emerged into the amazing sight of an oasis. Extensive well cultivated fields of maize and other crops, with vineyards and orchards surrounding a much civilised small town, stretched out before us as far as the eye could see.

Some members of the group took a short turbulent air trip from the town to see the stupendous scenery and the huge inscrutable hieroglyphics on many of the precipitous mountainsides, before the group resumed its journey.

After a comfortable stay in Arequippa; a lovely cultured and modernised city, another scenic flight brought us back to Lima from where, escaping with only minor involvement in yet another insurrection, we returned to Heathrow where grey skies greeted our return from an excellent and stimulating holiday.

Next morning back in Worcester, having taken delivery of my new car as arranged, done my routine clinic and picked up my 'better trinkets' from the cathedral crypt, I continued on my way home, where — after exchanging a few words with a neighbour — I gladly went into my house. Normally I would have hung my coat in the hall and got on with whatever domestic activity presented itself, but as the boots I was wearing were uncomfortable, I just put my bag and the precious package on the kitchen table and went upstairs for better shoes.

At the top of the stairs I was puzzled to see that the usually wide-open bathroom door was half-closed, but quickly assumed that the agents had been showing prospective buyers round the house, and went on only to stop again on seeing that the curtains in my bedroom were drawn closed. In the next instant my throat was gripped from behind, the stranglehold preventing me from breathing, and before I knew what was happening, I was kneed into my bedroom and pushed on to the bed.

The intruder, who wore a black patterned stocking over his head and face and exuded a pungent aromatic hot oil smell, lost no time in making his intentions clear and quashing my attempts at protest and struggle by wielding a heavy, rusty, hooked metal bar which he drew from his belt. I knew that even if I could shout no one would hear me, as my house was an end one and adjoined extensive convent gardens.

The creature put me through a long drawn-out maniacal usage, which he performed with relish. When at last the brute desisted and betook himself downstairs, shattered and disgusted as I was by the revolting ordeal, I suddenly had the added horrifying realisation that I had obligingly provided the intruder with my 'better trinkets' conveniently lying on the kitchen table beside my handbag.

As I could hear the man rattling about in the kitchen, and fearing that he might isolate me by ripping out the incoming telephone line near the kitchen door if I tried to phone, I only started my frantic phoning when I heard the door bang shut. Besides my desperate call to the police I called my next-door neighbour. She took the call for a sick joke, but collapsed on grasping the reality, and demanded a police chaperone pending her husband's return some days later.

The phoning done, holding my breath and prepared for the worst, I crept to the kitchen expecting to see the camouflaging outer plastic coverings of the package strewn around and no contents, but I could not believe my eyes or good fortune: the man had contented himself with clearing my handbag and must have thought the plastic carrier-bag beside it to be just shopping.

The relief at having been spared the horror of losing my valuables, minimal though they were, was enough to save my sense of humour.

It was soon obvious that the man must have been in the house for a long time before my return, as he had ransacked the cupboards and drawers, probably searching for the equivalent of the actual contents of the grocer's bag he had spurned. The black stocking he had used as a mask, and discarded on the stairs on his way down, was one I recognised as one of mine he had taken from my belongings when he had rummaged amongst them.

The experience had indeed been shattering; the throttling, the rough handling, the revolting assault and all the necessary medical tests and investigations following it were bad enough, but the curiously unsympathetic attitude with which I was met at the cathedral the next day was another unwelcome surprise.

I had not known that news of the event had been broadcast on the local radio and, on meeting the friendly Custos who had witnessed the reclaiming of my goods from the crypt the previous day, I flippantly said: "I've been raped since I last saw you!"

Aghast and very sympathetic, he must have relayed this alarming news to higher authority, whereupon I was approached by a severe-looking staff member, who insisted in a horror-muted voice that on no account was I to tell anyone that I had been the subject of that morning's news bulletin! This sudden command to silence was an unexpected shock. Perhaps the principle of 'unmentionability' had a value, but this was not obvious to me at the time.

Eventually the Worcester house was sold and I settled into my Hampstead flat where, needing to deal with some car problems, it was arranged that an insurance clerk would call on me. To my horror the young man who arrived exuded an unpleasantly familiar pungent aromatic hot oil smell similar to that of my rapist.

Quickly finishing the business matter, I hastened to get the man on his way and as the Worcester police had regarded the rapist's hot oil fumed aroma as suggestive of motorcycles, I asked whether he had come on a motorbike. The man's only reply was to ask why I had enquired. As the reasons were too complex, I just shrugged the matter off and changed my insurance company. Although I had considered discussing my observation with the local police, I dismissed the matter as too far-fetched.

Fairly soon after that occasion I was subpoenaed to attend court in Weston-Super-Mare as the rapist, who had repeated his outrages on several further occasions in the Worcester area, had at last been caught. Just before the date of the hearing, however, the subpoena was cancelled as the man ultimately pleaded guilty.

Though glad not to attend court, I would have liked to have been able to check whether my two aromatic visitors were the same man, but preferring to forget about the whole episode, I got on with trying to be of help in Penelope's difficulties.

FATHER AND DAUGHTER

Penelope, whose life was more difficult in many ways than anyone ever deserved, had received considerable moral help from various members of the Spiritual Centre at St. James' Church in Piccadilly. She had worked with them for 'Help at Christmas', the comfort for the homeless. Supporters of the independent St.John's Church in Downshire Hill in Hampstead, had also helped her.

Wanting to repay these kindnesses, she arranged to give a fund raising piano recital at Downshire Hill, and got a young artist friend to join her in the project. This young woman was to exhibit a number of her paintings.

Having forgotten how her father had ignored her school-time attempt at writing to him, and disregarding the Linnean Society era rebuffs, Penelope sent Roger an invitation to the recital.

As the invitation was an open one he just put it to one side. His second wife Caroline had died some years earlier, and as he was long retired and feeling lonely and dejected, when the day of the concert was sunny in Sydenham where he lived, he decided to attend.

On that evening I arrived in Downshire Hill with my good friends Bill and Peggy Parker in our two cars. While the Parkers were dealing with their car, I went on to the church with a box of supplies for the interval refreshments which I handed over to the little lady who was setting out cups and glasses. I soon recognised this lady. She was Shareen Spencer, the musical daughter of the English painter Sir Stanley Spencer, who had given Penelope a lot of help with music, and had also supported the girl who was exhibiting paintings. Shareen quickly told me that Penelope's father was "just along there" pointing down the aisle.

Going along towards the only other visible person in the building who had emerged from a distant door, I could see nothing recognisable about the dejected looking figure which approached. As there was no one else in the church the situation needed words, so, looking quizzically at the strange man I said: "Do tell me your name."

The puzzled and displeased deep voice that gloomily intoned his surname was unmistakable; it was indeed an aged and crumpled Roger. Laughingly I explained myself upon which Roger relaxed saying: "Oh yes!—I recognised you when you smiled!"

Not having envisaged an encounter with Roger, I had not thought, until we had all met, of the awkwardness such an encounter might be for Bill, but quickly tried to assure myself that it was more than thirty years since the days of past antagonisms and hoped that he would see it that way too.

In actual fact the Parkers' presence was an immense blessing throughout the whole evening; it eased the strained encounter that was possibly more difficult for Roger than for me. For Penelope it certainly defused the tenseness of the long-sought meeting with her father that had to be faced in the interval. Naval occasions provided a common topic of conversation for the two ex-naval doctors.

Roger, still a stiff and awkward man with a disapproving look about him, had at last to face meeting his daughter. He probably did not appreciate that it had been Penelope's efforts that had brought about the meeting, nor did he show any approval of the very polished performance with which she had entertained us all.

In spite of Roger's inevitably distant attitude, I was glad that we had all met and, wanting to encourage contact between him and Penelope, I offered him invitations, but understandably, he was not interested. He did, however, continue a strange and strained telephone contact with his daughter. His calls were mainly late-night, and annoying for Penelope in their timing besides being distressing in their content. These he followed by phoning me to verify Penelope's comments and statements—which he quoted incorrectly to me—later quoting my corrections inaccurately to Penelope. Roger's calls to me most often included reference to his sister Jan, whom he denigrated to me and was surprised that Jan and I were in contact with each other.

The fact that Rowland, Jan's and Roger's father, had made provisions for his daughter's security rankled with Roger. He did not want to accept that Jan had been genuinely fond of her only niece from Penelope's earliest days, and had maintained a pen-friendship throughout many years.

He would have been annoyed, had he lived, to learn that when Jan died intestate, actually two years after him, Penelope inherited her aunt's estate. This only happened because Stephen Williamson, Penelope's second cousin—having learnt her unusual married surname at the time of Roger's funeral—had taken the trouble to trace her in London so as to alert her to her claim.

Contact with Roger having at last been achieved, I looked in to see him briefly at his home from time to time, and had found him sitting at the breakfast bar of his kitchenette-dining room beneath precariously hanging remnants of floodwater stained ceiling. He appeared to be occupying himself by playing endless games of patience with grease-stained cards to the accompaniment of both radio and television blaring at him.

He told me how he enjoyed looking up at the sparrows and their antics in the steeply rising minute garden behind the house, and kept saying how clever 'his Caroline' had been to have found the little Sydenham town-house, with all of which I was happy to agree. After his usual offer of whisky, which I politely refused and, after enquiries into his well being and some further general conversation, I would leave, but felt glad that I had visited.

After several such visits I managed to get him to come to a family lunch party at my house that proved to be a happy event for which Penelope's outgoing nature had long craved. Great is the pity that this party had not taken place many years earlier.

That occasion resulted in Roger inviting Penelope to his home where, having concocted a simple meal which they ate at his breakfast bar, they had gone on to inspect his books and other trophies, and were both glad to find common interests and some basic similarities in their make-up, that day becoming the most heart-warming occasion Penelope had experienced with him.

Roger, at long last, began to realise that the lovely woman who was there beside him, bubbling with wisdom, humour and love, was his own daughter.

As the incredible fount of pride welled in him, overwhelming him with a depth of affection he did not know he was capable of, he tried to convey his emotion to her in his undemonstrative way, and only wished he had allowed himself to find out earlier what life really held.

Sadly, even after this one flash of affection, Roger's thinking either became progressively confused, or perhaps the fact that he had never contributed towards his daughter's upbringing or education was troubling his conscience; he seemed to be obsessed with the subject of wealth. His telephone conversations hammered at me persistently that I must be a wealthy woman, whilst pointing out that he hadn't done too badly either, that he "flew to the States on Concord," and totally ignoring my repeated responses that Penelope's and my circumstances were very modest.

Despite the fact that the apportionment of his estate between his own daughter and his two step-children had been gone into in many of the repeated financial telephone discussions; a third for each being my suggestion, he excluded Penelope from his will.

Perhaps like the mindless fool who, years ago had murdered Sergei in a demented quest for imagined hoards of crown jewels, Roger expected me to be backed by Russian reserves. Yes, by reserves, but of true Russian pride: not money. But why punish his one and only child?

Although the telephone conversations continued, they were becoming more confused with time, and as Roger was not likely to remember Penelope's birthday, I phoned to remind him of the imminent one on September 11th in 1991. As he had sounded more than usually disorientated when I spoke to him, I drove over urgently to see him, intending to persuade him to come back with me to my house, as he was obviously needing to be cosseted.

Fearing that he might even be too ill to answer the door, I was glad to find him relatively well when I got there. He, of course, refused my invitation but admitted to feeling that perhaps he should have more domestic help and, to my surprise, added that he had not realised before that I was "really a remarkable woman."

Between us we managed to improvise a birthday card and make an envelope for it with which Roger enclosed a cheque for Penelope, and insisted that it be posted rather than delivered by me. I undertook the posting. Roger thanked me for coming and for my considerate offer of hospitality, and gave me the hottest and most sincere kiss he had ever given me as I was getting into my car. Perhaps it was to thank me for the daughter I had given him, whom he had only so recently discovered to be the one real jewel in his life.

He waved me an unusual and affectionate goodbye and must have felt faint enough to need to lie down.

The letter never arrived and—knowing that there was a cheque in the un-delivered envelope—I made a post office enquiry. Meaning to warn Roger that there would be enquiries into the matter, I rang his number. To my sur-prise the phone was answered by Tony, his stepson, who told me the sad news. Neighbours, on returning from holiday several days after my visit, had been surprised to see the untended doorstep with Roger's long-emptied dust-bin still blocking the entrance and had raised the alarm. He was found long dead, having had a massive heart attack.

WIDE HORIZONS

Losing her father, whom she had only just begun to know, was yet another distress for Penelope, for whom life continued to be hurtful. Though her di-vorce had been essential it left her feeling abandoned and very alone.

She was an outgoing and affectionate person who longed to share her life with someone congenial. She adopted a recently abandoned family of three growing kittens and their mother, and continued to add to her many friends, amongst whom one day she met a young man with an unusual Welsh name.

He was Meredydd, the artistic third son of a Welsh mother and a Lan-cashire-born successful industrialist father. Defying the family life plans pro-scribed for him to take up accountancy after reading history at Oxford, Meredydd had taken up art. As is usual in the initial phases of any art career Meredydd's early days ran a chequered course with many trials and doubts but, having applied himself to the task with dedication, he went through his training brilliantly. On graduation he secured an envied museum-based ar-chaeological illustrator post with the British Museum, which he held suc-cessfully for many years.

In his student days the charms of a pretty Malaysian fellow-student had led to a marriage which, due to unexpected culture clashes and other difficulties, did not last long. Deeply affected by the divorce, Meredydd began to find life empty and pointless, and after his father's death (which added to his distress) he tried to ease his bereaved mother's difficulties by having her over from her Southport home for odd weekend breaks in his bachelor flat high above the heights of Hampstead Heath, where he normally used his free time develop-ing his talent for minutely detailed drawings.

Whilst Meredydd engrossed himself in art in his Highgate eyrie; in Hamp-stead on the other side of the Heath (their abodes were near to each other as the crow flies) Penelope, the petite blonde version of her gentle grandfather

Sergei, bustled about busily, her friendly face evoking happy smiles from everyone around. It had been one evening when she was at a friend's impromptu party to which someone brought along a somewhat reticent tall, dark and handsome Meredydd whose presence immediately interested Penelope; her inborn Russian perspicacity quickly recognised his Celtic mysteriousness.

They had chatted amicably and were soon pleased to find that they had many common interests. They were amazed they had not met while at Oxford as further surprises sprang up as time went on. They found they had grown up remarkably near to each other at exactly the same time: Meredydd in Cheshire and Penelope in Derbyshire. It further transpired that their parents, as children, had lived in the same part of greater Manchester called Eccles—well known for its genuine good-hearted folk and famous for its Eccles cakes—and an easy friendship was begun.

Meredydd's intuitive nature was curious to know more of the bright sparkle that was all about Penelope's person. When he learned she was part French and part Russian, he remembered a proud tale his father had told the three of them when they had been small boys and, quickly raising up his hand to hold the moment said: "Wait ... my father used to tell us boys how he had rescued a small Russian girl one day in Eccles!". Checking the likely period of that encounter, Penelope recognised yet another wild foredoom and countered with ripples of laughter: "That could not help but be my mother. They certainly were the only Russians in Eccles at that time and their presence had created quite a stir!"

They were soon amused trying to imagine their various parents as such young things!

The more they learned about each other, the more and many were the surprising coincidences that kept cropping up. They found they had both moved to London at much the same time, and that it was only strange it had taken all this time for them to meet. Before long, without touching on the actual problems, they were glad to be able to share the hurts they had each gone through in their divorces, and having talked about those pasts, it seemed much easier to forget them.

Their mutual interest and attraction grew, and though occasional conflicts occurred, they were happy to spend a great deal of time together. It looked as if life had begun to smile again for both, when—out of the blue and, of all undreamed of calamities to cap the many injustices and difficulties Penelope had been forced to face—breast cancer gripped her.

Meredydd's loyal care and love became her main support and sustenance throughout all the severest of the necessary treatments she had to undergo.

Deeply grateful for the merciful success of the intensive therapy Penelope was put through, we all watch her progress anxiously as doubtless her loving grandparents Vera and Sergei would have been doing. Sergei had regarded little Penelope and me as his two girls and had loved us warmly. The part he had taken so affectionately in the early months of his little granddaughter's life had given him great happiness; she had been the shining joy in those sadly brief last months of his life.

Had he lived, he would have been Penelope's loving guardian angel throughout all the stages of her growth and development. Although he would have often had to grieve on Penelope's account, the happy faces on that quiet sun-blessed spring day—some time ago by now—when she and Meredydd married would have given him and Vera great happiness.

My father would indeed have been deeply proud of both his grandchildren whom, sadly, he only knew when they were very young and who, though both faithfully and indistinguishably British, are indelibly lit by their Russian essence. His thoughts would doubtless have been turned to the fate of future generations of his line; whether in the face of the unquenchable world-wide turmoil which persists in spite of international endeavours for peace, their destinies might—like his own fractured life—be reshaped by further wars.

Chatting and going over memories one day with Penelope and Meredydd, I suggested the two of them might explore Russia and search out the former family havens; Crimea, central Russia, far Siberia, Tashkent, Vladivostock and even Nagasaki.

To Meredydd's puzzled enquiry: "Nagasaki? Why, what happened there?" Penelope laughingly replied: "Nagasaki!" "Oh, that truly is a 'must' because way back in 1901 Grandpa Sergei had been more than glad that, instead of going to Japan with Marie, Granny Vera had married him."

"They must have loved each other, then, just as we do now," but which of the two said it first did not matter as, to my delight, it was soon lost in a long kiss.

Chapter Six

Later Years

WINDSOR

The picture of that long kiss shone in my mind brightly: it looked as if a happy marriage was beginning for the two blissful young people, and every heartiest wish and blessing was hoped for them by me, now glowingly happy, and also by Lyn, Meredydd's absent mother.

By this time I was living in Windsor, where Lyn had been due to come down from Southport to stay with me for the occasion, but a sudden train strike prevented her arrival. Her good wishes were nevertheless sincere, and the progress of the honeymoon was trumpeted by a string of delighted post-cards from along its path.

Indeed the marriage thrived, and in time jogged along, though not without some of the hitches usual in most marriages, which, happily, were resolved and forgotten by the maturing Meredydd and Penelope.

Few marriages can be as completely happy as mine had been with Leonard. Had it lasted many more than its devastatingly short eight contented years, doubtless differences and troubles would have had time to creep in, but the blessed bond of mutual understanding and respect would have smoothed out any problems. Be that as it may, troubles did not creep in, and those years of happiness with Leonard changed my concept of life, and probably changed my personality in some ways too. Indeed they may have made me into what could be called a happy "late developer."

That contentment was true and deep enough to survive the sorrowing years of Leonard's going. Though much too soon, the fact that—for Leonard—it was a blessed way to go, was consolation indeed and the need to care for his son and family, though a demand on me, was part of the healing.

165

The whole smoothness and inevitability of my life with Leonard, together with his admission lovingly made quite late into those eight blessed years — that it was only some time after we had married that he had fallen in love with me — has made me muse laughingly that perchance some marriages may be made in heaven, or that perhaps arranged marriages, as of old, may be quite a good idea after all.

With time Penelope and Meredydd found that their personalities were very different. Artistic Meredydd lived in his mind and, unless engrossed in detailed drawing or intricate handwork, he escaped into reading or planning manuscripts or the like; all of which he tended to keep to himself.

Penelope — an outgoing creature who spoke to everyone she met, knew all the neighbours and loved all and every animal and bird — did manage to get her husband to join her in many of her interests. They went riding, took interesting trips abroad and each continued with his or her own occupations. Both loved their family of three affectionate cats.

Probably more than the recipient herself, I was consciously grateful to fate for the fact that Penelope eventually inherited some money, and that Meredydd, besides his work with the British Museum, had some means of his own.

Though Penelope had been very anxious to have children, and had largely divorced her first husband since he did not wish to do so, it was a mercy that they did not chance to achieve her longing as that was just when her cancer was developing. Had she become pregnant then, her chances of recovery would not have been as fortunate as they proved to be.

Various anxieties made me decide that I needed a family house. With these in mind I had cast my eye around, and a little house I had seen in Windsor seemed very suitable. It would fit in with my work quite happily and fulfil any requirements that might arise.

Kew properties were rising in value, and the appeal of the three-bedroom Windsor house grew progressively for me. Before too long, to my delight, my Kew flat sold and enabled me to buy the Windsor house I liked. This was in Edinburgh Gardens overlooking the Long Walk, and some years later gave me a grandstand view of the horrific sight of Windsor Castle on fire.

I was very glad to be in Windsor. I was doing clinics conveniently nearby and had developed a very warm friendship with a little Scottish lady, Margaret Carson, who was the widow of a Glasgow general practitioner. Margaret had come to Windsor as it was a halfway meeting point where she and her sister Jenny decided to share a house.

Jenny had retired from a long career in the Foreign Office and the two had enjoyed some three years of retirement, going on trips and cruises and being happy to do as they pleased. Sadly Margaret began to find that Jenny was deteriorating, and after a long struggle the diagnosis of Alzheimer's disease had to be accepted. Margaret tried to hide this fact from her friends and neighbours, making the next three or so years a nightmare, even more so when Margaret realised that she just had to get her sister into a nursing home.

Searching for a suitable home was devastating, as so many were impossible, whereas when she was visiting a pleasant place her heartfelt wish was to get into one of the inviting beds: she was exhausted almost beyond endurance. The horror of the deceit that had to be gone through to trick her sister into going into the ultimately chosen home was bad enough, but visiting her, when there was no longer a car, was another difficulty.

At the time of my arrival Margaret was becoming more used to the situation, and was glad of the new friendship and companionship. I too was glad of the friendship, and enjoyed having Margaret's company on many of my undertakings. The visits with her to see Jenny in her Crowborough nursing home gave me an insight into the ghastly condition to which the disease reduces human beings.

Edinburgh Gardens was a pleasant development of some sixty-odd houses and flats built in 1963 on the grounds of what had been a sizable country house. The YWCA had inherited the property, and having built a suitable establishment on part of it, they sold off the rest for much needed high-grade housing.

Edinburgh Gardens, as this development came to be called, held a very compatible community of relatively middle-aged, mainly retired or semi-retired, professional people and widows, who were socially very mixable. Bridge was played in many houses. All this sociability was very comforting for me, as I was recovering from quite a heart-break once again; a friendship which had meant a lot to me and was likely to grow into more, and had been one of the reasons for my move to Windsor, was again cut short by another sudden death.

In my Kew days I had had a few visits from a strange elderly man who had, over the years, been in contact with my mother and, since her death, had transferred his wish for friendship to me. He was Harry Ffaulks, who appeared to have had an extraordinary history. There had been a court case in which three brothers contested the inheritance of a family house. When this house was adjudged to the eldest, feeling unjustly deprived, Harry had stabbed the judge in the back as he left the court-house.

Harry's visits continued into my Windsor days and were resumed since my arrival in Coggeshall. He usually arrived with a large suitcase intending to explore the area. As his greatest interest appeared to be different religions, especially Eastern Orthodoxy, I arranged for him to be accommodated at the Greek Orthodox Monastery at Tolshunt Knights, and drove him around. During these jaunts more of his story came out.

It was then that I realised that the broken old man with me was the former brash Henry Best my family had known as a pupil at Sergei's Russian classes years ago. Indeed it had been Henry Best's exaggerated versions of my fathers memories, recounted innocently in the communal kitchen of his cheap lodgings, that had inflamed young Swallow's desperate mind to the bungled burglary which resulted in my father's death.

It seems that it was on Henry's release from prison following the stabbing incident that he had taken his mother's maiden name, and became the mysterious Welsh Harry Ffaulks who still resented having to pay rent to his brother, besides maintaining the decrepit rented house, out of his dwindling jobbing gardener's pay.

Another of the romances of that time suddenly developed for Margaret. Rudolf, a charming Austrian bachelor gentleman, who had been inveigled into taking on his niece's flat in Edinburgh Gardens, arrived and fell in love with Margaret.

That sunny summer I had great pleasure inviting Margaret to drop in for a cup of tea in the garden, together with the pleasure of ringing Rudolf and asking him along as well. There was an added bonus in the pleasure in his voice on hearing that Margaret was due, and Margaret's delight on seeing him. Margaret was too demure to invite Rudolf herself, although eventually. and with my chaperonage, she grew quite bold.

Rudolf, his brother, and family were all mountaineers, and had their own cabin high up on one of the highest of Swiss Alps where they all met. After some two happy Windsor years, on what proved to be Rudolf's last climb to this cabin, he overstrained his heart and came back to die of heart failure. Sadly Margaret's boldness had not grown enough for her to visit Rudolf in hospital, and Penelope and Meredydd proved to be the last people to see him alive.

Part of my various reasons for moving from Kew to Windsor was my friendship with Walter and Diana Lorch. This friendship had, surprisingly, been sealed by associations with Leonard's earlier days. Unbeknown to me, the Lorches, whom I should have contacted much earlier, had long lived nearby at Fulmer in Buckinghamshire, but whose existence I discovered by chance some years earlier in my Hampstead days.

I had been invited to a fundraising party in aid of Russian refugees, held at Sotheby's on an occasion when they had a Russian *ikon* sale planned. I did not exactly know where the showrooms were, so I took a tube (subway) to Bond Street where I quickly found the place and, being too early, had to wait around. I had studied as many of Bond Street's gorgeous windows as I could before the dank February evening got me shivering.

Whilst looking longingly at Sotheby's firmly shut door, I was surprised to see a group of people being allowed to slip in. When I saw another group approaching, I sidled towards them and looked enquiringly at the porter to see whether I too could be allowed in. My look was met with being asked whether I was one of the Balalaika players. I admitted that I wasn't one of the musicians, but was invited in and found myself in the extensive showrooms elegantly set up with displays of *ikons* of various ages, sizes and degrees of beauty.

After I had wandered around alone for quite a time, another lone lady arrived. We exchanged a few words, and wandered on while slowly the rooms filled up with other guests, who ultimately filled the rooms to an almost deafening capacity. As the evening drew towards a close—after great social interchange with ecstatic greetings, champagne and canapés—the two early arrivals met again and, both alone, were glad to talk to each other. Diana Lorch, my early sole '*co-ikoner*', admitted that her interest in *ikons* was the result of many business trips she undertook to Russia on her husband's behalf. She spoke Russian, and was charmed with what she had seen of Russia, and somehow the subject of Canada and its navy crept up.

To my astonishment Diana mentioned that her uncle was in the Canadian navy and mentioned his name, Roger Bidwell whom, to Diana's surprise, I knew. She was astounded to learn how closely her uncle had been associated with Leonard, my late husband. A further surprise was to find that we lived relatively near each other, and that we both had each other's names in our address books. A warm friendship quickly thrust open its welcoming arms.

This friendship was indeed great fun. Diana's husband Walter would ring and invite me to lunch, and on being asked when this was to be he would say: "Can you be here in half an hour?"

On arrival I would find a number of their fascinating friends there, friendship with many of whom has continued with the years. All the guests would be chatting happily whilst waiting around for Walter to barbeque a couple of chickens on his outdoor electric spit, an activity which would rapidly result in a gourmet meal. This would be accompanied by splendid wines, mixed in with arguments as to whether the lemon or other similar item he had used had been his or Diana's idea, and interrupted by telephone calls reporting progress of their entries into carriage driving competitions.

Many other such occasions were sprinkled over the years. Sadly in 2003 Walter, whose heart had begun to show signs of strain, was the first to go, leaving a very bereft Diana. Some fifteen months later, throughout which Diana had been supported by two caring daughters, together with a devoted son and their families, instead of eating a lovingly prepared supper (the arrival of which she had welcomed with a warm and happy smile) while sitting comfortably in her chair, she quietly died.

Time, which takes a toll of all of us, took its vengeance in Edinburgh Gardens and on my friend Margaret in unpleasant repeated little bites. Margaret and I had arranged a rota of keeping in vigilant touch by phoning each other at eight o'clock each morning. On quite a few mornings I needed to alert another helpful neighbour, Elizabeth; together with whom—and prepared for trouble—we found poor Margaret in very unhappy states on increasingly frequent occasions and a review of her health needed to be started.

Little by little Margaret improved, and eventually took an apartment in one of the widely advertised Country House Association (CHA) houses at Swallowfield near Reading in Berkshire. She thoroughly enjoyed her stay there, but after a while her health needed more care than offered by CHA, and she needed to move into a nursing home.

I had long been interested in the CHA apartments, and had visited one of the houses near Guildford. Though very charmed, there was not enough cause to take any action.

There had been a time when Penelope and Meredydd had talked of looking for a house for themselves in Essex. This made me take interest in Gosfield Hall, the CHA house in Essex. I found this really delightful, especially as there was a gorgeous apartment vacant in this truly Elizabethan mansion. Again there was no need to move, except that as a non-cook the idea of having meals put before me without having done any cooking, was a great temptation. Furthermore, the Lorches told me that close friends of theirs, Maren and Axel Mauder, lived in Gosfield village. Even so no action was called for, and life plodded on.

One of the charms of my Edinburgh Gardens house was that it backed on to former local school playing fields, giving it a splendid wide outlook all round. When one day I learned the fields were being bought for housing development, I was not pleased. Thoughts of that tempting apartment in the superb Elizabethan Essex house began to creep into my mind. Just to get a rough idea of things I got my house valued and let matters lie.

Before long I was surprised to find a note put through my door, a kind of flyer saying that an owner of one of the two-bedroom houses in Edinburgh Gardens needed a three-bedroom one, and was there any likelihood of a prospective vacancy? Doubtless it was the result of a little leaked information from a house agent, or a suggested means of approach from one such, without being indiscrete.

I followed up this enquiry and found that a young family needed more space for their growing children, but wanted to stay in the area. They had a prospective buyer for their house and were delighted to have had a wisp of hopeful smoke wafted discretely in their direction. To add to their dilemma the young family's prospective buyer wanted vacant possession by a relatively imminent date, thus thrusting the dilemma neatly into my astonished lap!

Early symptoms of some unexpected health trouble made the lure of the care offered by the CHA apartments very tempting. The prospect of selling the home added to this lure very strongly and I succumbed. I decided I could undertake vacant possession by the required date, if my prospective buyers would complete my sale correspondingly. An agreement was arrived at and I proceeded with my side of the deal. The jiggery-pokery, however, which my purchasers perpetuated, left me sorely beggared at the end of the transaction when I needed all the money I could muster. All this left me with a considerable distaste for the new owners of the little house I had formerly enjoyed.

Having undertaken to vacate my much-loved house in a matter of just a few weeks, I had to act swiftly. My first preference had been for Gosfield in Essex, but before a final decision I took a look at Swallowfield Park in Berkshire, where Margaret had enjoyed staying.

SWALLOWFIELD PARK

Swallowfield, though larger than either Gosfield or the house near Guildford, was somehow more open, more on the palm of one's hand, and more welcoming in its layout. It had been the house Henry VIII had given to each of his successive wives in their time and had been lived in by the Russell family up to as recently as the early 1960s. It had, in fact, been visited quite recently by a member of that family who was anxious to look at the nursery he had grown up in.

The day of the visit, however, had suddenly presented a problem. The occupant of the former nursery suddenly died during the night before the occasion. Making sure that the undertaker's visit preceded that of the honoured guest was indeed an anxiety for the administrators.

I quite liked Swallowfield Park, though it did not have the tone of Gosfield and the apartment available was not quite as seductive as the Essex one. It was only a one-bedroom flat as opposed to the two bedrooms of the other, but was less costly in the so-called purchase price.

This was a scheme whereby a sum of money was loaned to the association, from which a percentage was deducted annually to represent rent for the accommodation, on top of which a maintenance charge was levied monthly. Having been done out of a considerable portion of my available money, I had to consider costs and fortunately chose Swallowfield. Penelope was no longer thinking of living in Essex, and was against my moving there. I also did not know at the time to what extent the vast sum involved in the so-called purchase would be appropriated by the association, frittered away and devalued over the years.

All my friends raised their hands in horror, saying they would never see me again if I went into the inaccessible antipodes which Essex represented to them!

How much influence these protestations had on me I did not know, but I decided to stay in Berkshire, and took a very beautiful first floor apartment in Swallowfield where the remainder of my much-loved slowly accumulated furniture — which had fitted out my Queen Anne Buxton house — was accommodated very suitably.

On my early morning arrival at Swallowfield I was welcomed by one of the very friendly residents, Juliet McCreery, who though hampered by a severe limp, helped carry things which the obliging handyman could not load on to his well-filled trolley from the heavily loaded car. The absence of the administrators displeased, but did not surprise me; I had not been impressed by them. Juliet had been a Women's Royal Naval Service officer during the Second World War, stationed in Liverpool where she scrambled up the sides of in-coming ships to check their cargoes on their arrival in the convoys dispatched from Halifax, Nova Scotia by Admiral Leonard Murray, my late husband. She befriended me very warmly when she learned of my past.

Time proved that my first impression of the administrators had been accurate, but did not have to affect the day-to-day life and the interrelations of the residents. In contrast and in retrospect, the administrators at Gosfield had been quite a different proposition. Their warm, considerate personalities melded the residents together, and they appeared to go out of their way to be vigilant and caring for their guests' comfort and ease. Sadly the good lady of that pair died suddenly fairly soon into my CHA sojourn, and there was a reshuffle of administrators all round.

Many years have gone by since that arrival day, and CHA has changed from being Country Houses Association to CH Apartments and now is largely disbanded. Only, at most, two houses have remained residential. Some have been converted into wedding accommodation venues, and others were just sold off. How glad I am that I left when I did!

I know little of the fates of the delightful people whose company I had enjoyed. They have all had to face something like a year of anxiety, not knowing whether they must find other accommodation, or whether the association would weather the crisis. The financial disadvantage of the association's terms has been catastrophic for them.

Had people been able to end their days in their chosen accommodation, their basic original financial outlay should have lasted them thirty years, but the sudden eviction has left them without the ability to buy into adequate housing at current prices. House and accommodation prices have risen, while the capital invested in CHA has dwindled, besides being eroded. Fortunately most of the residents looked as if they had reserves, and though not necessarily happily, they appear to have re-settled their lives.

Taking a retrospective look at the nice folk I knew as they sat at their proscribed tables with their crisp tablecloths in the large L-shaped dining room, the ones who sat in the right hand corner away from the windows were a retired psychiatrist and his unsmiling lady wife Tilda.

Tilda's critical appraisal of all she surveyed was probably caused by ill health, as this sad lady soon died, leaving a husband who proved to be a very cultured and interesting man who has stayed on in what remains of Swallowfield under its new management.

The table in the left-hand corner by the entrance door to this part of the dining room was the domain of farming Major George and his charming and beautiful lady wife Juliet, who sadly was very disabled by a severely arthritic spine. This did not show in her demeanour, though it caused her a great deal of pain. Though George was obviously crippled with arthritic knees and hips, which had all been repeatedly operated on, he hobbled around indefatigably playing croquet and causing displeasure to other residents who failed to reserve the croquet ground before he had done.

George had farmed in the Henley neighbourhood and, on two days a week, continued to help his son to whom he had passed the farm on retirement. Between all these activities George officiated in many prestigious capacities in the military world from which he had originally retired. He ran rallies, reviews and arranged Beating-the-Retreat occasions and other such events for Swallowfield and elsewhere.

George had invited me to a British Legion occasion for a branch that was about to be disbanded. I reciprocated by inviting the members and their wives to a strawberry tea party at my flat. This proved to be a great success, and never before in my life have I had quite as many kisses in one day as I had at the end of that party. Each guest expressed his or her thanks and pleasure in sincere and warm kisses.

George and Juliet moved from Swallowfield at the beginning of its disruption. They found a residential nursing home in the Henley area where they repeatedly recommend I join them as they have found it both comfortable and pleasant—and even equipped with a good croquet lawn—but no room for archery.

The latter is no detriment in my view as I am not proud of the lumpy biceps in my right upper arm, developed in my archery attempts, although I enjoyed being a fletcher; and the arrows certainly needed frequent repairs.

An imposing-looking table, next to my small table, was occupied by another major and his wife. They were Ian and Gill, who were frequently visited by their very business-minded company director son-in-law who, to everyone's surprise, had been involved in the take-over of Meredydd's late father's and late uncle's widely-known business. Ian ran a lottery club for residents, and the finances of my newest soft-toy making venture.

This was a Wednesday morning session in the drawing room, when residents were invited to come and take part in making soft-toys to my patterns. These were made to sell on days when Swallowfield had its gardens open for visitors, and other such occasions arranged to raise money for the repair of some needy feature of the house or gardens.

These sessions were very happy occasions, even though those who could sew could not see, and those who could see could not sew, and those who could see and sew could, very genteelly, not remember what they were to do and the like!

The venture surprisingly raised something like £500 for the cause until its production began to feel old-hat, and sales began to fall off. New ventures such as the making of colourful Christmas stockings could not be delegated in quite as sociable a manner as it had been with the toys, and that venture fizzled out.

Four levels of bridge ran concurrently in the house. One money-raising weekly, multi-table afternoon occasion was arranged by Major Ian, and was attended by outsiders. This was neither very convivial nor profitable, and was ultimately abandoned. A high-grade serious level was played in rotating chosen apartments, a low-level haphazard kind was played by poor 'rememberers' and novices like me. An outside club was attended weekly by a few seeking to improve their game. At this club I was surprised to meet the fiancée of a widowed naval college classmate of my late stepson, Sandy.

To my surprise on arrival at Swallowfield, two of the lady residents there were called Nina. One day, when all three of us travelled together in one car, we nicknamed ourselves. I, the newcomer doctor was Quack; Nina Mallard became Ducky, and one lady whose apartment had a kitchen where she cooked for herself, defined herself as Cooky.

Ducky, who died just before the demise of the CHA, had been the romantic much-adored second wife of her brigadier second husband. They had resumed their early-life romance on both becoming widowed. The now again-widowed brigadier—one of Swallowfield's military contingent—has become another of the few who have stayed on in the remodelled household.

Cooky's story is sad, long, and very romantic. Besides having a stone-deaf daughter, now the widow of a stone-deaf man, this Nina—a widow and a long-time CHA resident—fell in love quite a few years ago with a male resident and they planned to marry. To everyone's distress the gentleman suddenly became totally blind. As the sudden blindness delayed the official marriage, an actual co-habiting became essential and raised quite a number of eyebrows. Sadly it was not long before Cooky was bereaved again, and it still saddens her that she cannot carry the name of the man she came to love very deeply.

She had dealt with the current CHA problem by moving somewhere conveniently near her daughter just when the wind-up problems were beginning.

Of the doctor contingent—besides the psychiatrist and the ophthalmic Quack—there was a senior and very wise and respected physician, Kenneth Buxton. Kenneth and his lovely, gentle, wife Agnes, had been missionaries in Africa for many years. Agnes died while they were waiting for a vacancy elsewhere. Kenneth left Swallowfield before the changes and died soon after. A very long established and esteemed medical historian Ferdie Cartwright and his delightful lady wife Paddy completed the medics. Ferdie, who was happy to end his days before the changes, had had one of his books translated into Chinese.

He had looked after the huge and beautiful library of the house, and ran money-raising book sales to which residents contributed their surplus books. Paddy was a wonderful friendly and smiling devoted gardener and splendid housewife, who silently and with the uncompromising support of a steel corset, suffered great pain, the aftermath of Poliomyelitis contracted during the infancy of her four now-adult daughters. In spite of her distorted frame Paddy was like a little garden gnome, who was to be seen busying herself contentedly in different parts of the extensive grounds.

Paddy quite often invited people into their apartment for morning coffee or pre-supper drinks when, among other home made delicacies, she would offer her guests home made sloe gin. On occasions such as these Ferdie used to join the party and show people some of his special books. He invited his visitors to take away and peruse one of his most recent publications and, having put on a very serious and academic severe face, he would then hand them his Chinese volume.

Pre-supper drinks were a fully established custom no self-respecting resident neglected. Everyone was invited into everyone else's apartment at least once a week, resulting in few people being in their own apartment during any 6-7 p.m. period. Makes of gin were discussed and compared. The merits of whiskies with water as opposed to being taken with sodas were talked about, and among the military and service ladies, relative ranks and prestiges were ruminated on.

I am very ashamed to admit that I have before now, refilled someone's whisky glass with a gin and tonic, or even put tonic into someone's whisky, or soda into their gin and other such misdemeanours. But even so, I have been feted for my parties and have enjoyed giving them. It was an apartment well suited for such occasions.

Among the ladies (the maiden ones were definitely relatively the quieter) was a tall, elegant and handsome lady, of variable mood, called Jean, who had quite a story to her life. She had been in the Foreign Office and had served in Japan and in Canada, and must have been very attractive in her youth, so it was not surprising that romance did not pass her by. It sadly seems, however, that more than once Jean's journey to the altar has been unfairly diverted by ladies less scrupulous than she had been.

As a result she has had to resort to a relatively contented life as a companion to a lady of means who ultimately took up residence at Swallowfield. This lady had arranged for very pleasant accommodation for Jean conveniently near to herself, and all was well until the sad day when the good lady died. Jean, who had no capital, no pension and now no home, was indeed in a difficult position.

Somehow arrangements must have been made (by solicitors or somebody) and CHA accommodated Jean in a cupboard of a room, as a bed-sit with access to a shared bathroom in the attic. She had to be content, and content she was and very thankful. The trouble, however, was 'face', the indignity of suddenly being in reduced circumstances.

None of the residents thought any the less of Jean, understood her problem and admired how well she faced the new state of affairs. She was allowed the use of one of the smaller drawing rooms if she had guests or needed to arrange a return pre-supper party, but her shoulder developed a large 'chip'. The depth and tenderness of this chip varied from day to day, and had found an unnecessary power of fancy, making Jean imagine that people looked down on her and even snubbed her, these fancies colouring each day's outlook and mood.

Another retired Foreign Office lady was Elizabeth, who never quite recovered from the fact that, some years before her arrival in Swallowfield, her former Chelsea flat had been burgled. Elizabeth had worked mostly in Burma, and had had a very brief marriage while out there. History relates that only a few weeks after the wedding her young husband, a BBC war correspondent, was lost at sea with the troop ship he was accompanying. To Elizabeth's perpetual distress, his loss has never been officially recorded.

Elizabeth, a small, pale and fleshless senior, elegant, lady with a slightly haughty attitude about her was, in reality, a very affectionate and lonely little soul. She needed to give her heart to someone in return for approval and friendship. Unfortunately, besides devoting herself to a number of people she called her 'God-children' she gave her heart to a resident widower.

This gentleman still carried the spirit of his beloved late wife Daphne in his heart and of whose Special Operations Executive (SOE) activities he was very proud. This man, Howard Bridge, though sad to be without his Daphne, had happy memories and a warm affection for many old friends and enjoyed the company of both men and women and lived life generally to the full. Unfortunately for Elizabeth he found her managing devotion tedious, and had to tell her so from time to time to her hurt. But she persisted. Elizabeth also gave her loyal heart to women. This again proved to be trying, inconveniencing and tedious.

Sadly all along it seemed that Elizabeth's concern was more for her own wish to please than for the pleasure or comfort of the person she hoped she was pleasing. One of Elizabeth's characteristics had been that she continually droned about her money problems which, she said, included fears she might fail to meet all the benefactions she wished to bestow. She found the added insecurity of not knowing how CHA would handle its financial breakdown very distressing, and eventually settled somewhere relatively economically. Howard died painfully from cancer of the jaw just as CHA was breaking up.

The young do not need to think that romance, love and sexuality are their prerogative. These ruling emotions all go on and grow in understanding and intensity, though sometimes without one or both, as long as people live.

A very dapper moderately-aged and relatively long-time resident colonel who, although only a Territorial, persisted in calling himself "Colonel," had been very devoted to a resident lady who had come from Guernsey. To Norval's and every body else's distress, but mercifully for her, this lady died on a plane in the air with a gin and tonic in her hand on the way to a Paris weekend.

My nephew John Seaford (Nicholas's son), the Dean of Jersey, on one of his very welcome visits to my Essex home

Norval recovered from the distress of losing his lady friend, and before long started paying great attention to me, the new arrival. It started with invitations to drinks.

These invitations grew more and more frequent and gradually became embarrassing. He would be almost in the nude when he opened the door to me, blaming the heat for the dearth of his clothing. His flat was on the top floor of the house and did get hot, so, regarding the association to be sufficiently casual, I ignored his lack of outfit. When, however, the nudity became total and was promptly followed by proclamations of undying love and its needs, the situation had to be stopped.

A firm but undramatic break had to be made in the openly friendly association. I had quite quickly become regarded by the other residents as Norval's preferred lady, encouraged to sit by him in the minibus and the like. An obvious sudden distancing would have caused titters.

The educational world was represented by two retired teachers; Peggy Jessop and Norma Turbett. These two delightful ladies had been friends for years, shared a holiday home in Spain, and had a very pleasant apartment where each had a bedroom with its own bathroom. They shared a splendid sitting room. This was very convenient as they were both very senior delegates in the world of education administration, and entertained many colleagues.

Early in their settling-in period they needed to notify the supplier of some big domestic item that they would be unable to accept delivery of on a proposed day, because they would be out. This statement resulted in a surprised: "Oh, do they let you out?" to Peggy's great amusement. This kind of misunderstanding of the nature of the establishment had its annoying side in many respects.

The ease of being able to entertain visitors by just stating the numbers invited and the exact date they would be due was one of the great attractions of Swallowfield. Friends from away could come; some came just for Sunday lunch, others came to stay in the reservable guest rooms. Penelope sometimes stayed for quite a while, using the second divan in my spacious bedroom, and Penelope and Meredydd enjoyed Sundays with croquet on almost alternate weekends.

There were trips to local theatres and cinemas arranged by Mark, the retired surgeon, and the fifth member of the medical contingent. Mark filled the house minibus roughly every six weeks, taking residents to carefully chosen entertainment events he had vetted before opening the booking list. The house arranged weekly minibus shopping trips; one week to Reading and the next to nearby Wokingham. Woe betide anyone not on time for the return journey; such culprits were left behind, and taxi costs were high. Fortunately I had my car and rarely used the Reading ride.

The village of Swallowfield was very small and un-village like. It consisted of one shop-cum-post office, and a very splendid newly-built doctors' surgery, the rest being made up largely of newly-built insignificant houses. It was a mile away from Swallowfield Park and did not include us in any activities that may have gone on in the area. Not much went on at the church from where the vicar visited us and held weekly services in the library. The church had been built at the periphery of the park grounds in Henry VIII's time because it was too dangerous to ride through the forest to the nearest church, which was at Windsor.

Generally there was a feeling of being isolated in the ageing mansion at the end of a bleak mile-long, rough drive. This was too short to drive and too long to walk, except as an enforced exercise, as it ran through grounds which were roughly grazed by a local farmer's stock.

I began to be oppressed by a feeling of boarding school restrictions developing in spite of, or perhaps because of, various changes of administrators and chief executives of the CHA.

One day two of my good friends from Hampstead came to lunch, and the three of us chatted, happily remembering the many things we used to enjoy doing together. This reminded me of all the many possibilities London offered, and we three agreed that it would be wise for me to start thinking of planning some way of getting back to the city. Though it hadn't been discussed, the unformed ghost of a thought of the possibility of taking a part of the big house one of my visitors lived in, hovered vaguely in my mind and we parted on the note of "let's start looking."

ESSEX

On the day following this decision Penelope arrived full of excitement: she and Meredydd were about to buy a house in Coggeshall in Essex. My thoughts immediately ran to the lovely apartment I had seen those years earlier at Gosfield, and the possibility of transferring to that section of the CHA. I set about looking into the matter after I had been taken to look at Coggeshall and the property my family was considering.

Although I liked the town, it is possible that my lack of enthusiasm for their particular prospective property may have given Penelope and Meredydd second thoughts, but anyway there was a pause in the proceedings. Some time later there was renewed excitement, they had found something they really liked and were getting on with buying it. In this new light, I renewed my investigations.

Nothing stays the same in this world as time goes on, and nearly three years had gone by since my original interest in Gosfield. The super flat was no longer vacant. The administrators were of a different type. Besides all of this there was only one very small apartment available, but the attraction of good storage facilities for holding my large excess furniture would still be available if I took an apartment there. This storage capacity was in a part of the house likely to have originally been a priest-hide. In it the items could comfortably await their acceptance into Penelope's new home.

While pondering on the matter I discussed the idea with the Swallowfield administrators. It proved not to be possible to just transfer, a new contract had to be negotiated. Down payments were all considerably higher than before, and of any such, three per cent would be immediately deducted for five years of prospective occupation, even if the proposed resident only stayed one year or less. Not a worthwhile proposition.

So I took a ride around Coggeshall, got local house agents' names and tried to arrange a viewing day only to find that there was very little property available. I did, however, prepare a list big enough to warrant the journey, and came to have another look at the town. One little house seemed, in my ignorance, worth a second look but I postponed arranging for this, hoping that a wider choice might open up. Nothing seemed to come up so I took a second look and decided that I would take it. It was very near Penelope, had a car parking space in an enclosure, and a reasonably fitted-out kitchen.

Having arranged for a survey to be carried out, I started pricing furniture removers and gave my notice to CHA. As it was only a few days into February I expected that month to be included in the statutory six months' notice required to terminate a resident's contract, but, annoyingly, the six months had to start from March, tying me to Swallowfield until the end of August.

One Saturday evening I was surprised to have a call from the surveyor of my prospective property who rang to ask whether I intended continuing with the purchase of the house he had surveyed. I said I intended to do so, but asked why he was enquiring and whether he, who was himself a house agent as well as a surveyor, had any preferable entities to suggest. He said he had none; he had just been wondering.

This sounded a very altruistic thought to phone about across the country, and I promptly checked the state of affairs with my list of agents. None had anything in the proposed price range. Reluctantly one agent admitted he had a few properties in the next bracket and agreed to send particulars. Among these a couple looked worth viewing and I again set forth on the two and a half hour drive to view.

I was completely charmed by the first cottage I saw; it had a welcoming atmosphere about it. It was old and low, and stood by the river with its ducks, geese and swans to the west, besides a communal garden with a riverside lawn stretching to the east. There was a very sheltered east-facing patio by the back door and a large high-walled shared car park to the side. A more romantic cottage would be hard to find.

Assured by the vendors that they had not been flooded, a price was agreed and appropriate steps were taken, together with a call to the surveyor to thank him for having alerted me to this totally preferable property. Returning to Swallowfield with glowing accounts of my find, my spirits were not too dampened by people's warnings about the wisdom of living near a river and the danger of floods.

By mid-July No. 3, Riverside Maltings became mine. As I was still tied to Swallowfield, Penelope and Meredydd camped in the cottage, equipped with my garden furniture and camp beds, while their own house continued to be adjusted to their needs. During those six or so weeks I came several times with carloads of easily movable items to ease the campers' discomfort. On these occasions I brought down friends to show off my find and, besides taking a look at the progress in Penelope's house, to consider and discuss what adjustments I would need with the apparently only available builder. He, however, was not likely to be free until he finished working for my daughter.

To anyone I met around the little Riverside Maltings development of nine houses I announced myself as "the new Number Three," but as most residents were away at work during the day, the only person I met turned out to be someone's "daily."

Eventually September 1st came and a huge pantechnicon lumbered up the long and rutted service drive to Swallowfield Park. Loading had to be carefully planned; items for delivery to Penelope needed to be at the back for unloading after my equipment for the cottage would have gone in. As the archway leading to the garages where the items for Penelope had been stored was too low for the van to go through, the removal men decided, against my advice, to load my furniture from the house first. This meant that, on arrival in Coggeshall, the big furniture intended for Penelope's house had to wait in the road during the unloading into my cottage. As the cottage had three floors the process took a long time and was very exhausting for the men.

To add insult to injury, when the reloaded van belatedly reached Penelope's Church Street house, it was found not to be ready to take the main big things. These, consequently, needed to be packed into Penelope's garage. As this was round the corner on a different road from the main house, the furniture had to be shuffled around again before reaching its further storage.

Everyone was grateful for the fact that it was not raining but, understandably, the men were becoming bad tempered and it was getting dark. I only heard later of the double reloading the men were forced to undertake, and though my sympathy for them was sincere, there was no longer anything I could do about it.

On the last of my visits to my new house before moving in, I had come with yet another of my friends, Joyce Manser. Joyce was a lady with a sad history who had had to leave Zimbabwe disastrously due to its troubles, and had been perching at Swallowfield for quite a considerable time. As time had gone along Joyce's husband, who had been a prosperous property developer and a skilled craftsman and chandler, had become ill and needed to be in a nursing home. Their son, who had stayed in Zimbabwe to try to sort out his own business and try to salvage some of his parent's property, eventually joined them. He had developed liver disease for which he hoped to get treatment in England, but sadly he soon died.

As Joyce and I walked around to look at the communal riverside lawn, I saw a gentleman getting out of his car in his car port and went along announcing myself as "the new Number Three." The gentleman was a little taken aback by this sudden approach but recovered in a short while and called after us as we disappeared towards the river, offering us cups of tea. Glad to accept the invitation we came into what proved to be Ken Aberdour's lovely house.

Ken was a retired doctor (a much-loved and honoured retired consultant radiologist who was deeply grieved by his beloved wife's recent death) who entertained his unexpected guests very nobly. The house certainly looked as if no guests had visited for quite a time: nor indeed had they, for his dear suddenly-taken Jean had not been there to entertain anyone for some eighteen sad months. Teacups and saucers had to be reached from a high-up cupboard, a tray found and sweetmeats searched for.

Polite enquiries followed: "What kind of tea would you like?"

"Just whatever you have on the go," from me was countered by Ken's whimsical: "Would you like Gunpowder?"

Confirming that it was Gunpowder Tea he was offering, Ken re-climbed the steps to reach for the accepted unknown tea while Joyce and I exchanged curious and amused glances. Proceeding into the lovely sitting room, we looked through the wide expanse of an almost wall-to-wall patio door into a huge expanse of developing garden with flower beds around an extensive paved area leading to a bridge by the riverside, which led to a further stretch of garden with lawn, sheds and greenhouses.

It had been the possibilities offered by this garden, with the river Blackwater by its side, which had persuaded Ken and Jean to abandon the big house they had lived in and loved for many years in nearby Wickham Bishops. Little more than six hard working busy settling-in months had gone by when, some ghastly forty or less minutes of the agony of a ruptured aorta suddenly killed Jean. Ken half-died that day too.

A slightly reluctantly brightening Ken continued to entertain his sudden guests. He showed and explained the many treasures tastefully displayed around the room, played his exquisite music box, and then suddenly asked whether I was interested in evening classes. I was indeed interested, and said I had arranged for a bridge course in the nearby small town of Witham, and that I had planned to attend the next meeting of the local National Association of Decorative and Fine Arts Society (NADFAS.)

Ken promptly pointed out that I had been given the wrong day of the week for the meeting, put me right and gave me excellent directions how to find the right place on the right day.

We had chatted about the charm of my cottage and its age and touched on many of the aspects of the interests Essex presented, when Ken asked whether I might be interested in joining an evening local history class about Coggeshall, for which registration was in progress. Since I was interested, he offered to book me in and the beginnings of a lovely friendship were laid down.

Ken, a kind and wise man of a physique reminding me of my late father, but who sadly has back and other health troubles (though he insists on being very athletically effective) has a brilliantly active and retentive brain.

As time has gone on I have learned that he belongs to an endless number of learned societies, attends cultural lectures, classes and meetings on several days each week, Besides all this he is secretary, treasurer or chairman of myriad and various prestigious associations, together with attending concerts, theatres, ballets and every opera that Glyndebourne produces. His activities are endless.

All this, and his greatly loved profession, Ken has attained purely by his own effort, as his early life had started in difficult circumstances.

To my surprise and pleasure Ken has, by degrees, invited me amongst many other widows to take part with him in quite a number of his undertakings. All this gave me a good introduction to the locality, especially as I joined him in the hardest of voluntary jobs: the distribution of election pamphlets, something I had done with Leonard in our Buxton days.

RISING WATER

As usual, settling in to my diminutive new home took longer than expected, as had been the case with the finishing of the re-organisation in Penelope's house. As a result of the Church Street delays, Penelope and Meredydd stayed on at my unadjusted place for the three months to that first Christmas, which, ultimately were glad to celebrate in their new home.

With the brightening days forecasting spring, they set to attending to their garden, whereas I began to wish I had more than just the small triangle of soil at the front of my house just below the bridge parapet. Though more limiting than I had realised when I had welcomed it as a token garden, having planted up the odd tub here and there, I was content. My help, however, was apparently welcome anytime in Ken's garden where, besides a lot else, there were roses to be dead-headed and weeding to be done.

The second summer was also sunny and hot, but as autumn drew on the river swelled from time to time, and though my house did not get flooded, the two parts of this refurbished and redeveloped old building nearest to the water did get some water, and people began remembering years when there had been floods.

As the rains grew heavier with the months, one October Sunday when, as a loyal member of the Essex Historic Buildings Group, I drove to my "guiding duty"—a whole day's undertaking at Cressing Temple—through the heavy rain which had persisted through the night, I was troubled to see diverted traffic areas and found roads I needed to drive through to be seriously flooded. Even so, I managed to reach my destination. Though a pre-booked party did visit Cressing's ancient barns, no other visitors came through the persistent rain and amongst others, I set off for home at about 2 p.m.

Having to turn back half-way along my first preferred homeward route, I chose another, when again I was stopped. I found myself amidst a long string of stock-still cars facing a wide sea that covered the land and roads around the low-lying village of Bradwell, thus cutting the A120 main road from Braintree to Colchester. Again I tried a different route. In this, after much queuing and slow creeping through a road that bypassed the blocked A12 main road between Chelmsford and Colchester, followed by an ultimate bold "swooshing" through a frighteningly deep flood which others were being wary of, I approached my house some considerable time after six that evening.

To my surprise I saw a crowd standing on the bridge beside my house, and a small child walking out of my front door. This was my "helping lady" Gwen's grandson. Gwen, a long-time resident of Coggeshall who was wary of floods, had wisely alerted my family of the danger on finding my imperilled house untended.

All of her family, and Penelope and Meredydd, were hurriedly trying to get as much as they could of my furniture and effects off the ground floor up the awkward and restrictive stairs.

They had struggled hard most of the day and had achieved wonders. Council men piled sandbags in places they considered appropriate, but the water slowly rose and kept on rising, though the rain seemed to be easing.

As they were all very tired, Gwen and her family—to whom I was heartily grateful for their forethought and toil—were sent off home with repeated sincere gratitude for their help. Penelope, escorted by Meredydd, went home while it was still possible to walk up the road, but Meredydd returned and

I survey the damage to my home in the aftermath of the flood. (Photo courtesy the Essex Evening Gazette)

stayed with me in the marooned house with the water beginning to seep in from unexpected places.

Since, at that stage, only a little water was getting into the actual house, we went along to help Ken with his problems. Other kind neighbours from higher up the hill joined in the rescue, enabling most of the movable pieces of Ken's valuable furniture to be moved upstairs. The women mostly helped move books from the lower shelves in his library, and bottles from the lower rungs of his wine stores, and tried to salvage his groceries.

Though the rain had seemed to lighten, it did not stop, and the river continued to swell. The higher it rose, the more it was dammed by the sturdy arches of the very solid bridge alongside my house, making the water swirl around its wider open northern end into the road and across it into the Maltings car park and buildings.

As the wide car parking area filled up, the rushing water did its unsuccessful best to flow out at the far end of the enclosure, through the narrow, high-walled paths at the sides of Ken's house and to the side into the communal garden flanking the river at the back of the beautiful small houses of the refurbished Maltings. There it was met by the rest of the overflowing river.

As the outflow was so restricted and slow, and the surge through the wide car park gate was persistently torrential, the water level in the enclosed car park rose swiftly. Ken could see it steadily creeping up the outside of his glazed front door. As the outside water reached towards knee height, it started seeping in through the front door cracks as well as those of his back door and, as it crept up on to his top terrace, it seeped in below and around his wide garden-facing patio windows, as well as flooding into the fronts of the four car-park-facing houses.

When, eventually and mercifully, the weight of the water became too much for the ten-foot tall old brick wall surrounding the car park, it forced some thirty or so feet of its north face out into the adjoining garden, allowing the water to escape in another direction.

The accumulated water cascaded in a torrent, carrying away with it flower tubs and all kinds of debris. With this release the flood level began to fall, and instead of coming in, water now ran out of Ken's house and out of the others into the relieved area.

In my house, water had entered the kitchen area from the low-lying small house (a refurbished former lean-to shed) that adjoined mine from the north. This had filled up from the car park lake, and water soon began to seep up through a badly placed central heating pipe in the sitting room. Towards midnight the rain eased, and water flowed out of the house using such outlets as an old cat-flap, carrying away things like oven gloves, tea cosies and the like.

Travel news on the radio spoke of the troubles on roads and of the problem of the flooding on the A12 in the Blackwater area.

Weary but relieved to see the carpet lying on the floor instead of being afloat, Meredydd was glad to find the bed he had used in past times on the top floor. I too was glad to be able to squeeze my way between the piled furniture in my bedroom towards my bed and tumbled quickly in to sleep. About 3 a.m. both Meredydd and I found ourselves vetting the situation on the ground floor and, relieved to find peace, returned to our beds and sleep.

At about 6 a.m. I was roused by the roar of gushing water. Flouncing out of bed I called to Meredydd who, in just his underpants, rushed down to join me as we gazed in horror at a depth of some four or more feet of water covering the ground floor. Water was rushing in through the windows and my lovely *chaise-lounge*, too big to have been moved, was floating towards us in the water.

Our first instinct was to wade out to the electric meter to switch that off before the water should reach the fuse box. Beyond that we just did not know what we could do, besides snatching up whatever we could grab? Radio News proudly proclaimed the victory of the road department over the flooding; the A12 had been cleared: but at whose cost?

As we stood in shattered disbelief, a high wheeled tractor swished over the bridge and down into, and on through the lake around the house, and up the road towards the town. The wash in its wake knocked down the bridge parapet in front of my house, its huge coping stones falling against my door with a shattering clamour and water surge.

Coats, clothes and documents in ground floor cupboards were soaked; filing cabinets were under water, kitchen items like cookers, fridges, freezers, washing machines and grocery cupboards were devastated, lights failed and there was no heat. The only thing left to do was to wait for the rain to stop, and to hope that the water would drain away with time.

Meanwhile people brought out canoes to play with, and children paddled at the shallower edges of the drain polluted floodwaters. One of my neighbours had a horse, and knew that it needed to be fed, as it was stabled somewhere in a loosebox. As the current of water through the car park gate was too strong to walk through, she eventually (and with help) scaled the ten-foot wall and waded to solid ground above water level where, to the bystanders' amusement, she donned the clothes she had brought with her in a bundle strapped to her back.

Eventually the water drained away and the hideous clearing started. People could not stay in their houses and moved away. Though Ken's house had suffered badly, as it lies higher than most, it was habitable and he accepted me as a lodger in my plight.

I ate and slept at his house, but spent the day in a bit of my slightly cleared bedroom, from where I did my best to try to sort out what I could. All the while I was dealing with insurers, demolishers, repairers, prospective flood-protectors and all the other horrid jobs that have to be faced at such a time, as well as sifting through as much as possible of the wrought havoc.

Eventually the river section of the environment department built up flood protection on the riverbanks, and the houses had individual flood protective devices fitted. It took a good year before walls dried out and got re-built where necessary. After these were re-plastered, and replacement items arrived and got fitted, and re-decorations finished, people began to creep warily back into their strangely altered homes.

It is surprising how bad memories get erased. Three happy years have passed since those nightmare times, lit for me by the company of friends and Ken's wise and stimulating example and companionship. But please, no floods!

What any future years might bring, nobody can know, but I hope to see many more happy English summers in which to ponder on this world's troubled tableau.

As, over the centuries Russia, mainly through her navy, has had associations with Scotland, it is possible that there may be Scottish genes amongst the present brew. This may account for ease with which my Anglo-Russian mantle can so easily appear to be that of an Englishwoman.

EPILOGUE

This story began as a tribute to my father, but I quickly realised that it is to both my parents that I owe the nature of my make-up. It is my hope that as the tale unfolds, the reader can sense my gratitude for the moral and spiritual legacies my brother and I inherited. It would have been easy for Sergei and Vera to have settled into the life of the disconsolate exile, deprived of their wealth and social status, barred from their beloved country, with nothing of material value to pass on to his children.

What they left both my brother and me has been an understanding of our family history, and an appreciation that with determination, sacrifice and effort, all adversity can be overcome. It is only now in my later years that I realize it has been this gift that enabled both Nicolas and me to surmount our troubles and that Penelope's share in this inheritance has helped her overcome her difficulties and that their share of it will help Nicholas' heirs in the future.

If this account of my life has proven to be merely an interesting story, I shall not consider the effort a failure. If it proves to be an inspirational story, for any reader, I shall be content to feel that I could pass on my father's gift in this way and that once again his spirit has triumphed.

Index

Aberdour, Kenneth, 182–83
Addis, Caroline. *See* Rigby, Sonny
Admiral Murray. *See* Murray, Admiral
    Leonard Warren
Admiral Toys, 133–35
Alexandrov (*Zavodi*) Mills, 18, *19*
Applebee, Moya, 113
Ariadne, deceased sister, 13–15, *14*, 140

Bardsley, John, 40, 50
Basra, 88, 93
Bedford, Henry, 44–45
Best, Henry, 43, 167–68
Bietti, Prof., 56
Biondo, Dr. Michele D'Azaro, 56
Bloomsbury Set, 153
Bosphorus, 2
Brammer, George, 75
Buxton, 109–14, 126–30, *127,* 133–36
Buxton, Kenneth and Agnes, 175

Carson, Margaret, 166, 169–70
Cartledge, Mrs., the gambling
    housekeeper, 103–6
Caucasus, retreat to, 20
CHA, 170–72, 174–77, 179–80
Charnley, John, 47
Clarke, Prof. LeGros, 94

Coggeshall, 180–88
Country Housing Association. *See* CHA
Crete, 62–64
Crimea, evacuation of, 1–3, 8–15

Disley, 53
Divorce: Nina's, 96, 110; Sandy
    Murray's, 135, 142; Nicholas', 139;
    Penelope's, 151, 162, 166
Dodd, John, 57
Droogy, spaniel, *36*–37, *47*

Eccles, school etc., 32, 38,
Edinburgh Gardens, 168–70
Elysée, Marie Josephine. *See*
    Matousseyvitch, Marie

Ffaulks, Harry, 167–68
Flooding, 183–88

Gaertner, Miss, secretary, 110–11, 113
Grasmere, 48
Grecian Slipper, 74
Greece, dowager Queen of, 57
"Green" Russians, 22–23
Gunpowder production, 18

Halifax Riots, 122–23
HMS *Calypso*, 25

Hogg, Quentin (Lord Hailsham), 75
Hopkins, Padre, 65
Huxley, Sir Julian, 147, 151–54
Huxley, Lady Juliette, 153–54

Istanbul: arrival at, 3; return to 118

Jackson, Roger (Warwick), 45–46,
   77–79, 81–88, *84*, 92–96, 158–62
Jackson, Rowland and Trudi, 78
Jolly, cairn terrier, 102, 105
Jones, Emmett Lee, 59–60

Karpenko, Mrs., housekeeper, 105
Kew, 126, 166–68
Kidnap attempt, 3
Kronschtadt, floating dock, 2–3

Laski, Harold, 100
Lazaret, prison hospital, 67–70
Lees, Elisabeth, 116
Leonidova, Lyda, 91, 155
Linnean Society, 147, 159
Littler, Allan, 110
Liza, Nanny, 2, 16, 20, 22, 24, 28,
   42–44, *99*
Longbotham, George, 44
Longbotham, Kathleen (Seaford), 41,
   49–51, 136–40
Long march (from prison camp), 71–74
Lorch, Diana, 168–69

Malvern Girls' College, 115
Manchester Courier, 111
Marriage: to Roger, 83–88; to Leonard,
   128
Matousseyvitch, Alexander
   Nikoleyevich. *See* Shoura, Vera's
   brother
Matousseyvitch, Marie, 2, 8–10, *9*, 12,
   15, 20, 22, 24–25, 42, 55–56, 90–92,
   98, 103, 113–14, 131
Matousseyvitch, Admiral Nikolai, 13, *16*
Matousseyvitch, Aunt Natasha, 2, 9–10,
   15, *17*, 22–24, 44

Matousseyvitch, Mitya, 55
Matousseyvitch, Vera (Shcheyteenin),
   11, 10–13, *14*, 20–23, 30–33, *34*,
   35–40, 44–46, 55, 81, 91–93, *99*,
   101–7, *106*, 113–15, 127–30
McCreery, Juliet, 172
Menton, Riviere, 55
Mereddyd, Penelope's second husband,
   162–64, 179–87
Miles, Bertram, 43, 45, 155
Milwitz, prison camp, 67
Moffett, Jim, 75
Monton, 35
Moorfields, 57–61
Muir, Patrick, 53–54
Murphy, belt factory manager, 30
Murray, Admiral Leonard Warren,
   119–30, *121*, 124–26, *129*, 133–36,
   134, *135*
Murray, family of Nova Scotia, 118–19
Murray, Jane, *129*
Murray, Jean (Scott), 120–23

Nagasaki, 10, 164
Nansen passports, 29
National Health Service: ophthalmic
   service first established, 96; full
   service begins, 109–10; helps Rusty,
   146
New Glasgow, Nova Scotia, 119, 129
NHS. *See* National Health Service
Nova Scotia, 118–19

Oxford, 59, 74–76, 80, 94, 117, 123,
   144–45, 162–63
Ozerki, *18*

Parker, Bill, 80
Parkfield school, 115
Parkin, Alice, 112; tragic death, 143–44
Pendleton belt factory, 30, 34
Penelope, 88–92, *90*, 109–10, 115–18,
   144–51, 158–64, 179–87
Peru, 91, 155
Pictou County, Nova Scotia, 119

Platt, Sir Harry, 47
Port Arthur, 13
Prisoner of War (Nicholas), 65–74
Protopopov, Capt. Paul (Pavil), 8
Pyatigorsk, 20

Radio, used in POW camp, 70
RAMC, 61
Rathbone family, 75
Rape, 156–58
Reddaway, Frank, Invitation to England, 3–4, *28*, 35,
Rigby, Sonny, jilted husband, 80, 107–9
Riviera, 55
RNVR, 77, 79, 93
Rome, "eye" studies, 56
Roughley, Charles, 32, 155
Royal Army Medical Corps. *See* RAMC
Royal Naval Voluntary Reserve. *See* RNVR
Ruby Rose, nannie, 108–15
Russian names, after saints, 17
Russo–Japanese War, 13–15
Rusty, Penelope's first husband, 145–51

Settle Speakman, 33
Seaford, John, 51, 138, 141–42, *177*
Seaford, Nicholas (Shcheyteenin), *34, 36, 47;* as a soldier, 62–74, *69,* 136–38; marriage breaks down, 139–42
Shcheyteenin, Olga, 7–8

Shcheyteenin, Prince Orest, 5–8, *6*
Shcheyteenin Sergei, 2–7, 12–13, *14,* 15, 18, 20–*21*, 25–33, *31*, 35–42, *36, 43*–44, *47,* 54–55, 90–93, *99*, 142; murdered, 97–101
Shoura, Vera's brother, 2, 10, 15, 23–25, 55, 91, 131–32, 155
Sowler, Col. Harry, 111
Sowler, Doreen, 112–13
Stalag VIIIB, 66–71
Stockport, 52–53
St. Petersburg, 5, 10, 15–17, 32, 110
Studio, 33, 35–37, 39, 54–55, 92, 98, 100, 102–5, 130
Swallow, the murderer, 97–101
Swallowfield, 171–79

Teheran, 131
Tiki Times, 67–68, 72
Trifanoff, Irene, 131–32
Tsezarevitch, Russian flagship, 13
Tuapse, 23–26

Wallis, Max, 65
Whitnall, Prof. Samuel Ernest, 75
Willison, Alice, 88, 102–7, 130
Windsor, 165–71
Winks, Violet, 33
Winmarleigh House, 27–29, *29*
Worcester, 154–58

Zakharov, Vasilii, vii–viii

CPSIA information can be obtained at www.ICGtesting.com
Printed in the USA
BVOW071709090613

322819BV00001BB/15/P